ETHICAL OIL

ETHICAL

ALSO BY EZRA LEVANT

Shakedown: How Our Government Is Undermining Democracy
   in the Name of Human Rights

Ezra Levant

OIL

The Case for Canada's Oil Sands

MᴄCʟᴇʟʟᴀɴᴅ & Sᴛᴇᴡᴀʀᴛ

Library and Archives Canada Cataloguing in Publication

Levant, Ezra, 1972-
    Ethical oil : the case for Canada's oil sands / Ezra Levant.

ISBN 978-0-7710-4641-4

    1. Petroleum industry and trade – Moral and ethical aspects. 2. Organization of Petroleum Exporting Countries. 3. Petroleum – Purchasing – Moral and ethical aspects. 4. Petroleum industry and trade – Environmental aspects. 5. Human rights.
I. Title.

HD9560.5.L45 2010   178   C2009-905146-X

We acknowledge the financial support of the Government of Canada through the Book Publishing Industry Development Program and that of the Government of Ontario through the Ontario Media Development Corporation's Ontario Book Initiative. We further acknowledge the support of the Canada Council for the Arts and the Ontario Arts Council for our publishing program.

Typeset in Electra by M&S, Toronto
Printed and bound in Canada

ANCIENT FOREST
FRIENDLY

This book is printed on acid-free paper that is 100% recycled, ancient-forest friendly (100% post-consumer waste).

McClelland & Stewart Ltd.
75 Sherbourne Street
Toronto, Ontario
M5A 2P9
www.mcclelland.com

1 2 3 4 5   14 13 12 11 10

To my family, for their patience and support

CONTENTS

THE SHOCKING TRUTH ABOUT THE OIL SANDS

C anada's tar sands are the largest industrial project in the world. We're not talking factory large or city-block large. We're talking as big as the entire state of Florida large – 140,000 square kilometres of toxic sludge, where more than a hundred oil companies work around the clock to literally boil the oil out of the ground.

What they don't turn into open-pit mines – like something out of Mordor, in *The Lord of the Rings* – is left as giant toxic lakes, which the oil companies cynically call "ponds." They're so large, they're even visible from space, so it's no wonder that migrating birds sometimes stop to rest on them. Those unlucky enough to make that mistake – and scientists estimate that the number will be in the tens of millions – will only do so once.

It's not just birds that are in jeopardy. Fish are too. Deformities are commonplace; one fish was recently found downstream from the oil sands with a grotesque second jaw. Aboriginal peoples, who have lived in the region for centuries before the white man came with fossil fuel imperialism, say that the fish just aren't the same anymore, and the rivers themselves smell of poison. Whether those rivers will even survive is an open question: to boil each barrel of oil out of the tar sands takes five barrels of water. And new tar sands plants will add more than 1 million barrels of oil a day in production. Do the math yourself: the mighty Athabasca River is about to become a small, dirty creek.

Of course, what's poisonous for fish and fowl is poisonous for people too. In Fort Chipewyan, a village of twelve hundred souls just downstream from the tar sands, half a dozen cases of a rare bile duct cancer, called cholangiocarcinoma, were confirmed by John O'Connor, a soft-spoken doctor who ministers to the largely Aboriginal town. By tragic coincidence, Dr. O'Connor's own father passed away from the same affliction.

Is six cases of bile duct cancer unusual for a village of twelve hundred? Put it this way: it's so rare, your chances of getting it are one in one hundred thousand. And Fort Chip has it six times out of twelve hundred people. That's about as likely to happen in nature as playing a game of golf and getting eighteen holes in one, in a row. No wonder that when Dr. O'Connor blew the whistle on the tar sands as the culprit, he was hit with a series of ethics complaints designed to muzzle him – all of them filed by "doctors" working for the federal government. There's just too much money at stake in the tar sands to let one physician's conscience stop "progress."

And then there's the tar sands' dirtiest little secret: it's the filthiest oil in the world when it comes to greenhouse gases (GHGs). No other method of oil production in the world comes close to the tar sands in terms of CO_2 emissions. The tar sands aren't just poisoning the Aboriginals in Fort Chip. They're poisoning our very planet – and threatening to turn Canada into a climate criminal.

It shouldn't be surprising. The oil sands are brought to you by the same people who gave us the *Exxon Valdez*, the world's largest oil spill. Where normal people smell pollution, they smell money. But don't think any of that money is actually spread around. What isn't expatriated back to the oil companies' U.S. corporate headquarters goes largely untaxed – the inevitable result of having Prime Minister Stephen Harper, the son of an Imperial Oil executive, setting tax policy. It's not just the oil that's flowing to the United States. It's the money too.

What's left behind, besides environmental catastrophe, in the oil sands headquarters of Fort McMurray are all the social ills of a boom town – the violence, the mistreatment of women, the addiction problems, and an artificially high cost of living that makes almost anyone with a job part of the working poor.

It's not good enough for a country like Canada to care only about financial goals. A country, like a person, has a soul too. The tar sands are turning our collective soul as black as bitumen. It's time to do the moral thing, for a change. We've got to shut down the tar sands to save Canada.

Wow. The oil sands are embarrassing. Not just for Albertans but for anyone in Canada who cares about the environment, or Aboriginal rights, or our international reputation.

Except, it's not true. Every single fact in the preceding pages is false. Every one of them.

The tar sands – or the oil sands, as they're more commonly called nowadays (tar, a product of distilled coal, just isn't accurate, no matter what certain anti–oil sands group claim; this is bitumen in Alberta's ground: a thick oil) – are, in fact, huge.

They are believed to represent the largest single deposit of petroleum reserves on the planet, with, by some estimates, between 1.7 trillion and 2.5 trillion barrels of oil inside it.[1] The recoverable oil in Alberta's north has the potential to deliver a stable oil supply to the world for the next one hundred years.[2]

The oil sands do cover an area the size of Florida. But only 2 per cent of that area will ever be mined. The rest of the oil sands are just too deep – they'll be steamed and pumped out of the ground, not unlike the way normal oil is. Forests will still grow and critters will still frolic on the land high above the drilling. And even the 2 per cent that is mined will be reclaimed once the oil is pumped out – it's the law in Alberta, and the first oil sands mine reclamation projects have already been certified. They're gorgeous hiking trails now, with forests and pristine lakes.

It's true, there is oil seeping into the rivers north of Fort McMurray and sometimes the air smells like sulphur and the water is bitter. And that's how it's been for millennia – Aboriginals traditionally used the thick bitumen that bubbled out of the ground to waterproof their canoes. There is so much oil oozing naturally into the environment that sometimes the water quality adjacent to an oil sands operation is cleaner than the water upstream, where a seam of bitumen exposed on the riverbank has been leeching into the water for thousands of years.

That double-jawed fish supposedly deformed by Alberta's water? When it was finally inspected by scientists, they discovered it was a dead goldeye whose naturally bony tongue had punctured through its decomposed jaw floor, as commonly happens with dead goldeye. Stinky water? You bet – a natural phenomenon that early European explorers wrote about in their journals too.

Tens of millions of dead birds? No. About sixteen hundred died once when Syncrude's high-tech scarecrow system temporarily stopped working. That's a lot of birds, to be sure. But it's a tiny fraction compared to the hundreds of thousands killed by wind turbines each year[3] – or the billion birds killed in North America each year by housecats.[4]

Well, how about water usage? All the oil sands companies combined are only permitted to use a maximum of 2.2 per cent of the Athabasca River's flow. In practice, they typically only use 1 per cent – but even that is reduced in low-flow periods, under a water management law. And only oil sands mines use river water – most oil sands operations drill for oil underground. They don't use river water at all, and 90 per cent of the non-potable water they do use is recycled again.

Okay. But what about those half-dozen cases of bile duct cancer? When Dr. O'Connor raised the alarm, Fort Chip's citizens panicked. He had confirmed their worst fears. Health Canada kicked into high gear too, immediately launching a massive cancer study in the area. But they found a strange road-block: O'Connor himself, who refused to turn over his patient files, even though he was required to do so by law. After obstruct-ing the study for months, O'Connor finally relented – and his files showed that there had only been two rare cancers in town, not half a dozen. Other cancer diagnoses were completely fab-ricated. O'Connor simply made them up, a fact revealed by investigators from the College of Physicians and Surgeons. O'Connor has never been muzzled – in fact, while the college was bound by its obligation to keep the investigation private, O'Connor hit the talk-show circuit, telling and retelling his fibs, even starring in a movie.

Well, what about U.S. oil companies like Exxon? It's true, Exxon's subsidiaries are indeed in the oil sands. But it's not true that they're simply taking the oil and the money. Oil companies get the smallest slice of the profit pie, with the bulk going to Canada's provincial and federal governments in the form of taxes and royalties. And, of course, an enormous amount stays in the community in the form of salaries for employees and contracts for suppliers. And not just in the West: more Ontarians are now employed by the oil sands than by the Big Three automakers.

The oil sands combined emit just 5 per cent of Canada's total greenhouse gases – less than, for example, the emissions from all of Canada's cattle and pigs. Oil sands technology continues to improve – to produce one barrel of oil sands oil takes 38 per cent less emissions now than it did in 1990. But when everything is taken into consideration, oil sands oil actually has a smaller carbon footprint than other sources of oil, like Nigeria, where huge amounts of natural gas are simply burned off into the air as the oil is produced.

And that gets to the biggest oil sands lie of all: that Canada's oil miracle is somehow immoral, even criminal. Oil is an international commodity; if an oil-thirsty country such as China or the United States can't buy oil from one country, they'll buy it from another. So even if the oil sands were to completely shut down, the world wouldn't use one barrel less. It would just buy that oil from the oil sands' competitors: places like Saudi Arabia, Iran, Sudan, and Nigeria.

Over the past few years, Canada's oil sands exports to the United States have displaced 80 million barrels of Saudi oil annually. That's 80 million barrels less each year from a misogynistic, theocratic dictatorship that has used its oil money to bankroll terrorists. And at the end of the day, that's the real test of ethical oil: not comparing oil sands oil to some impossible, ideal standard but comparing it to its real competitors.

That's what *Ethical Oil* is about: trying to separate the propaganda coming from anti–oil sands groups like Greenpeace from the facts, and using those facts to decide which oil is more environmentally clean, more peaceful, more democratic, and more fair. That's the true test of moral oil.

Oh, and speaking of Greenpeace? They're sure tough on the oil sands. But you'll never guess what that $340 million per year transnational corporation has to say about oil and gas production in countries like Saudi Arabia and China.

Let's take a moral inventory of the oil sands. And while we're at it, let's take a moral inventory of oil sands critics like Greenpeace too.

The question is not whether we should use oil sands oil instead of some perfect fantasy fuel that hasn't been invented yet. Until that miracle fuel is invented, the question is whether we should use oil from the oil sands or oil from the other places in the world that pump it. That's what this book tries to answer.

Chapter 1

WHAT ARE THE OIL SANDS AND WHY ARE THEY IMPORTANT?

For decades, the way that oil production worked is that oil was discovered in a liquid state and was pumped out of the ground just like water. It was then refined into usable products like gasoline. That's how it still is in countries like Saudi Arabia and Iran and in the conventional oil fields of Canada and the United States. But conventional oil fields have been depleted over the years; the International Energy Agency estimated that existing, conventional oil fields are losing production at a rate of 6.7 per cent a year.[1] With world oil prices steadily rising because of new energy demand from the emerging industrial economies in India and China, scientists have turned their attention to unconventional sources of oil – like the oil sands.

The oil sands are just what they sound like: oil mixed with sand and clay. Bitumen has the thickness of peanut butter, so it's not exactly ready to be pumped and piped like the Saudi stuff. The process of removing the oil from the sand in an economical way has bedevilled scientists for decades, and until recently it was considered an experimental project. Only in the past ten years have technology and higher oil prices come together to make the oil sands economically viable.

It's so unconventional that for thirty years the U.S. Securities and Exchange Commission, the government regulator that oversees the stock market, has had a policy that forbade oil companies from including oil sands oil as part of their "proven" reserves on their balance sheets.[2] That's how new oil sands oil is – until recently, the world just didn't believe it could work.

But if the oil sands had a slow start, they've made up for it with amazing growth in the past few years. More than one hundred oil companies are now working or planning to develop the oil sands, and Fort McMurray, once a sleepy outpost in Northern Alberta, has grown into the third-largest city in the province, a boom town of one hundred thousand people. It was because of the oil sands that the value of energy companies on the Toronto Stock Exchange finally exceeded the value of banks. That's big.

The oil sands are the reason why Canada is now the number-one exporter of oil to the United States, pushing Saudi Arabia down to number two in 2004 – the year the U.S. Department of Energy finally included oil sands oil in its estimates for global oil reserves. In 2008, Canada shipped 715 million barrels to the United States, far more than the 550 million barrels the Saudis sold. From 2003 to 2008, the oil sands had helped cut Saudi imports by 80 million barrels a year.[3] The oil sands aren't just a huge economic force. They're changing the calculus in foreign affairs and national security too.

Oil sands have been discovered in other parts of the world, such as Venezuela's Orinoco oil belt,[4] but Alberta's political and economic stability make it the most important alternative to Organization of the Petroleum Exporting Countries (OPEC) oil in the world. It's hard to believe, but Canada's oil sands represent more than half of all publicly accessible oil in the world – that is, oil that isn't controlled by a government monopoly. That's why companies from around the world are setting up shop in Canada. If you're an investor in oil – and anyone with a pension fund probably is – you're an investor in the oil sands.

But while the oil sands are an enormous economic and energy opportunity, they're a great public relations opportunity for critics of oil too. For one thing, they're ugly, or at least the handful of open-pit mines dating back to the first oil sands installations are, since they're vast digging operations conducted by incredibly large shovels and trucks. They've been the subject of dramatic photo shoots by the likes of *National Geographic* magazine, and the ugliness of those mines are now a staple in fundraising letters for every environmentalist group in the world. Oil sands porn sells magazines and gets donations, but it's not exactly a substitute for a serious discussion about the pros and cons of oil sands oil compared to OPEC oil.

But any industrial project brings negative side effects with its benefits. Ugly photographs are part of the story, but they're not the whole story. Putting the oil sands into perspective means understanding not just how Alberta operates, but how the rest of the world produces oil too. And it also means getting behind some of the tactics and agendas of those who wish dearly to see the oil sands stopped and shut down tomorrow to find out what's really going on. As with any politically charged, economically transformative issue, there are hidden agendas and vested interests beneath the surface; the truth about the oil sands isn't always what it seems. A good place to start is comparing the ethics of the Canadian oil sands to other oil-producing countries – countries that don't allow *National Geographic* or other journalists free rein to report on them or activists to protest their behaviour.

Chapter 2

THE VERY SHORT LIST OF DEMOCRACIES THAT SELL OIL

I t's a fact of life: if Americans don't fill up their cars with Canadian gasoline, their gas is going to come from another oil-producing country. Even environmentally friendly cars like the Toyota Prius still need to get their gasoline from somewhere.

The oil sands have made democratic, peaceful Canada the number-one source of U.S. oil. But the rest of America's international oil suppliers are pretty ugly. With few exceptions, the other countries on the top ten list are the world's dictatorships, human rights abusers, and warmongers.[1]

After Canada, Saudi Arabia is the biggest source of U.S. oil imports. Saudi Arabia is an Islamic feudal state named after the Saud family that owns it – some seven thousand princes[2] known for their lavish lifestyles and idleness. For those not lucky enough to be a member of the royal family, Saudi Arabia is one of the world's most repressive regimes, where the Koran is strictly enforced as the official constitution, where 6.4 million foreign workers[3] are brutalized, and where political dissent is forbidden.

A major sponsor of world terrorism, Saudi Arabia is where Osama bin Laden made his money – and it's also where fifteen of the nineteen 9/11 hijackers came from. Needless to say, a country that doesn't value human life doesn't care much about plants and animals either – environmentalism is the punchline to anti-American jokes in Saudi Arabia, not a pillar of their oil industry. This fascist theocracy shipped 551 million barrels of oil to the United States last year.

In third place is Mexico, nominally a democracy but a democracy with endemic human rights abuses and corruption. They sold 433 million barrels to the United States last year.

Venezuela, run by socialist strongman Hugo Chávez, is next, followed by corrupt Nigeria, strife-torn Iraq, undemocratic Angola, and torture-loving Algeria.[4] The world's nastiest regimes, like Iran and Sudan, can't legally sell oil to the United States directly because of economic sanctions. But with major oil consumers like China and Japan taking up the slack, those sanctions are essentially meaningless. Moreover, for every barrel of oil that doesn't come out of the oil sands, another barrel must come from somewhere else. The less oil that comes from Alberta, the better it is for every other exporter in the world, including Iran and Sudan.

The list of countries that export oil to the United States is a rogues' gallery. But the rankings of the world's oil reserves – a good predictor of where oil is going to come from in the future – is even worse. Out of the top ten countries with the largest reserves, Canada is the only liberal democracy, other than the fledgling democracy of Iraq.[5] There's no way to avoid the conclusion that oil comes from the world's worst places, and there's no reason to expect that to change.

It's one thing to condemn Canada's oil sands and to publish ugly photos of them. But for ethical oil consumers, unless there's a better alternative, demonizing Canadian oil isn't just useless – it can be counterproductive, by driving consumers into the hands of oil producers who are worse by every ethical measure.

That's exactly what happened in February 2010, when an anti–oil sands lobby group called ForestEthics persuaded two retail giants to direct their suppliers to use non–oil sands oil.

Michael Besancon, senior vice-president of the fashionable supermarket chain Whole Foods, declared that "fuel that comes from tar sands refineries does not fit our values." According to ForestEthics, Whole Foods "eliminated tar sands-linked fuel at one of its distribution centers and committed . . . to replace all fuel supplies connected with Canada's tar sands." And Bed Bath & Beyond, another international retailer, "has agreed to make the tar sands an issue in the bidding process it follows for selecting transportation providers."[6] Okay, but given that two out of every three barrels of oil in the United States is imported,[7] where should Bed Bath & Beyond insist its truckers buy their oil from? And is it even possible for truckers to know where fuel from a particular gas station comes from? If scoring political points against the oil sands is your goal, coming up with a practical answer to that question isn't important. But if your goal is to genuinely buy morally superior oil, the question remains unanswered.

According to press reports, Whole Foods switched some of its oil purchases to Marathon Oil, a U.S.–based company.[8] But while Marathon does indeed pump a lot of oil from the United

States, it also owns a 20 per cent stake in a major oil sands development – and it operates in dictatorships like Equatorial Guinea and Libya.[9] Does that "fit" Whole Foods' values?

It's an important question to ask because critics of Canada's oil sands complain that the oil isn't just environmentally dirty but somehow has moral failures, that it is inherently evil. It's an attempt to denormalize the oil sands, to make them so morally repugnant that any debate about them is over before it starts.

But if we were to stop oil sands development, as ForestEthics demands we do, where would the oil come from? Canada would have enough oil for itself from conventional Canadian oil fields, but what about America? Let's look at some of the other countries on the list – competitors to the oil sands whose oil would quickly substitute for any decrease in production.

In Chapter 7, we'll compare the environmental impact of oil from different countries. But the number of pounds of carbon dioxide per barrel of oil – one of the key environmental criticisms of oil sands oil – is a narrow measure of ethics, and it's a pretty tenuous one at best. If we're comparing ethics, country to country, there are a lot more revealing – and more important – factors to measure.

SAUDI ARABIA

If Saudi Arabia didn't exist, it would take a science-fiction writer in an apocalyptic mood to invent it. Saudi women are treated as the property of men, with fewer rights than children and only slightly more rights than animals. They are forbidden from driving cars; they cannot travel abroad without a man's permission; and they can't even have elective surgery without their master's consent.[10]

That doesn't sound like Whole Foods' values, does it?

Men have it better in Saudi Arabia, of course, but Allah help them if they're gay, or even eccentric. An international group called Human Rights Watch (HRW) has documented men being arrested and flogged for wearing women's clothing.[11] In a medieval theocracy like the Saudis,' such heresy is a crime, the crime of "suspicious behaviour" and "imitating women." And, according to Amnesty International, Saudi Arabia executes gays simply for being gay. Amnesty has documented this barbaric punishment, carried out in full medieval style: a beheading and a crucifixion.[12]

Even children are not spared Saudi Arabia's merciless "justice." Teenaged "criminals" are beheaded with swords in the public square; children as young as thirteen have been sentenced to more than one thousand lashes.[13]

Question: How many press releases do you think ForestEthics has sent out about the ethics of Saudi oil? If you guessed zero, you're right. Too bad – not only could Saudi Arabia's endangered forests[14] use the help, but its women and children could too.

A full ethical inventory of Saudi Arabia would take a whole book, but no list of that country's morals would be complete without a mention of the most grotesque "crime" in Saudi Arabia: the crime of being raped. That's right. Rape victims are routinely prosecuted and punished by the government, after having already been violated by real criminals. According to HRW, one rape victim who was convicted of "illegal mingling" had her sentence – six months in prison and two hundred lashes – doubled when she complained to the media.[15]

Saudi justice is done in secret; it's built around confessions, which "provides an incentive to interrogators to obtain it by any means, including torture and deception," writes Amnesty International.

An appalling justice system is just the start of the problems with Saudi oil. The oil itself is produced by a workforce largely made up of foreign workers whose employment conditions often border on slavery.

There are literally tens of thousands of members of the Saudi royal family, and many more privileged members in the Saudi kingdom who don't care much for actually doing any work. But since someone still has to work all the Saudis' oil fields and clean all the Saudis' palaces, the kingdom relies heavily on "guest workers,"[16] mostly from those parts of the Middle East and Asia not blessed with oil riches. Many of them don't make it out alive. In fact, Saudi Arabia's legal system, with its basis in sharia law, seems to catch an extraordinary number of non-Saudis. Of the more than 1,600 prisoners executed by Saudi authorities between 1985 and 2008, more than half – 830 of them – were foreign workers, compared to just 809 executed Saudi nationals.

It's not just men on oil rigs. One and a half million Asian women are employed as housekeepers in the kingdom, and they have, according to Human Rights Watch, no rights at all: not to protect themselves from abuse, not to a lunch break, and not to even insist on a regularly delivered paycheque. Most domestic workers report working fifteen to twenty hours every day of the week, usually with only a one-hour rest break or, just as often, no rest at all. Of those foreign workers surveyed by HRW, not a single one was given a day off or paid leave by their employers. Nearly half of the cases studied by Human Rights Watch "clearly amounted to forced labor, trafficking, slavery, or slavery-like conditions."[17]

Greenpeace's fundraising letters label Canada a "climate criminal" because of the oil sands. But if Canada is a criminal, what word is left to describe Saudi Arabia?

IRAN

Of course, the holy kingdom of Saudi Arabia is far from being the only oil-rich nation with jails full of innocents.

Let's talk about labour unions, something taken for granted in the oil sands. For the crime of peacefully organizing a bus union, Iranian labour activist Mansour Ossanlu was sentenced to five years in detention and while in prison was blocked from getting the medical treatment he needed. And in Iran's prisons, "torture and ill-treatment of detainees" is "common," according to human rights investigations.

Like in Saudi Arabia, it's not just labour freedom that's curtailed, but any sort of personal or religious freedom too. Suspicion of adultery or being gay are all considered high crimes in the Islamic Republic of Iran. And convictions in Iran are no small matter: this is a country where justice often means a sentence of death by stoning, crucifixion, or limb amputation.

Simply being a woman in the land of Islamic revolution means a life of fear. For example, the odds are that much higher that you will one day find yourself hauled in, and convicted, on charges of "adultery." After all, women are only allowed, by law, to have one sexual partner for their whole life, namely their husband. Men, naturally, have no such limits: they are allowed to take up to four permanent wives and are permitted to have as many "temporary" wives – prostitutes or mistresses, who they can temporarily "marry" for as briefly as a few hours – as they like. Men are free to divorce any wife, temporary or permanent, without any preconditions, while often women are denied access to divorce.

And just as in Saudi Arabia, adultery is a capital crime in Iran – punishable by stoning. Yet even in this final, barbaric act, women are discriminated against: Article 102 of Iran's penal code requires that during stoning – when the community gathers round to throw stones at the convicted person, buried in a hole in the ground – a woman be buried up to her chest and a man be buried only up to his waist. What's the difference? It happens that Article 103 says that if the condemned person is lucky enough to get themselves out of their pit before the stones kill them, they get to live and won't be stoned again. Obviously, for a woman buried right up to her chest, with her arms trapped underground, that just doesn't happen.

Of course, the mullahs aren't without their compassion: according to Article 92, when a woman convicted of flogging is pregnant or breast-feeding, and the clerics rule that the flogging might hurt the baby, the punishment can be delayed until it can be done without harming the infant. How thoughtful.

How does Iran's treatment of women compare to Fort McMurray's? Well, let's put it this way: Fort McMurray's most powerful politician is Mayor Melissa Blake. As a single mom living with her fiancé, she would be stoned to death in Iran.

And if anyone, anywhere had any doubt about the arbitrary and brutal nature of Iran's authorities, the bloody events of the summer of 2009 surely put those doubts to rest. The presidential election in Iran was rigged in favour of the incumbent, Mahmoud Ahmadinejad. When peaceful protestors dared to gather in the streets to stand up for what few democratic rights they had left, the government crushed them with arrests, beatings, and even murder. Ahmadinejad didn't even try to hide it: Iran admitted to arresting four thousand demonstrators in the weeks after the election.[18] Pro-democracy protestors languished in prison for months, reporting torture and rape by Iranian authorities. Many pro-democracy activists will never get a day in court: in the weeks that followed the election, Amnesty International documented an "execution spree" of staggering proportions.[19]

Of course Iran doesn't just get away with blatant, brutal, and widespread human rights violations because it has oil: Canada and Norway could never get a pass the way Iran does. It gets away with its brutalities because one of its biggest customers is China.[20] A serious human rights abuser in its own right, China doesn't care about what terrible abuses the Islamic Republic is up to. What they do care about is that Iran is their second-largest supplier of much-needed oil (Saudi Arabia is number one). Having oil partners like China – and nuclear partners like Russia – isn't just an economic benefit to Iran. It's political cover. With two allies in its corner at the UN Security Council, Iran can be sure that, despite its nuclear weapons program and its bellicose rhetoric of attacking its neighbours, it will never suffer the kind of international sanctions that South Africa did in the 1980s. Iran has friends in low places.

RUSSIA[21]

Certainly the emergence of Russia as a capitalist country in the last two decades has done wonders for its oil production: from 1993 to 2009, the number of barrels of oil Russia produced increased by 40 per cent,[22] ranking it one of the largest producers on Earth. But the more oil Russia produces, the more it follows the menacing, human rights–abusing lead of other oil-producing giants like Iran and Saudi Arabia.

In fact, no other G8 country relies so heavily on energy for taxation as Russia does. Russian export taxes are designed to catch about 90 per cent of the revenue collected from every barrel of oil shipped for export.[23] And a good chunk of that goes to build Russia's violent power: 40 per cent of Moscow's budget goes to its military or internal security, not surprising given the background of Vladimir Putin as a devoted agent of the KGB.[24]

Under the leadership of Putin, Russia has entangled itself in some brutal foreign skirmishes. In 1999, Putin blamed a series of terrorist attacks in Moscow and Volgodonsk on Chechen separatists, though there is credible evidence that they may have been staged attacks coordinated as a pretext for an invasion. A 2001 Amnesty International report recounted "indiscriminate" bombing and shelling of civilian areas by Russian troops, and the explicit targeting of Chechen civilians, including medical personnel.[25] The United States Holocaust Memorial Museum put Chechnya on its "genocide watch list" after seeing evidence of "massacres of civilians" by Russian troops and torture.[26] The exact death toll of what is known as the Second Chechen War has never been verified, though 25,000 to 50,000 civilians are estimated to be dead or missing.[27]

During another of Putin's wars, in 2008 in South Ossetia, the Russian military was accused of more war crimes.[28] Russian soldiers were reported to have indiscriminately attacked civilian houses. Prisoners captured during the conflict were subjected to torture and abuse to extract confessions. Roughly 192,000 people were displaced by Russia's war; about 30,000 of the ethnic Georgians displaced have still been unable to return home, with 18,500 facing "long-term displacement."

Putin isn't much for dwelling on such trivialities: journalists in his country who have made efforts to uncover the real story behind Russia's questionable behaviour have been silenced in the most aggressive ways. Anna Politkovskaya, a top journalist who had written investigative pieces critical of Russia's actions in Chechnya, was gunned down in an elevator in her apartment building; her killers were never found.[29] In 2009, Politkovskaya's lawyer was assassinated in Moscow; no one has been charged in his murder.[30] Politkovskaya may have been the most high-profile murder of a journalist critical of Putin's regime, but it was far from the only one. Between 2000 and 2007, twenty-one journalists have been murdered on the job in Russia, according to the press freedom organization Reporters Without Borders.[31] Often, the culprits are never prosecuted.

Enemies of Putin's regime aren't safe even when they're outside the country. Former KGB and FSB officer Alexander Litvinenko, who wrote tell-all books spilling secrets about Russia's human rights abuses and crimes – including pointing the finger for those terrorist bombings blamed on Chechen separatists directly at the government – was given political asylum in the United Kingdom. That wasn't far enough from Moscow evidently: in 2006 he was mysteriously poisoned by a radioactive isotope placed in his teacup that experts said could only have come from a laboratory in an advanced nuclear power such as Russia.

This is becoming a pattern. Two years earlier, Ukrainian politician Viktor Yushchenko angered Putin when he challenged Moscow's favoured candidate in an election for prime minister of the Ukraine. Poised to win, Yushchenko turned mysteriously ill in the middle of the campaign. He claimed it was the work of government agents, supported by Russia. Austrian doctors were able to confirm he had been poisoned by a dioxin known as TCDD; his body had more than one thousand times the usual concentration. Though he survived, his previously young and handsome face is now grey, pockmarked, and severely disfigured from the poisoning.[32]

If you write a book condemning Alberta's oil sands policies – as many have done – it could be a best-seller and you'd be rich. Write a book condemning Russian policies and you could end up dead.

Which source of oil do you prefer?

NIGERIA

While Russia, Iran, and Saudi Arabia at least make the attempt to hide their human rights abuses behind the closed doors of their brutal prisons or under the fog of war, Nigeria is far less artful about the way it spills blood. There, the government simply resorts to plain, old-fashioned massacres.[33] In November 2008, a post-election riot turned into a bloodbath. Human Rights Watch has called for an investigation into what happened on November 29, when police and military in the Plateau State were issued a "shoot-on-sight" directive by Governor Jonah Jang. The consequence: 118 cases of arbitrary killings, all taking place between seven in the morning and lunchtime.

A country that doesn't care much for its own people won't care at all for the environment. Nigeria produces just under 2 million barrels of oil per day – 50 per cent more than Canada's oil sands.[34] Half of Nigeria's production goes to the United States. But Nigeria also has one of the world's largest reserves of natural gas, though much of it – 593 billion cubic feet a year – is wasted, simply burned off. That flaring is economically foolish: Nigeria estimates that it could sell that much gas for U.S.$1.5 billion a year. It's also a significant emitter of carbon dioxide, a greenhouse gas. And in Nigeria, hundreds of oil spills happen every single year. Roughly two thousand sites in that country have been registered as contaminated by the National Oil Spill Detection and Response Agency—and the government may be underreporting the real number. Between January and June 2008, 418 oil spills were reported to the authorities.

According to the World Bank, oil and gas make up 97.5 per cent of Nigeria's exports – pretty much the only thing of economic value in the country and the source of almost all of Nigeria's tax revenues. You'd think that being Africa's largest oil producer might lift Nigerians out of their grinding poverty, but you'd be wrong: gross domestic product per capita is just $1,400 a year, and more than half the population lives on less than a dollar a day.[35] So where does all the oil money go? And, while the question is being asked, where did all of Nigeria's foreign aid go, including tens of billions of dollars in loans from developed countries that were recently forgiven?

The answer is: it was stolen. According to a Nigerian government agency called the Economic and Financial Crimes Commission,[36] from 1960, when Nigeria became independent, to 1999, when civilian rule was restored, a whopping $366 billion was stolen through embezzlement, bribes, or outright theft.[37] As London's *Telegraph* newspaper put it, Nigeria "is a country where people equate their politicians with thieves and where, apart from the federal government, there are 36 state governments and 774 local administrations, all of which are tempted to take their cut." Just one kleptocrat, Sani Abacha, stole between $1.6 billion and $5 billion during his five-year rule. Five billion dollars spent on such basics as clean water or immunization might have done something about Nigeria's life expectancy – at less than 47 years, it's ranked 212th in the world.[38]

From 1960 to 1999, Nigeria produced, on average, 1.39 million barrels of oil per day.[39] So, 40 years × 365 days a year × 1.39 million barrels a day = 20.3 billion barrels of oil. From that, $366 billion was stolen – or about $18 per barrel. Put another way, that's $300 per second stolen ever since Nigeria became independent.

Because of Nigeria's wasteful practice of simply burning off any natural gas they find along with the oil, Nigerian crude has one of the highest carbon "footprints" of oil produced in the world – and then there's the environmental cost of shipping that oil from Africa to America. According to a 2009 study by the U.S. government's National Energy Technology Laboratory,[40] because of its flaring, Nigerian crude had the highest greenhouse gas emissions per barrel, at the production stage, of any source of crude in the world – 10 per cent more than Canada's oil sands. But then, ForestEthics isn't likely to risk holding demonstrations at Nigeria's oil installations. They don't want to end up being dealt with the same way that Jonah Jang dealt with people he considered troublemakers.

Nigeria has it all: the corrupt government that butchers its own people, the environmental degradation, and world-class poverty. But if Bed Bath & Beyond has its way, its truckers will substitute Nigerian oil for Alberta oil. Better change the name to Bloodbath & Beyond.

Venezuela

Venezuelan president Hugo Chávez doesn't have much to worry about when it comes to activists complaining about his country's sizeable oil industry. It's not that environmentalists might not find something to complain about. In fact, studies by the U.S. government's National Energy Technology Laboratory have determined that the "ultraheavy" bituminous oil extracted in Venezuela might actually emit more greenhouse emissions than what's produced in Canada's oil sands, though the lack of proper data from Venezuela makes it impossible to verify.[41] Rather, it's that Chávez has pretty well outlawed complaining about anything his government does in his new, socialist Bolivarian Republic.

Since taking office in 1999, Chávez has forced television and radio stations to air government propaganda any time he tells them to. In the last decade, this has added up to more than two thousand presidential speeches, including one that lasted more than seven hours. That doesn't leave a lot of time for investigating environmental or human rights issues.

Not that many news outlets would want to try it, anyway, after what happened to Globovision, a national TV station that's proven to be a thorn in the side of Venezuela's bully boss. After the network dared to raise questions about the government's response to an earthquake in May 2009, the National Telecommunications Commission opened an investigation into the station, claiming its reports might "generate alarm, fear, anxiety or panic in the population."[42]

Pretty soon, Chávez won't need to rely on such tactics: he'll be able to officially send in the police. In July 2009, the Venezuelan Attorney General introduced new legislation outlining punishments for so-called "media crimes." That doesn't mean stealing televisions or droning on the airwaves for half a day about what a great president you are. It means making it illegal for anyone to broadcast or print what the government considers to "harm the interests of the state" or what might "mislead or distort news, generating a false perception of the facts or creating opinions, if this affects social peace, national security, public order, mental health or public morale."[43] The punishment? Up to four years in prison.

Rounding up critics of the government would be nothing new for Chávez's government, though. Human rights groups have documented hundreds of cases where political activists who dare to speak out against the government have been arrested and, often, killed.[44] The country's main democratic opposition, the Coordinadora Democrática, says that as many as 350 of its supporters have been apprehended around the country and claims to have evidence of police fabricating evidence against many of its protest leaders. Amnesty International cites reports of authorities using "excessive force" and failing to "follow correct procedures for detention."

And then there's Chavez's treatment of Venezuela's Aboriginals. The Yukpa are a favourite whipping boy of the government. When human rights groups tried to press for the Yukpa's indigenous land rights against landowners in Machiques, the Chávez government harassed and detained the human rights activists. An elderly father of one of the Yukpa's leaders, meantime, was beaten to death by armed men.[45]

Nor has Venezuela ended up looking like the workers' paradise that Chávez's socialist supporters might have hoped for. When it comes to unions, the government only seems a fan of those willing to uncritically support El Presidenté. In 2004, for instance, the country's National Electoral Council ordered the largest public health worker union in the country to halt its elections the night before the vote because it was unhappy with how the campaign was unfolding. When the union proceeded with the election anyway, without incident, the council refused to recognize the result for seventeen months. And while the health union waited for approval from the government, Chávez signed a collective bargaining contract instead with a brand new, pro-government health workers organization that had never once held a leadership election.

Chávez may try to sound like he's pro-worker when he's rambling on in one of his forcibly televised manifestos, but it's just talk. In fact, the number of collective bargaining agreements in Venezuela has plummeted under Chávez, from 854 in 2004 to just 538 by 2006, mainly, say human rights groups, because the Ministry of Labour regularly blocks any collective bargaining with unions whose elections aren't officially blessed by the National Electoral Council. The president has even publicly denounced "the venom of union autonomy" and called for organized labour to act as his operatives, "the industrial arm" of his political project.

Is this a morally superior source of oil to Canada's oil sands?

SUDAN

Remember when we used to read all those headlines about the bloodshed in the Darfur region of Sudan? The headlines have stopped, but the killing hasn't. There are few places in the world as bloody as Sudan. Despite its oil – or perhaps because of it – it is one of the worst places to live.

The fighting in Darfur continues without rest. Human rights groups report that in 2008, attacks on villages by government militias actually increased, with between 270,000 and 300,000 people displaced by violence during the year. Armed attacks by opposition groups routinely trigger waves of extrajudicial executions, arbitrary arrests, unlawful detentions, and torture from the government's National Intelligence and Security Services and the police, according to Amnesty International.[46]

The evidence of war crimes committed by the Sudanese government, against its own people, is so overwhelming that in 2009, prosecutors at the International Criminal Court issued an arrest warrant for Sudan's president, Omar Hassan Ahmad al-Bashir.[47] It's not hard to see why. When Al-Bashir senses his enemy, usually in the form of the opposition Justice and Equality Movement (JEM), is nearby, he scorches the earth and everyone on it. In 2008, his army bombed the villages of Abu Suruj, Saraf Jidad, Silea, and Sirba in West Darfur in an attempt to regain control of the northern corridor of West Darfur from the JEM. The entire area was cut off from humanitarian organizations for months, though the attacks displaced an estimated thirty thousand people that the United Nations and other aid groups could not reach. The assaults were "indiscriminate and the government's forces and security services looted and burned villages," reports Amnesty International. Dozens of civilians were killed, and there were reports of rape by soldiers during and after the attacks.

When the JEM tried moving on Omdurman, one of Sudan's largest cities, in May 2008 but were repelled by government forces, Al-Bashir's troops combed through the city with orders to arrest and detain anyone – men, women, or children – who looked even remotely Darfuri. Hundreds were rounded up, and there were reports of executions, torture, and other abuses. One woman and her nine-month-old infant were thrown into an underground detention centre for two months.

And when government gunmen tried entering Kalma, the country's largest refugee camp with ninety thousand displaced citizens, to search for illegal weapons and drugs, residents refused to co-operate. In response, the gunmen surrounded the camp and opened fire with machine guns and mortar shells.

Any access into or out of the camp was denied to humanitarian agencies or to wounded people seeking medical care. In the end, at least forty-seven people were killed.

While North American and European leaders fret over whether Greenpeace thinks they're being nice enough to fish and plants, Al-Bashir has laughed off the arrest warrant for war crimes issued by the International Criminal Court. He responded by ordering the expulsion of ten non-governmental organizations (NGOs)[48] from his country: groups like Oxfam, Care, Save the Children, and Doctors Without Borders that had been working in famine relief and disease control, efforts the government itself neglected. Those aid agencies that weren't expelled from Sudan ended up having their assets seized. By 2009, 2.2 million Sudanese were facing starvation and·disease.

Of course, much like their OPEC peers in Saudi Arabia, Sudan has crimes such as women wearing pants.[49] In the sharia state, even when war rages all around, such things can't be allowed.[50] "Tens of thousands of women and girls have been whipped for their clothes these last 20 years. It's not rare in Sudan," Lubna Ahmed al-Hussein, a UN worker in Sudan, said in 2009, after waiving immunity for UN workers when she was arrested for the same fashion crime.

How does one measure such a persistent genocide? It would be macabre to try to put a number on it. But if we're trying to compare the ethics of different oil-producing regions in the world, that's what we have to do. Here's one metric: how much human blood is shed in Sudan to produce each barrel of oil? If we're measuring how "dirty" or "nasty" oil is, shouldn't we look at things that are dirtier or nastier than carbon dioxide? It would be awfully shallow not to.

According to the United Nations, 300,000 people were killed in the Darfur region of Sudan between 2006 and 2008 as part of the government's genocide campaign and another 2.5 million people have been displaced.[51]

While Sudan does consume a portion of its own oil production, most of it is for export – that's where all the cash has come from to wage the war in Darfur. Sudan exports about 350,000 barrels of oil per day – a quarter-billion barrels in the approximately two-year span when most of the murdering was going on in Darfur. These are rough numbers, but dividing that much oil by 300,000 victims works out to 850 barrels of oil per murder. With 185 ounces of blood in the average human body, that's about a fifth of an ounce of blood per barrel – 6.5 millilitres, or just more than a teaspoon. It's about as much blood as you could fit inside a tube of eyeliner or lipstick.

A barrel of oil from Alberta's oil sands accounts for about seventy-five pounds of CO_2. Fair enough: *mea culpa*. Oil from Sudan, meanwhile, has even more CO_2 in it, thanks to all the flaring they do to extract it – and a teaspoon of blood. It would be nice if Greenpeace gave a damn about this, but it's just so much easier for them to work in a democratic, liberal jurisdiction like Alberta, where most of the oil companies are owned by ethical shareholders, rather than take on government-owned oil companies in a faraway Muslim dictatorship.

CANADA

Amnesty International has a file on every country in the world – including Canada. It also has a strong local presence here too – unlike Saudi Arabia, where Amnesty isn't even permitted to visit. But what's so encouraging about Amnesty's human rights "to-do list" for Canada is how much of it is actually about other countries. The very first item on Amnesty's Canadian "human rights agenda" is actually an American issue: it wants Canada to protest and demand the closing of the U.S. prison on Guantanamo Bay, Cuba, started by President George W. Bush and continued by President Barack Obama. And it wants Canada to guarantee it won't hand over suspected terrorists to their home countries where they might be denied legal rights or face torture. Amnesty International isn't worried about Canada abusing human rights: it wants Canada to take a more active role in stopping other countries from abusing human rights. Countries like Saudi Arabia.

Another top agenda item: "The federal government should adopt a comprehensive strategy to advance human rights in all aspects of Canada's relationship with China."[52] There it is again: calling on Canada to help spread its own human rights values around the world. You know you're dealing with the world's Boy Scout when Amnesty has got to fill out its human rights agenda by borrowing criticisms it's made against other countries. Amnesty also wants Canada to "stand firm against the death penalty." Canada doesn't have the death penalty, of course. Human rights activists want it to persuade other countries not to execute prisoners too.

It's no surprise human rights activists can come up with so little to say on the matter. Canada is one of the most hospitable places in the world to live, offering democracy, a stalwart commitment to the rule of law, and economic freedom. There is no torture, no slavery, no state-sanctioned rape, no murdered journalists. It's the country that gave the world UN peacekeeping. No one in their right mind would suggest that in a comparison of countries around the world that Canada isn't a leader in moral behaviour.

There is a reason that a quarter-million immigrants,[53] from the Middle East, Africa, Europe, and Asia, settle in Canada every year and hundreds of thousands more wish they could. Canadian values are the very embodiment of the thing we call ethics: the moral codes chosen freely by free people. Like every other country, Canada can always improve its human rights record. But on every key measure, from women's rights, to gay rights, to Aboriginal rights, to the sharing of the oil wealth equitably among workers, to environmental protection, Canada is hands down the most ethical major exporter of oil in the world.

And yet, today Canada finds itself being accused of severe immorality. A country that has been a leader in ethical leadership is suddenly cast as a "criminal"[54] or "unethical"[55] for the way it produces its energy. It lacks "moral vision and leadership."[56] How can this be? Has the world been wrong about Canadian values all along? Was Canada's ethical leadership on the world stage not the product of a humanitarian and liberal worldview but an accident just waiting to be spoiled by the corrupting influence of oil? Or is it possible that Canada's approach to energy is being measured by an entirely different yardstick: an unconventional version of "morality" that weighs values entirely differently? The accusations of those who fight Canada's energy industry so fiercely are so out of sync with the reality of the Canada the world has known for centuries, so illogical, that it's worth asking – actually, it's critical to ask – whether there might be something else behind those attacks. Because, as it turns out, there is.

Chapter 3

THEN WHAT? THE SAD CASE OF TALISMAN IN SUDAN

To understand how an upstanding world citizen like Canada can suddenly find itself being accused of being more immoral than countries like Russia, Saudi Arabia, or Venezuela requires an understanding of the way that activism works. People who campaign for the environment, or for human rights, have many targets on this planet to pick from and only so many resources to devote to each. The way they pick their targets isn't always based on who's doing the worst things. In fact, it usually works the opposite way. A good way to illustrate the backward nature of cause-crusading is to look at what happened to Talisman Energy.

In the fall of 1998, a mid-sized Canadian oil producer called Talisman Energy did what oil companies often do: it conducted a takeover. The company Talisman bought was another Canadian firm, called Arakis Energy.

Arakis owned, among other things, a 25 per cent share in a Sudanese oil project that was still under construction. The project was a four-company joint venture called the Greater Nile Petroleum Operating Company (GNPOC) that was developing oil fields and building a pipeline to the coast and a terminal to load the oil onto tanker ships. Arakis's partners in the project – who would now become Talisman's partners – were three state-owned oil companies: China National, Sudan's Sudapet, and Malaysia's Petronas. In other words, Talisman found itself doing business in a very nasty part of the world and partnered with two and a half dictatorships (Malaysia being the half). The oil business is like that: it's filled with some pretty unpleasant characters.

Talisman became the operator of the consortium. It quickly finished building the project, and by the summer of 1999, GNPOC was producing oil at an impressive clip of 150,000 barrels a day,[1] just as world oil prices were starting to rise.[2] Things got even better: by 2002, production was up to 240,000 barrels a day. The four companies made a healthy profit, and the government of Sudan was positively rolling in cash. In a country where per capita gross domestic product (GDP) was about $100 per month,[3] the economic boon offered a chance to lift millions of the world's poorest people out of misery. By 2008, oil represented 95 per cent of Sudan's exports and most of its government revenues.[4] By 2009, Sudan's proven reserves were a whopping 5 billion barrels of oil, and the country had been invited to join OPEC. It had hit the big time.

Of course, the first thing Sudan's dictatorship did with its petrodollars was build up its military. U.S. president Bill Clinton had imposed sanctions on Sudan in 1997, citing Sudan's "support for international terrorism, efforts to destabilize neighboring governments, and perpetration and sponsorship of pervasive human rights violations."[5] But there were plenty of countries all too willing to take Sudan's new-found wealth. Khartoum went on a spending spree, buying armoured vehicles and attack helicopters from Russia and artillery from Belarus and plenty more from whomever would sell to them. Sudan's military budget grew 45 per cent in just two years, from 1999 to 2001. The government spent more than half of its oil windfall on weapons.

Now, Sudan has never been the closest of friends with its neighbours, but the enemies it really worries about are internal. Sudan has had some form of civil war going on for more than a century – Winston Churchill himself fought there in 1898 and wrote a best-selling book about its warring factions.[6] Save for a few ragtag NGO charities, Talisman, based in peaceful Calgary, Alberta, Canada, was pretty much the only liberal institution in the country.

Talisman's state-owned partners had no problem with Sudan's militarization – in fact, besides being a co-owner of GNPOC, China acted as a major arms exporter to Sudan, selling them everything from T-59 tanks to anti-aircraft guns.[7] T-59s are a Chinese version of a Russian tank first built in the 1940s. They're hardly a leading-edge weapon. But when you're fighting against defenceless civilians or lightly armed rebels, a sixty-year-old tank will do just fine.

While Sudan's government did well off the deal, it's fair to call GNPOC a Chinese project. They own the biggest stake, at 40 per cent. And then they earn back most of Sudan's share too, by selling Sudan weapons. China also happens to be the largest buyer of Sudanese oil, sopping up 55 per cent of the country's exports.[8] They now operate the GNPOC facilities too.

It wouldn't be too much of a stretch to call Sudan a subsidiary of China. And in return for Sudan's fealty, China is

Khartoum's protector, vetoing any attempts by the United Nations to sanction Sudan for its Darfur massacre.[9]

As Sudan got richer, and its military got stronger, its abuses of the human rights of its own people got bolder. This didn't bother Sudan's Malaysian or Chinese partners, but it became a huge problem for Talisman, a publicly traded company headquartered in a country that places a high value on freedom of the press, human rights, and a culture of corporate accountability.

As Sudan's behaviour got worse, and as the world's democracies started to isolate Khartoum diplomatically, Talisman found itself in the hot seat as one of the only pressure points that Western politicians still had on the regime in Khartoum. Mere months after Talisman's investment, Lois Wilson, a Canadian senator who was formerly the president of the World Council of Churches, called for pressure to be put on Talisman if peace negotiations in Sudan were unsuccessful by the spring of 1999.[10] Of course, Talisman wasn't a party to those peace negotiations, but Wilson knew that if Talisman could be cajoled into lobbying against Sudan's excesses, they would have a better chance of being listened to than an impotent Canadian politician. Certainly China wasn't about to complain. Nor was Malaysia. Talisman went to Sudan to pump oil. But it was soon forced by politicians and public opinion to be the West's human rights ambassador too.

And Talisman tried. In what must have been a bizarre conversation, Talisman's CEO, Jim Buckee, met with senior Sudanese government officials in 2000 to press GNPOC to adopt a code of conduct that respected human rights. Buckee and his vice-president, Jacqueline Sheppard, flew to Beijing and Kuala Lumpur to meet with the presidents of China National and Petronas and to press them to adopt the same liberal ethics Talisman had suggested to Sudan's government. It surprised no one that the pleadings of two Canadian oil executives were unable to accomplish in Beijing what hundreds of massacred students at Tiananmen Square could not accomplish. If the full force of the U.S. sanctions (and cruise missile attacks ordered by Clinton against Sudan in 1998) weren't enough to make Sudan liberalize itself, surely Talisman lacked the persuasive power too.

Talisman couldn't convince its thuggish partners to respect human rights, but it could at least practise what it preached. By September 2000 – barely a year after buying Arakis's stake – medical clinics, paid for by Talisman, started popping up in the areas of GNPOC's operations. They built five such clinics, drilled four new high-capacity water wells, and maintained another twenty-eight along the pipeline route.

Talisman built a sixty-bed hospital in the town of Heglig, with four doctors and a twenty-four-hour emergency ward. They built four schools and subsidized sixty-five thousand acres of farmland. Talisman provided two thousand artificial limbs for amputees in Khartoum – hardly a standard expense for a Canadian oil company to incur. And then there were the women's entrepreneurial workshops in the Shagara and Mayo refugee camps – quite a change for women used to living under sharia law.[11]

Even though Talisman couldn't get its partners to abide by a code of ethics, it implemented one of its own in its operations. According to its Corporate Social Responsibility Report issued in April 2002, Talisman set up its own Human Rights Monitoring and Incident Investigation Program and opened twenty-one files – a bit of a risky endeavour in a fascist country. Talisman even made some progress lobbying Khartoum: the

Sudanese government allowed Talisman to publicize the amount of revenue the government itself made from the oil fields, a novel act of transparency in a secretive dictatorship. And when Sudanese helicopter gunships killed twenty-four civilians at an emergency food relief centre in February 2002, Buckee wrote a letter of complaint directly to President Al-Bashir – which likely would have incurred a death sentence had it come from anyone else.

Talisman had clearly made life better for many people in Sudan, but it wasn't enough. The public pressure against the company for even operating in the country was just too much. Sudan may have been impervious to sanctions, but Talisman wasn't – the constant threat of punishment by the Canadian and U.S. governments depressed Talisman's share price, despite its economic successes in Sudan. Anti-Sudan protesters had found GNPOC's soft spot. Buckee had decided that he preferred being an oilman to being a public relations agent for one of the world's most odious regimes. So in October 2002, Talisman announced that it would sell its Sudan assets to India's state-owned Oil and Natural Gas Corporation. "We say welcome to the Indian company," declared Sudan's energy minister, Awad al-Jaz.[12] Of course he did: life would actually be easier for him without Talisman's constant nagging to answer to anymore – nor their human rights investigators. "This deal was done with the consent of all and everybody is happy," said al-Jaz. Well, Talisman was at least happy to put an end to being the world's diplomatic scapegoat, and India was happy to buy into a profitable oil field (India also buys Sudanese oil). But how about the thousands of Sudanese who had come to rely on Talisman's network of social services – and their human rights advocacy?

Talisman completed its sale in 2003. Incredibly, it continued paying for its social infrastructure until 2008, at a cumulative cost of $14 million.[13]

The last, big, socially conscious Western company was hounded out of Sudan. And at precisely the same time, Sudan's ethnic cleansing of Darfur began in earnest.[14]

Was it a coincidence that, at the same moment Sudan's only on-the-ground watchdog was driven out by noisy activists in North America that the Sudanese government ramped up its genocide in Darfur? If Talisman had remained on the ground, would their presence have restrained Khartoum? No one knows. But one thing is clear. By driving Talisman out of GNPOC, Western human rights activists put a new boss in charge of GNPOC: China, a country with one of the world's worst human rights records. Would China, the country with the world's highest execution rate, really care if Sudan killed a few tribespeople to pump oil? Would the country that killed 50 million of its own people in Mao's Great Leap Forward really quarrel with Sudan if it wanted to massacre 300,000 of its own?

As Human Rights Watch noted after Talisman left, "[China National] and Petronas . . . have shown little interest in corporate responsibility, however; they are state-owned corporations based in countries, Malaysia and China, whose governments have shown little interest in human rights accountability."

Was anyone unaware of that fact before they helped hound Talisman out of Sudan? Talisman was hypersensitive to criticism; it spent millions of dollars in social services and human rights on the ground; it spent an enormous amount of management time wrestling with ethical issues that were more properly the domain of diplomats. Didn't the activists who were on

Talisman's case – people like Lois Wilson and Human Rights Watch – ever ask themselves, if Talisman left, "Then what?"

In HRW's report on Talisman, there's this little gem: the Chinese oil company "did not respond to Human Rights Watch correspondence mailed or faxed to its Sudan office and in care of the Chinese embassy in the U.S." Talisman was in constant contact with HRW and other groups who expressed concerns about Sudan. China National wouldn't even respond to their letters. So HRW's report "concludes that the [remaining] companies are inappropriately operating in Sudan and should suspend their operations unless and until the steps recommended below are taken by both the companies and the government of Sudan."

Are they serious? They can't even get their letters answered, but they think that the government-owned oil companies of China, India, and Malaysia are going to simply pick up and leave a lucrative investment?

There is a sense of postpartum depression in HRW's lengthy report card on Talisman. It's almost as if they'll miss having a Western, liberal company to kick around. It's not as easy to tackle an oil company headquartered in Beijing, where there is no freedom of the press, freedom of assembly or mobility rights – the building blocks of political activism. The only reason the onslaught of the NGOs worked against Talisman was precisely because it was a liberal company, sensitive to public opinion. By definition, it would be the vulnerable partner in GNPOC – the only one they could drive out.

HRW adds a hilariously wishful anecdote to its report: "The head of one advocacy group warned PetroChina investors with this sound bite: 'If you want to be tarred with this radioactive slave stock then we will do that.'" Really? HRW has yet to write a 581-page report, like they did about Talisman, condemning PetroChina (a China National subsidiary). Says HRW, "the anti-PetroChina coalition represented possibly the most effective example of shareholder activism since the South Africa divestment campaign." Perhaps HRW's donors believe that bravado. But PetroChina is now the world's richest company, by stock market value. How is that a success?

Reg Manhas, the Talisman executive who was in charge of corporate social responsibility during their Sudan years, has a more realistic view. With "large state-owned companies directly competing for resources against western publicly-traded companies," he wrote after the sale to India, "divestment is a blunt instrument that only creates pressure on those companies from which divestment is even possible (generally western, publicly-listed companies)."[15]

This is the critical thing to understand about how activist groups operate: when they call for boycotts, or demand divestment, they can only have any real effect on the organizations that care about those things. Talisman did; as a Canadian company with public relations considerations and corporate social responsibility principles, it preferred to abandon the challenge of Sudan rather than keep trying to do its best under the circumstances. Human rights and environmentalist groups rely on fundraising to keep them in business, and few donors are foolish enough to give money to lost causes: campaigning against PetroChina or the Sudanese government won't bring in much revenue. But a campaign against a Western organization that's vulnerable to public pressure actually offers the hope of progress, which is why activists spend so much of their efforts on pursuing the most ethically conscious actors rather than the irredeemable ones. The result is that they get things exactly backward: they smack-down the good guys and leave the bad guys be. Activists may have succeeded in moving a socially conscious, publicity-sensitive firm like Talisman out of Sudan, but they didn't change a thing on the ground. In fact, they probably made matters worse.

Thanks to the efforts of so-called ethical groups, life is a lot harder for people in Sudan. And it's not just Talisman that learned a hard lesson: any other Western, liberal company has learned from Talisman's experience that no matter how many millions of dollars an oil company spends improving the lives of locals, and no matter how hard it lobbies for human rights, there will be no pleasing NGOs like Human Rights Watch. After all, they've got PR campaigns to run, and as they've admitted, it's a lot easier targeting the Western companies than dictatorships.

Human Rights Watch and a dozen copycats have ensured that good companies will stay out of bad places. How that helps the poor souls of Darfur isn't clear.

One company that hasn't succumbed to global pressure the same way Talisman did is Total S.A., the large French oil company doing business in the Asian dictatorship of Burma, also known as Myanmar. Burma is a totalitarian country under the command of China, just like Sudan is. And, just like Sudan, it was also hit with trade sanctions by President Clinton.[16] But for whatever reasons, Total has been immune to the pressure to divest – so far. In their ethics report, Total does what Human Rights Watch doesn't do – it asks the question: if Total were to leave, then what?

"If we decided to leave," says the Total website dedicated to their Burma operations, "we would immediately be replaced by another company who might not apply the same social or ethical standards. There would be no real impact on the State's revenues or on the political debate, but there would certainly be a negative effect on its people. As long as we believe our operations . . . can contribute to the welfare of the people of Myanmar, we are committed to staying in the country and to demonstrating that our presence is more beneficial for the Myanmar people than our absence could be."[17]

Like Talisman in Sudan, Total runs a suite of social services that has nothing to do with the oil and gas business, and certainly has nothing to do with making money. The fifty thousand Burmese who live near Total's operations – covering twenty-five villages – receive social services that other Burmese can only dream about, including ten doctors, six agricultural advisers, and four veterinarians with nearly forty vet assistants. For comparison, the doctor-to-patient ratio under Total's program is more than ten times what it was before they arrived. Not surprisingly, infant mortality rates have plunged and are far below the national average.

Total has built forty-five schools, doubling the number of children who receive formal education, with a teacher/student ratio of 1:25 – better than many Canadian classrooms. Total has brought micro-credit banking to Burma, and has given out nearly fifteen hundred loans. Most incredibly, Total has actually set up a modest form of democracy in Burma, with a series of permanent town hall–style forums that are used to guide Total's socio-economic program and act a forum for human rights concerns too.

These achievements sound incredible; which is why Total invited Bernard Kouchner, the co-founder of Doctors Without Borders, and a personal acquaintance of Aung San Suu Kyi, the

Nobel Peace Prize–winning Burmese democracy activist, to inspect their work. Kouchner is an unlikely defender of a global oil colossus; he's a lifelong left-wing activist whose radical past includes helping to lead the French protests of 1968. He has personally gone to war zones from Rwanda to Lebanon to do relief work. But after inspecting Total's Burma operation, he actually said it was "so successful that it may make others [in Burma] jealous," and Total should consider expanding its program beyond its areas of operation. "It is easy for do-gooders to criticize these efforts," said Kouchner, "since they are far from the danger." Kouchner didn't think Total should stop doing work in Burma. He thought they should be doing more.

Kouchner did have a criticism for Total. He said they should publicly express their political opposition to the Burmese government, and that in addition to doing their work as an energy company and a social service provider, they should do the work of international diplomacy too. There is case to be made for Total speaking out publicly for political reform. But there is something rather precious about politicians and diplomats outsourcing that work to private companies. Surely, of all the things Western politicians can do, using the bully pulpit to criticize Burma is the easiest – it doesn't take talent or money or patience, like running social services for fifty thousand people does. In 2007, Kouchner became France's foreign minister, a post he holds to this day. To his credit, he has made democratic reforms of Burma a priority and hasn't pulled a Talisman on Total.

Total calls their presence in Burma a "sustained commitment," which sounds a lot like the environmentalist call for "sustainable development." Total could surely sell its stake in Burma for a healthy profit; but like Talisman's exit, it's almost a certainty that the acquirer wouldn't maintain Total's social programs. Ironically, the U.S. sanctions on Burma would positively ensure that only companies of the moral character of China's state-owned oil giants would buy it.

So what do Talisman's exit from Sudan and Total's decision to stay in Burma have to do with the Alberta oil sands? The obvious point is how brutal life is in many of the world's oil-producing countries. But there is a less obvious lesson too: international do-gooders don't often look past their immediate tactical goals to see the bigger strategic issues.

Sudan lost a liberalizing force when Talisman left; and so would Burma if Total left. Those two dictatorships wouldn't be any worse off, but their citizens would be.

And that's the problem with the international campaign against Alberta's oil sands. If the anti–oil sands lobby had their way, and oil sands production was slowed or even stopped, then what? The world's oil-thirsty countries would simply replace their ethical oil from Alberta with unethical oil from nasty places like Saudi Arabia and Iran. The world would not be a better place – in fact, it would be worse.

If the oil sands were somehow shut down, it would be an economic disaster for Canadian families, as hundreds of billions of American energy dollars were paid instead to the idle princes of Saudi Arabia, the corrupt politicians of Nigeria, and the bellicose strongman in Venezuela. But that awful price wouldn't make the environment any better – none of those countries has environmental standards equal to Canada's. And then there are the other measures of ethics, from democratic rights and freedom of the press to the treatment of women.

Human Rights Watch has gone pretty quiet about the oil fields in Sudan. They got their way, driving out Talisman – and that made things worse. If groups like ForestEthics got their way and Canada's oil sands were shut down – and replaced by other, nastier sources of oil – what would they do then? The earth wouldn't be any cleaner; forests wouldn't be any safer; and the world wouldn't be using one drop less of gas.

But a lot of good people would be hurt, and a lot of nasty regimes would have a windfall.

The lobbyists at ForestEthics would probably find a new way to keep the donations coming in. But the rest of us would live in a poorer world – poorer economically and poorer morally.

Chapter 4

IF AMERICA DOESN'T BUY OIL SANDS OIL, WHO WILL?

Development of the Alberta oil sands was made possible through the triumph of science and the motivating force of high world oil prices. But their location had a lot to do with it too: they're just a pipeline away from the world's biggest consumer of oil, the United States. That's where every drop of Canadian exports goes.

But what if the United States decides that it no longer wants oil sands oil? What if a thousand retailers get on the bandwagon with Bed Bath & Beyond and Whole Foods? What if gas stations refuse to stock oil sands oil too?

Or, in a more likely scenario, what if President Barack Obama brings in a tax on oil sands oil, or other punitive regulations – as he's promised to do with his "cap and trade" plan, effectively restricting exports from Alberta? Having the United States as your sole customer is pretty great when everything's going well; but if they ever stopped buying oil sands oil, that would be a problem.

Or would it?

To be sure, the oil sands are dominated by Canadian and American oil companies. But increasingly, companies from Japan, Korea, and India are either building, buying, or shopping for oil sands projects of their own.[1] And China – rapidly catching up to the United States as the largest consumer of oil – has calmly been making acquisitions in the area for five years. China National and Sinopec have had stakes for years, and in 2009 massive PetroChina dropped $1.9 billion in its splashiest buy yet – all approved by Canada's Industry Department, despite some public concerns about a foreign government owning such a strategic asset (all of China's oil companies are partly owned and fully controlled by the government).

But – at least for now – such strategic concerns are misplaced. With no pipelines going anywhere but the United States, it's not like Chinese companies could suddenly divert their oil elsewhere, in a strategic strike at Canada or the United States – and even if they tried something extreme or destructive, the oil sands are geographically in Canada and could theoretically be expropriated on grounds of national security.

China is not investing in the oil sands as a military trick; they're looking to put their enormous currency reserves into something other than U.S. treasury bills, and oil sands projects are a good bet – a strategic asset that will surely throw off cash flow for decades to come. As U.S. debt spirals and the price of oil holds, look for tens of billions more in Chinese investments to come knocking on the door in Fort McMurray.

But what if the United States pulled a Talisman on the oil sands? What if all the retail boycotts and all the political pressure from environmental lobbyists was just too much, and the United States did take punitive measures against the oil sands – perhaps even leading to an exodus of U.S.–based firms?

Well, there already is a proposal for an oil sands pipeline flowing from Alberta to supply Asia-bound tanker ships on British Columbia's Pacific coast. Right now it might not make economic sense to build: in addition to building a costly new pipeline, there's the cost of shipping all that unrefined bitumen across the planet too. Who would choose to do that, if they could simply pump it straight to U.S. refineries? But that math would change in a flash if punitive new U.S. regulations came in. A pipeline to the Pacific would allow massive importers like Japan, India, and China to buy from someone other than Saudi Arabia and Iran. Right now, Canada imports more than $40 billion in goods and services from China each year but only sells around $10 billion back to China in return. A pipeline carrying a million barrels of oil a day to China-bound tankers would add $30 billion worth of Canadian exports to China, nearly eliminating our trade deficit with them.

Like Talisman's ouster from Sudan, an American boycott of the oil sands wouldn't shut down the wells. If anti–oil sands groups succeed in convincing the United States to block Alberta oil, it would just mean different companies, from different countries, would pump the oil, while different customers from other markets would buy it – companies and markets immune to American PR campaigns. Not asking "then what?" about a U.S. energy tax on the oil sands could mean giving a country like China even greater access to one of the world's most stable, plentiful reserves of energy while leaving the United States increasingly more reliant on imports from unstable or unscrupulous partners. It would mean the United States handing over its most important strategic energy supply to its growing global rival.

Chapter 5

A MORAL CHECKLIST FOR OIL COMPANIES

So how do companies like Bed Bath & Beyond and Whole Foods know whether the oil they buy "fits their values"? How did they measure the morality of the companies they were buying from? They didn't, really – they took the word of an anti–oil sands lobby group. But is there some independent way to measure the ethics of oil?

Measuring the morality of a company, let alone an entire industry, is difficult. It's tough enough to rate the ethics of an individual person; now try doing it for thousands of people acting together. How can you get more precise than "thumbs-up" or "thumbs-down"? Could you measure ethics on a scale of one to ten, so you could compare different companies? How?

Critics of the oil sands have tried in their own way to quantify their objections, mainly through measuring the environmental side effects of the oil sands – typically with things like how much water is used in the process, how many trees are cut down, and how much pollution is emitted. The most common measurement used by oil sands critics is the emission of carbon dioxide (CO_2) – not a pollutant in the traditional definition of the word but a factor in the theory of human-caused global warming, which suggests that CO_2 from industrial processes is warming up the atmosphere.

Those measurements aren't a bad way to start. Each of those criteria can be assigned a real number, which makes comparisons to other energy sources practical. But surely there are other factors in corporate morality besides the amount of water going in and the amount of CO_2 coming out. What else should we measure, and how?

It's the most important question to ask, for obvious reasons. If your measurement of morality ignores an oil company's role in supporting terrorists, you'll rank oil from Saudi Arabia a lot higher than if you gave points for promoting peace on your list. Same thing for the equality of men and women: if it's not on your list, you'd probably be happy with oil from Sudan and Iran. Whole Foods didn't even list their criteria – their opposition to the oil sands was more of an expression of personal esthetics and political fashion. But that's not ethics – that's politics.

Sometimes, though, making sensational headlines seems to be the only ethical criterion for some lobby groups. Take the U.K. leftist group Platform, which released a report in early 2010 on the oil sands, calling them "blood oil."[1] It was a deliberate homage to the theme of "blood diamonds," the African-mined diamonds that are the root of so much violence in that continent. It's a powerful phrase, but Platform's report didn't really measure the bloodiness of oil from around the world, which would have actually been a very useful moral guide. It just used the phrase "blood oil," without bothering to provide any real justification for it, as an insult – and a surefire way to make headlines. That's Platform's job – it's an activist group that likes to whip up political sentiments. But by declaring the oil sands to be bloody, while not saying a word about actual bloodshed for oil – in places like Iran, Sudan, and Nigeria, for example – can Platform really be taken seriously?

That's the thing about corporate ethics: if you're not measuring the right things, good intentions can really cause you to veer off course. Following Platform would steer a conscientious consumer away from Canadian oil and toward Saudi oil. That's not moral.

So if we can't rely on the Platforms of the world, who can we rely on? There are experts out there who do nothing but rate corporate ethics, and some have come up with elaborate lists of up to three hundred questions they ask to make their determinations. Make no mistake: these measures are taken very seriously. Covalence SA, one of the major ranking firms, based in Geneva, was ranked in 2009 by *Ethisphere* magazine – a business magazine focused on corporate ethics – among the 100 Most Influential People in Business Ethics; Covalence's research is transmitted by the world's biggest business news organizations, Bloomberg, Capital IQ, and Thomson Reuters, to institutional investors including governments, pension funds, and mutual funds. The information becomes part of the investment-decision matrix for some of the most powerful market movers out there. More than that, it becomes an official part of the record, influencing how the wider world perceives various corporations: those who do well in these ethical rankings promote their standings, and the rankings, lending them ever greater weight. Measuring the ethics of industry has become an industry itself.

The capitalist icon Dow Jones, for example, has a Sustainability Index that ranks and measures hundreds of companies based on "long-term economic, environmental and social criteria." Dow Jones uses hundreds of criteria, including "climate change strategies, energy consumption, human resources development, knowledge management, stakeholder relations and corporate governance."[2] The DJSI is designed to allow investors to screen out "unethical" companies and to track the financial success of ones deemed green and peaceful enough to make the list.

Trouble is, many of DJSI's questions reflect their own biases and political fashions. For example, their "operational eco-efficiency" questions require companies to disclose their greenhouse gas emissions, like carbon dioxide, but not more traditional measures of pollution, like sulphur dioxide or airborne particulates, elements of smog that actually affect air quality. Such a bias means the DJSI could quite feasibly end up giving higher ecological marks to an industrial factory that belched out sooty, lung-scarring smoke than to an organic farm whose livestock emitted the natural gases that animals do.

The DJSI tries to measure employee freedom, but again it prejudges how employees must use that freedom. Companies with labour unions score higher than companies without them, even if employees have the right to organize, but choose not to, or if they choose a more modern approach instead – like employee share-ownership programs. And the DJSI absorbs the bias of third-party observers too: part of their ethical assessment of companies is based on what's written about the firms they rate in various media articles, which are bound to occasionally include unchecked factual errors or simply a journalist's grudge. DJSI even uses "stakeholder commentary" – an impossibly vague catch-all that could include everything from the comments of disgruntled ex-employees to competitors.

If Dow Jones's approach doesn't suit you, there are plenty of others in the ethical rankings business. Covalence SA gets 95 per cent of its data about the companies it tracks from the Internet.[3] "Every day," the company explains, it "receives 3,000 Google alerts that are dispatched among analysts for selection and codification." Covalence hires student interns[4] each year to do the groundwork, sifting through the thousands of emails that mention the companies they track.

Like Dow Jones, Covalence's method has no shortage of flaws. There's the built-in bias of using Google as the universe of ethics. Here's a quick illustration: Exxon, the largest American oil company, has nearly 7 million mentions on Google and a large number of Google news alerts every day. By contrast, Saudi Aramco – by far the largest oil producer in the world, four times as big as Exxon – has fewer than 600,000 mentions on Google. It's four times bigger than Exxon but has less than one-tenth of the Google coverage. And then there's the English-language bias of Google; Saudi Arabia's underdeveloped Internet and lack of a free press; and the fact that Covalence interns don't read Arabic anyways.

That's a bias problem that goes far larger than Covalence. Take the mighty New York Times. Saudi Aramco was mentioned on just eleven occasions in 2008 by the Times, four of which were because an Aramco ship was seized by pirates. In Canada, Saudi Aramco was mentioned just seven times in the Globe and Mail (three for the pirate hijacking), and in the United Kingdom, the Daily Telegraph mentioned it just three times (once for the pirates).

Exxon, over the same period, was mentioned 227 times in the Globe, 218 times in the Times, and 43 times in the Telegraph.[5]

That's quite something, given that Saudi Aramco is the largest oil company in the world, when measured by oil and gas production, or reserves. Aramco has 260 billion barrels of oil in the ground, plus 263 trillion cubic feet of natural gas.[6] It pumps 8.9 million barrels of oil each day, plus millions more in gas and liquefied natural gas. ExxonMobil's oil reserves are a tiny fraction of that, 12 billion barrels,[7] and its daily production of oil and gas was equivalent to 3.9 million barrels per day.

But that's the thing about scrutinizing the ethics of the world's energy sources. Most of them, being foreign state owned, are hidden behind natural barriers to scrutiny: a language barrier; a lack of a free press; and the fact that the truly massive oil companies in the world are owned by governments, often dictatorships – so they don't issue annual reports or submit to public audits or shareholders meetings, the source of so much information on the likes of Exxon.

Covalence only codes information in English, French, German, and Spanish – not Arabic, Farsi, Chinese, or Russian. That guarantees that news about the ethical conduct of most of the world's largest oil and gas companies simply isn't even considered by Covalence. Not that there's much on the Internet to go by; most citizens of OPEC nations can only dream of a news media that wasn't under the thumb of the government. So when the world's largest oil companies make their profits – or make their oil spills – it's not announced in press releases, and journalists and NGOs can't lob "gotcha" questions at shareholders meetings. Because there are no shareholders meetings.

But the problem with Covalence's rankings is even bigger: as a matter of policy, they refuse to treat some sources of information as more reliable than others. Any source is considered equally and everything counts.[8]

Covalence publishes a list of the countless sources they weigh. It can actually be quite hilarious: their interns give the same weight to oil and gas news from sources like the Socialist Party UK, websites like gay.com and vegetariani.it, and the Girl Scouts of Northern California as they do to information from the Sierra Club, *The New York Times,* and Harvard's Kennedy School of Government.

In other words, any company that simply floods the Internet with self-serving spam can cancel out academic-quality research into environmental quality or civil rights. Covalence even counts emails from individuals – no matter their expertise, bias, or vendetta – to influence their studies. Any rambling blogger with an axe to grind that shows up on a Google search can counterbalance the most serious think-tank. Covalence even lists a blog called Ella Does Squamish as a source.[9] (According to photos on the website, Ella was a dog living in British Columbia.[10])

Even fake online nicknames count. Covalence lists "crap-713three" as a contributor on the same spreadsheet as the UN's well-regarded World Health Organization.

It's not really science. It's gossip that weighs Ella the dog as highly as Amnesty International.

Based on this strange ranking system, Covalence publishes an annual ranking of thirty oil and gas companies. In 2009,[11] they put StatoilHydro, the Norwegian company with an interest in Alberta's oil sands, right at the top. Suncor was second, British Petroleum was third, and EnCana was fourth – all of which have major stakes in the oil sands too. Shell ranked at twenty-five and Exxon at twenty-eight.

Saudi Aramco? It's not even on the list. Neither is the massive National Iranian Oil Company, or Pemex, or Venezuela's

PdeVSA. In fact, not one OPEC company is on the list. The only state-dominated company ranked is China National Offshore Oil Corporation, placing sixteenth.

By comparison, Talisman Energy is ranked nineteenth. If this were 2001 and Talisman still owned its Sudan stake, that ranking might even be justifiable. But since leaving Sudan, Talisman has made itself one of the oil-patch ethics leaders, voluntarily submitting to all sorts of reporting and disclosure standards. It's a participant in the UN's Global Compact, a group of companies that have basically pledged to be social service providers around the world. It's included in the Dow Jones Sustainability (North America) Index and is the first Canadian company to join the Voluntary Principles on Security and Human Rights Plenary Group.[12] Talisman has gone from being the bad boy of Canadian oil companies to being a do-gooder of the first order. If it's possible to call an oil company a human rights activist, Talisman is it.

Yet they were beat by China Offshore, a major branch of the communist state's national energy enterprise. How could that be? A review of Talisman's corporate responsibility report reads like a Green Party election platform, full of principles about promoting "security and human rights," "trust and respect," and of moving "beyond traditional indicators of good governance into industry-leading practices in corporate respon-sibility."[13] China Offshore, with talk of creating a "bright future for our country and people, and to forge ahead in the harmoni-ous development of people, society and the environment,"[14] reads like the blueprint of a Stalinist five-year plan. Which, come to think of it, is exactly what China Offshore is.

It's owned 70 per cent by the Chinese government, some-thing you could guess just by reading its own list of proud accomplishments in its annual report. For example, China Offshore boasts[15] that its employees get a full five days a year off – but only if they are "conforming to relevant conditions." What liberals! Like many multibillion-dollar oil companies, China Offshore says it considers it important to give something back to the community. Its annual report highlights its generosity: a donation of u.s.$5,800 to the grindingly poor country of Kazakhstan – where China Offshore probably extracts $5,800 worth of oil every thirty seconds. That was so uncharacteristically generous of it that it considered it worthy of writing up in its annual report. It even brags that fully 12 per cent of its employees are women. That's pretty low, but in fairness it is higher than the 0 per cent women that Saudi Aramco would report, if Saudi Aramco bothered to do an annual report.

The five days off a year and $5,800 charitable fund comprise the list of good things – the things China Offshore wants you to know, no matter how scanty they may look compared to the quarter-billion dollars Exxon donates to various charitable causes every year.[16] But there are some things that even the tone-deaf buffoons writing China Offshore's propaganda are smart enough not to even attempt to spin.

China Offshore is one of sixty-nine Chinese companies working the military dictatorship of Burma.[17] While Total S.A. in Burma spends money building schools, clinics, and democracy, bringing Western humanitarian values to the totalitarian state, China Offshore brings its own values, from Beijing. It's the closest thing to being back home.

In China, when an oil company wants to drill on land, it just goes ahead and drills – and if peasants on top get a few yuan in compensation, they should consider themselves lucky. There are no property rights in China, and all the big oil players are majority owned by the government. When China Offshore comes for your oil, you can't complain to the government – China Offshore *is* the government. When it's operating in Burma, it behaves in the same way. Given that the Burmese junta is a client state of Beijing,[18] that's no surprise.

When China Offshore moved into Burma in a big way, it discovered plenty of oil – and a lot of little Burmese entrepreneurs making a living pumping it. Arakan Oil Watch (AOW), a human rights NGO focused on the western Arakan State in Burma, reports that in one particularly resource-rich region, where crude oil lay close to the surface and was easy for locals to pump on a small-scale base, which they used to help supplement their meagre incomes from farming and fishing, China Offshore simply showed up and confiscated the real estate. Local owners were just cleared out and offered a comical U.S.$31 for their land, regardless of the size or value. AOW estimates that five hundred to one thousand local oil drillers were put out of business, simply brushed aside by China Offshore like they were stray cats. With such callous disregard for the rights of locals, it's no surprise that China Offshore has created what AOW calls "wanton pollution of rice fields and water systems."

If you think that a ranking system that omits OPEC countries and puts China Offshore ahead of Talisman is broken, you're not alone. But Covalence's crazy Google system – and its perverse results – has landed them a lot of blue-chip clients,[19] from Coca-Cola and Alcan to BMW and the World Wildlife Fund. Covalence doesn't just have an audience, it has paying clients – some of the world's biggest multinational are forking over top dollar for Covalence's research.

There are plenty of other companies out there who will give you their ethical opinions for a price too. The confidently named Spanish company Management & Excellence S.A. (M&E) does a bit more than just Googling the companies they track. They rely primarily on companies' self-reporting of various criteria. In other words, it's partly a test of the companies' ability to fill out forms well.

M&E uses four hundred standards set by different agencies or laws, ranging from the Securities and Exchange Commission rules, to the U.S. Sarbanes-Oxley governance standards, to UN agencies. They even incorporate other ranking sources, like those of Dow Jones.[20]

M&E conducts an onsite audit of companies,[21] and ranks them, report card–style, from AAA+ to D. Clients are shown the proposed scores before they're published and are allowed to object – which raises questions about M&E's independence but probably avoids errors too.

M&E uses more relevant data than Covalence does. But there is something disconcerting about a company that holds itself out as an independent judge of corporations and then propositions those same corporations to become clients. For a fee, M&E promises to help promote the good news about a company, "using our strong media contacts."[22] Say, what are the ethics of being both a referee and a player at the same time?

Like Covalence, M&E publishes a ranking of "most sustainable" oil and gas companies. Their 2008 rankings[23] put Petrobras, the Brazilian oil company, at the top, with a score of 92.25 per cent. Unlike Covalence, M&E ranks OPEC producers. "Companies with the poorest governance and sustainability practices generally controlled the largest oil/gas reserves," they wrote, noting that the Saudi, Venezuelan, and Abu Dhabi companies received a score of zero for governance – but together control 430 billion barrels of oil. Not a single Canadian-owned company was ranked.

Examining what goes on behind these unusual, and highly questionable, ranking methods is extremely important to understanding how we can get such a distorted view of the ethical behaviours of different energy producers. The flawed methodologies, the biases, the conflicts of interest, they're all obvious reasons we need to be circumspect about these kinds of lists. This isn't just a story about oil companies. It's also a story about a self-proclaimed ethics industry that has sprouted up to take advantage of legitimate public concerns about oil ethics. These corporate analyses are so whimsical that two different rankings of the same industry can come up with precisely the opposite results. Some rankings are just an exercise in oil companies filling out forms and checklists; sometimes they're useless Google searches; sometimes the ratings agencies actually allow themselves to be hired by the oil companies. It's become a game, not a genuine moral investigation.

In order to get an idea of how a real-life ethical evaluation might look, rather than a jury-rigged ranking, let's compare two oil companies.

ExxonMobil is the largest U.S. oil company. PetroChina is China's largest oil company. In fact, based on market capitalization – the value of its shares, according to the stock market – PetroChina is the largest company in the world,[24] worth U.S.$366 billion. That's 73 per cent more valuable than Microsoft and nearly double the market capitalization of Wal-Mart. Perhaps the clearest way to compare the ethics of these two energy behemoths is to compare how they dealt with catastrophes: the *Exxon Valdez* oil spill in 1989 and PetroChina's chemical explosion in the northern Chinese city of Jilin in 2005.

The unhappy story of the *Exxon Valdez* is one of the world's most famous industrial accidents: while dodging icebergs, the crew of a large oil tanker ran aground in Alaska, spilling 38,800 tonnes of oil[25] – or about 257,000 barrels. No one was hurt, but 35,000 bird carcasses and 1,000 dead sea otters were found. It wasn't the biggest oil spill in history – it's not even in the top fifty, by volume. (For comparison, ten years earlier, two very large tankers collided in the Caribbean, spilling 287,000 tonnes, or 2.1 million barrels, of oil – eight times bigger than the *Valdez*. And even that mega-spill is dwarfed by a blowout of the Pemex Ixtoc 1 offshore oil rig in 1979: for nine full months oil spilled into the Gulf of Mexico,[26] totalling 3.3 million barrels – or the equivalent of thirteen *Exxon Valdez*es. And then there was Saddam Hussein's environmental weapon against the Allies in the first Gulf War: the dictator simply opened up the taps, dumping 11 million barrels of oil into the sea, in a bizarre environmental equivalent to the nuclear doctrine of "mutually assured destruction." That's like forty *Valdez*es.)

The *Valdez* got far more attention, though, because it was on the American coastline, not out at sea or in a faraway country; because the media had easy access to the site; and, frankly, because it's Exxon, and not Saudi Aramco – who, for all we know given its lack of a free press, has had even larger spills that remain unreported to this day.

But probably the biggest reason that makes the *Valdez* incident so famous is that Exxon itself responded to the spill with the largest environmental cleanup in history.[27] Exxon hired 10,000 workers, 1,000 boats, and 100 planes and helicopters to battle the oil slick and clean up the birds and others – a number larger than most countries' armed forces. The total cost of the cleanup to Exxon was $2.1 billion – a number that grew to $3.5 billion[28] once fines and punitive damages were added in.

And none of that begins to calculate the PR damage done to Exxon's image. The ecosystem in Alaska has recovered over the past twenty years, but not Exxon's reputation.

It wasn't the spill that was the largest in history – not by a long shot. It wasn't the ecological damage that was the largest. It was the corporate responsibility that was the largest in history. That's actually why the name *Valdez* is famous. The word *Ixtoc* should be synonymous for oil spills. But when you're an oil company owned by the Mexican government, you really don't have a lot to fear from the Mexican government if you break every environmental law in the book – and then there's the fact that Ixtoc was out in the middle of the sea, not easy for CNN to camp out for weeks with video cameras.

Now, compare all that to the massive explosion at PetroChina's chemical factory in Jilin City[29] in 2005. Six workers died in the blast and scores more were injured. Ten thousand nearby residents were evacuated.[30] One hundred tons of poisonous benzene and other pollutants poured into the Songhua River that runs through Harbin City, forcing authorities to shut off running water to the 3.8 million residents for five days. Toxic waste formed an eighty-kilometre slick in the river that oozed along, crossed over into Russia, and finally ended in the sea.

The first response by PetroChina, and their government masters, was the one favoured by dictatorships that are thin-skinned when it comes to criticism: they deny there's a problem. That was the official Soviet line in 1986 when the Chernobyl nuclear reactor caught fire, and it's been communist China's default response to other public safety crises, such as SARS and other epidemics.[31] In Jilin, company and government officials waited for more than a week before telling the public what had happened. Their initial story was that the explosion released only some carbon dioxide, not toxic chemicals, and that the government order to shut down Harbin's water supply for five days was simply for pipeline "maintenance."[32]

That's a pretty typical arc for any story involving corporate or government responsibility in a dictatorship. Step one is to simply stay silent for as long as possible. When that no longer works – such as when an eighty-kilometre toxic slick has reached a city of 3.8 million people – the next step is to lie about what's going on. Step three is to confess to the whole sham and noisily demand accountability. Step four is to announce the execution of a scapegoat – thus short-circuiting any genuine investigation into what went wrong and who's to blame.

At least one victim of step four was Wang Wei, the vice-mayor of Jilin City, who was in charge of environmental protection. On the morning of December 7 – more than three weeks after the explosion – Wang was finally planning to set off to investigate the explosion but was found dead at his home.[33] Whether Wang was killed because he actually had some culpability into the matter, or because he might have actually planned to conduct a genuine (and embarrassing) investigation, or because he simply was of the right rank and proximity to serve as the official fall guy is not certain.

What is certain is PetroChina's punishment: a $125,000 fine[34] – or the profits that the company earns in about four minutes of operations.[35]

And we also know for certain that there was no massive cleanup effort – no equivalent to the Exxon army that deployed immediately and stayed in Valdez for four years. Exxon's ten thousand bird-scrubbers were not replicated, though labour in Jilin or Harbin would have cost a mere sliver of what it did to hire people in Alaska. There were no lawsuits, for there are no independent courts in China, and suing a government-controlled enterprise is a ticket to the gulag.

Comparing Exxon's response to *Valdez* to the way a state-owned, unaccountable, non-transparent enterprise like PetroChina reacts to a major ecological and humanitarian disaster illustrates company ethics in a vivid way that so-called corporate ethical rankings simply cannot. So what did the world's self-appointed eco-saviours have to say about China's own version of *Valdez* on a river? (That's actually too generous a comparison, for *Valdez* killed and injured no one – and no one was murdered in a cover-up.) What did Greenpeace have to say about all this?

"We urge the Chinese government to make even greater efforts in protecting the local people and the environment," said Kevin May, toxics campaign manager of Greenpeace China. Really? Even "greater" efforts? But there were no efforts made whatsoever – innocent citizens weren't even told what was going on for a week. The government "should, for example, conduct a comprehensive environmental impact assessment of the pollution," May said, "and, on that basis, draw up a plan and implement effective cleanup."[36]

Six dead, dozens injured, ten thousand evacuated, 3.8 million without water, and the Greenpeace rep can't even bring himself to criticize the government? No condemnation at all – just a helpful suggestion to study things and make up a plan for cleaning things up? To do an "even greater" job next time? The only thing missing from May's talking points was praise for the glorious efforts of the Communist Party and praise for Chairman Mao.

Did PetroChina learn anything from its experience in Jilin? Did it change its approach to public safety, or pollution, or even just transparency? Ask the people of Chengdu, a massive city of 11 million people, where just two years later, PetroChina started building a $5.5 billion ethylene plant.[37] In a dramatic display, hundreds of Chengdu residents took to the street in protest – a criminal act in a country without freedom of assembly. "What Chengdu people demand is very simple," one protestor told *The New York Times*. "This is a policy closely related to people's interest, so why was [environmental and safety reviews] not open to the public?" Where were those "greater efforts" that Greenpeace China had called for? That's easy: they didn't happen. Why should they? PetroChina paid virtually no price for its environmental and humanitarian catastrophe. It didn't face the public outrage that Exxon did for its less harmful disaster, despite its massive restitution efforts.

Just contrast the complete lack of democratic consent, let alone public participation in health and safety and environmental matters. This is the reality of the world's largest corporation. You'd think Greenpeace would care.

PetroChina's parent company, the China Nation Petroleum Corporation, has also been implicated in the deaths of thousands of Sudanese in Darfur, according to Amnesty International and the UN.[38] So why does PetroChina get an A for Effort while Exxon gets slandered? Why has *Valdez* become synonymous with corporate crime, but Jilin is an unknown point on a map? Why did Greenpeace help spin things for the Chinese government but continues to rage against Exxon, even today, fifteen years after its Alaskan spill was cleaned up?

The fact is that all these judgments and rankings about ethics say far more about the judgers and rankers than about the oil companies themselves. For a lot of groups, including Greenpeace, this is more a matter of ideology than one of environment or ethics: Exxon is a leading capitalist company in a leading capitalist country. In 2008, Exxon made more money than any other publicly listed company – a whopping U.S.$45.2 billion.

But with mighty profits come mighty taxes, and in 2008 Exxon paid some $36.5 billion in income tax, plus $34.5 billion in sales-based taxes, plus $41.7 billion in "other taxes and duties."[39] In other words, that one company paid more income tax than the bottom 50 per cent of all U.S. taxpayers combined.[40] And if you add in Exxon's other taxes and duties – for a total of more than $113 billion each year – that's more than the entire budget of the state of California.[41] And Exxon contributes to Americans' prosperity with more than just corporate taxes: most of Exxon's $477 billion in revenues are spent on everything from equipment to employee salaries – each of whom, in turn, pays their own taxes. Exxon doesn't just operate as a moral company in times of crisis. Just by being there, it provides nearly eighty thousand jobs directly and countless more indirectly.

This is not a love letter to Exxon. It's a comparison of the actual virtues and vices of Exxon, one of the most demonized companies in the world, with its proper comparators – PetroChina, Saudi Aramco, and the other super-majors. The choice the world has is not between Exxon or nothing, or the Alberta oil sands or nothing. It's between Exxon or PetroChina, between the Alberta oil sands or Saudi Arabia.

Which company would you rather have operating in your city? That's a question you probably couldn't have answered in any useful way by the world's official ethics measurers. In the end, it's up to each of us to decide what the important criteria are, instead of outsourcing our moral judgment to someone else. We've each got to decide what's important to us – whether it's carbon dioxide, terrorism, or the treatment of minorities.

Before the Dow Jones Sustainability Index, Covalence, and M&E came along to apply their eccentric methods in ways that ranked ethical corporate behaviour, we once entrusted the job of arbitrating moral quandaries to our religious leaders. To their credit, the Canadian group Kairos – a coalition of a half-dozen large liberal churches in Canada, including the United Church, Anglicans, Catholics, Mennonites, and Quakers – has taken on the task of judging the oil sands using more traditional Western values. At the very least, judging oil sands operators based on criteria more substantive, and established, than what the world's bloggers have to say about them would seem to promise a more helpful perspective for those of us who put more stock in Judeo-Christian notions of ethics than some arbitrary framework drawn up by a bunch of Swiss consultants.

Kairos is a pretty serious outfit with a pretty serious interest in the oil sands: it had more than twenty staff[42]; in 2008, its annual budget exceeded $4 million,[43] $1.5 million of which came from the Canadian government. Its largest single project, its most pressing concern, according to its annual report, is Energy Justice, with a focus on the oil sands. Kairos did manage to scrape together $148,000, or 3.7 per cent of its budget, for "anti-poverty" grants. But apparently it's too busy pondering the morality of the oil sands to bother with all that "feed the hungry, clothe the poor" business.

As part of its Energy Justice campaign, Kairos sent a fact-finding delegation to the oil sands in the summer of 2009. Mind you, calling it "fact-finding" is a bit of a stretch: months before they went on their junket, Kairos blatantly declared its determined opposition to the oil sands in a lengthy paper called *Christian Faith and the Canadian Tar Sands*,[44] published in September 2008 – nearly a year before they actually studied the place first-hand. Shoot at the oil sands first, ask questions later.

Nevertheless, Kairos outlines some respectable criteria by which it proposes to judge the morality of oil sands energy. The paper lists four core values to be considered: justice, peace, sustainability, and democratic decision making (Kairos called it "participation"). It's pretty tough to disagree with those criteria, even if they're defined rather creatively. At least Kairos proposes a broader and more reasonable definition of oil ethics than just the number of pounds of carbon dioxide per barrel of oil.

Kairos explains that measuring justice means "access to affordable energy." Now, economists would say that this is strictly a matter of supply – the more of something there is, the lower its price; more oil from Alberta means cheaper oil overall. "Do the tar sands promote a fairer distribution of energy between rich and poor, both within Canada and in the broader global community?" asks Kairos. "Do they promote a fairer distribution of wealth in general between rich and poor?"

It's a biased question, implying that there is something immoral about wealth, as if economic success is rooted solely in luck, or sharp dealing, rather than ingenuity and hard work, but in some oil-producing nations, poverty can be directly linked to corruption and unfair play. So, let's accept Kairos's first criterion, more or less: no oil-producing region or company can actually set the price of oil, but surely an ethical producer of oil would treat the workers on the lowest rung with respect and allow them to share in the profits of the venture.

Kairos's second criterion in its evaluation of the oil sands is peace. "Do the tar sands promote peace either directly or indirectly? Do they promote violence and conflict directly or indirectly?" That's an even better one; it should probably have been a higher priority than the economics of oil. It's one thing to be poor but free and safe; it's quite another to be subject to fear, violence, and even death. Most of the world's oil reserves are found in dictatorships, especially the brutal, hostile dictatorships of the Middle East. Surely the violence associated with producing a barrel of oil has an enormous impact on the ethics of that barrel. Given the stark contrast between Alberta's blissful peace and OPEC's strife, these are easy points for the oil sands.

The third criterion Kairos lists is "sustainability and the integrity of Creation" – otherwise known as environmentalism. "What kind of ecological impact do the tar sands have?" it asks. "Do humans have the right to make such drastic changes which may have dire consequences for the rest of the creation?"

Again, the question is loaded; it has its own answer built right in – it begins with the premise that the oil sands really are making "such drastic changes" that may have "dire consequences." Still, even with that spin, the oil sands have a fighting chance when stacked up against some of the dismal environmental track records of OPEC nations. That is, after all, what Kairos is ultimately trying to get at, isn't it? It's asking how the oil sands compare to other sources of oil in the world, as opposed to how they rate relative to some magical, imaginary energy source that appears, manna-like, from the hand of God?

Kairos's fourth criterion has to do with democratic participation in decision making. "Particular attention must be focused on those who have historically been marginalized in decision making and power-sharing, such as those living in poverty, women, Indigenous people and racial minorities," says Kairos. "Do the tar sands aid or diminish the ability of Canadians to share in decisions about their energy future? Who is making decisions about the tar sands development? How are men and women differently involved in decisions about the tar sands, in sharing their benefits and dealing with the negative outcomes? How have Indigenous people been consulted and involved in decisions about the tar sands?"

Those tests sound awfully challenging, or at least they probably did when written in Kairos's headquarters in downtown Toronto, before Kairos's trip to the oil sands. When Kairos staff landed in Fort McMurray a year later and realized that, in fact, the oil sands are Canada's largest single employer of "Indigenous people,"[45] and that women have an extraordinarily high participation rate in oil sands work, they probably wished they had chosen a different criterion – or at least one in which the oil sands companies didn't exceed the ethnic diversity of Kairos's staff themselves.

Kairos asks one final question, a wonderful display of anti-industrial utopianism: "Could Canada do without the tar sands? Could it produce and export less oil and gas?"

Of course it could. It's not necessary to our economy – Canada has more than enough oil, without the oil sands, to meet our own domestic energy needs. Sure, if anti–oil sands groups, like Greenpeace and Kairos, had their way, the eighty thousand or so people who work in Fort McMurray, and thousands more across the country, would be out of work. That includes fifteen hundred Aboriginals; perhaps Kairos thinks its exquisite political correctness – calling them "Indigenous peoples" – would make up for putting them out of their jobs. Of course, the end of the oil sands also means countless billions of dollars of private sector income, and public sector taxes, that would be lost, defunding schools and hospitals.

But other than indulging an anti-capitalist fantasy, how would shutting down the oil sands help improve any of Kairos's criteria for Energy Justice?

Canadians wouldn't be short of energy. But the rest of the world would have a lot less – especially the United States, where Canada is the number-one source of oil, ahead of Saudi Arabia. Reduced supply means higher prices – something that would affect the world's poor most of all. Doesn't that contradict Kairos's first criterion – access to affordable energy?

There would still be access, of course – dozens of other countries would jump at the opportunity to replace the oil sands' lost production. But would those other sources meet Kairos's other criteria any better than Canada does? Does the world's largest oil country, Saudi Arabia, really beat the oil sands in terms of peace? Does Nigeria truly share the wealth with its workers better than Canada does? Do Mexico and Venezuela really treat their Aboriginal peoples better than Canada does? Of course we know they don't.

But instead of answering those questions, Kairos takes aim at the very system that delivers the higher standard of human rights, security, and prosperity the group claims to seek, indulging in a socialist assessment of who's making the profits: "The critical question for the churches is, who are the main beneficiaries of this wealth? What portion, if any, of this wealth is accruing to poor people in Canada?"

If any? The majority of oil sands wealth is taken by the government – in royalties, in corporate taxes, and then again in taxes on the thousands of people who work there. In fact, at the time of their report, $1.5 million of Kairos's own budget comes from taxes, a hefty chunk of which comes from oil. You wouldn't think that a church founded by a man who eschewed wealth would be so obsessed by just who was making what money. But then, any church group that spends less than 5 per cent of its budget on poverty programs strayed off course long ago.

Kairos grudgingly acknowledges that many First Nations bands have "benefited significantly from jobs and other economic spin-offs" in the oil sands. But others "further away" haven't. Besides being blindingly obvious, what exactly is the point? If every last First Nations band in Canada doesn't get to work in the oil sands, does that somehow undermine the morality of those who do?

Kairos's criticism of Newfoundlanders and other Atlantic Canadians who have found rewarding work in the oil sands is equally bizarre. Atlantic Canada was "hit hard in recent years by the closing of the fisheries and coal mines," noted Kairos, so thousands migrated to Fort McMurray. Kairos's complaint (and it always has a complaint): "the economic and social impacts on the small communities have been unprecedented as young educated residents and many men have left in search of sources of income. . . . The very survival of some East Coast towns is in doubt."

Got that? If you're in Newfoundland and unemployed or even just poor, Kairos thinks it's immoral for you to leave to find work. Better to be idle and survive on government entitlements. Forget the economic punishment that would entail; what about the social and psychological pain that comes from unemployment or even having a low-income job? Is it the Christian view of Kairos that it is better for people's souls for them to lounge about idly than to work hard for an enormous paycheque? And can it really be serious to argue that it's an ethical failing of oil sands producers that they offer so much opportunity for Canadians?

Talk about seeing the glass half-empty: instead of looking at the bright economic hope given to tens of thousands of Atlantic Canadians, Kairos is looking at the places they left. That's the point, though – they could leave, to earn incomes they could never find at home. Isn't that what a success story looks like?

Likewise, Kairos bemoans in the gravest of tones the influx of workers from abroad that have flocked to the oil sands. Does Kairos know better than those workers what's best for them? There are plenty of other hot spots in the world where foreign workers are in demand – like Saudi Arabia or Dubai. Are those places really better for foreign workers than life in Canada? Because if poor migrant workers aren't coming here, they're either going somewhere else – or languishing in poverty at home.

It's like Kairos was so desperate to find bad news about the oil sands, it literally had to invent it.

If Aboriginals, Newfoundlanders, and foreign workers are all going gangbusters in Fort McMurray, how about the women Kairos was concerned about? "Overall only 28% of jobs in the oil and gas industry are held by women (compared to an average 47% in other sectors of the Canadian economy)," writes Kairos. Is Kairos seriously trying to compare the oil sands – really, a form of mining – with being a clerk at a retail store or a bank?

Of course, the only meaningful comparison would be to compare women's participation in oil industries in other parts of the world like, say, Saudi Arabia. Women aren't even allowed to drive in Saudi Arabia, so it's pretty certain that the number of women driving trucks in Saudi oil fields is approximately zero. Strolling through the other OPEC countries – Iran, Algeria, Kuwait, Libya, and so on — is there any oil patch in the world that is even close to 28 per cent women? Or how about the simple fact that the most powerful politician in the oil sands – the mayor of Fort McMurray – is a young woman, Melissa Blake. If Blake even stepped into the streets in Saudi Arabia without a burka on, and without the supervision of a man who was her relative, she'd be beaten by the mutaween – Saudi's violent religious police. Is that a better way to produce oil?

Instead of oil sands, Kairos proposes an economy run on solar and wind power – something that no country in the world has successfully achieved. The technology is so prohibitively expensive that without massive government subsidies industry simply won't build it. And then there's other, obvious issues, like the fact that every car on the road runs using an internal combustion engine. Nonetheless, Kairos throws its ethical support behind the theoretical possibility of a solar-powered future.

And yet all that pie-in-the-sky optimism about emerging technologies evaporates immediately when Kairos assesses Alberta's plan for "carbon capture and sequestration" (CCS) – a $2 billion program designed to pump CO_2 underground, rather than to let it escape into the atmosphere. "CCS is still in its infancy, unproven in its ability to work and its high cost for the foreseeable future suggests it is unlikely to become a major solution to the industry's greenhouse gas emissions," Kairos says. It may well be right. But every one of those criticisms can be applied to Kairos's fantasy solar-power solution too.

We might have expected as much corrupted morality from Kairos just by taking a look at how it ranks the importance of its campaign issues. Besides spending scarcely a fraction of the resources it devotes to its war on the oil sands to actually helping the needy, Kairos focuses on just a handful of other countries it considers areas of concerns. China, where it just happens that Christians are persecuted for their faith,[46] isn't on the list; neither are any OPEC countries, including Saudi Arabia, Iran, and Venezuela. But the democratic states of Israel and Colombia are – Colombia because it's the only South American country to resist Hugo Chávez's socialism, and Israel because it's just plain easy to pick on. Kairos even describes ways that its members can use shareholder activism to punish companies that operate in Israel's West Bank.[47] It says nothing about boycotting any other country in the world. Apparently the only way Alberta's oil sands could be morally worse, judging by Kairos's priorities, is if they were located in the Jewish state.

Kairos isn't the only church that has left theology behind and embraced amateur economics and geology as a way of delivering a predetermined ethical verdict against the oil sands. Not to be outdone, Bishop Luc Bouchard of the Catholic Church's Diocese of St. Paul wrote a lengthy report of his own.[48] It's hard to be an expert in everything, and while Bishop Bouchard is surely an expert in Catholicism, the same can't be said about his command of the oil sands facts.

"The proposed oil sands projects, if all were to be activated, would remove an area of boreal forest eco-system equivalent in size to the state of Florida," he writes. But that's simply not true; only 2 per cent of the oil sands, by area, are strip mined; the rest is pumped out of the ground like regular oil – with minimal disturbance to forest life. Did Bishop Bouchard even run his report by someone who works in the industry before publishing it – not for ideology, but just to catch the factual whoppers?

Or this: the bishop predicts that by 2011 – next year – the oil sands will emit 80 megatons of CO_2, "far more than all of

Canada's passenger cars. The oil sands plants will then account for 15% of all of Canada's greenhouse gas emissions."

Well, the oil sands had better get cracking: in the next year, to make the bishop's wild prediction come true, they've got just a few months to ramp up emissions from 29.5 megatons to 80 megatons – almost triple. But even the bishop's stats for cars is wrong: according to Environment Canada, in 2007 Canadian cars and SUVs accounted for 86 megatons.

The bishop demands "water removed from the Athabasca should take into account the probability of low flow." Good idea – so good, that's exactly the water management regulations that are in place in Northern Alberta now.

Emitting carbon dioxide is "damaging to Canada's reputation," so future developments "must be paced" to meet the Kyoto Protocol, he writes. No other country in the world has reduced emissions to meet Kyoto; nor has any other industry in Canada, for that matter. Is the bishop saying that only his flock should suffer an economic slowdown – even though the greenhouse gas emissions of the oil sands is just 5 per cent of Canada's total?

That's the unseemly thing about the faddish interest in the oil sands exhibited by some publicity-oriented clergy. There are bigger problems in the world than the oil sands. Each of the complaints lodged by the bishop, and all of the criteria listed by Kairos, are laughably mild in Alberta compared to other places in the world. To criticize Fort McMurray's treatment of women while staying silent about the subjugation of women in Saudi Arabia, Fort McMurray's chief competitor, isn't just foolish and unfair, it's immoral in itself. To criticize Fort McMurray's environment – cleaner air and water than any major city in Canada – without commenting on the toxic swamps that infest, say, OPEC's Nigeria – is to show a staggering level of unseriousness about solving the world's real problems. It is nothing less than bizarre that the real global polluters and ethical abusers are ignored, but industry leaders in Fort McMurray are slandered. It's a shame that the fashionability of denouncing the oil sands appears, for Kairos and Bishop Luc Bouchard, to take priority over acknowledging that for Aboriginals, for women, for the environment, for Canadians, for migrant workers, for the poor, and for peace, the oil sands represent a more decent way of producing petroleum than any other realistic alternative out there. But evidently, it does.

It's also evident that as much as it would be easier for all of us to outsource our moral analysis to the self-appointed arbiters at ratings agencies or clergy, the stakes are simply too high to risk the poor or misguided judgment of others. The reality is that if we are going to arrive at a truly meaningful judgment of the oil sands ethics in a realistic context that values real human rights, real prosperity, real peace, and real environmental stewardship over the actual alternatives offered by the world's tyrannies—and not some fictitious solar-powered Utopia—we simply have no choice but to make the effort to inform ourselves of the facts, and determine the ethics of the oil sands according to our own, less politicized standards.

Chapter 6

SAY ONE THING, DO ANOTHER: ETHICAL FUNDS AND THE OIL SANDS

Paul Monaghan and Colin Baines were ecstatic, and it showed. The two middle-aged bankers from Manchester, U.K., had been planning a spectacular photo-op for their employer, Co-operative Investments – a British credit union – for months, and everything was going according to the script. After a seventeen-hour trip to Northern Alberta, Monaghan and Baines and their entourage of London-based reporters were greeted warmly by the chief of Alberta's Beaver Lake Cree Nation. The bankers were dressed identically in blue Oxford shirts and bland corporate neckties, standing out like pink sore thumbs as they mingled with Cree dancers in colourful traditional clothing. The two knew they looked out of place, but that was the whole point: to show the very un-bank-like lengths that Co-operative was willing to go to be socially responsible.[1] The contrast of the two pasty nerds with the singing and dancing Aboriginals was precisely what the trip was all about. It's that carefully crafted un-charisma that has made the bank so successful with progressive customers back home.

That's Co-operative's shtick: a big bank that values the little people. The bank's website is just as clever: its domain name is www.goodwithmoney.co.uk – get it? Monaghan and Baines had brought along reporters who lapped it all up. It was a clash of cultures, but instead of the British coming to colonize the Indians, as they had done 150 years ago, they were coming to given them a cheque: to help the Beaver Lake Cree in their massive lawsuit aimed at nothing less than stopping all oil sands production in its tracks.

Co-operative spends a lot of money on showy PR demonstrations of its righteousness, much more than its six-figure donation to the Beaver Lake Cree. It's all just a drop in the bucket for Co-operative, whose investment arm alone has £18 billion under management.[2]

And the Beaver Lake Cree were more than happy to sing for their supper. Their chief, Al Lameman, even made a cameo appearance in London for a Co-operative-sponsored rally – and he made sure to bring along his ceremonial headdress for the cameras. Four hundred years after Pocahontas was brought back from the New World to London for some exotic show and tell, Co-operative was still playing the condescending "noble savage" card for PR purposes. And if Lameman had to dress up for the part, well, it was a small price to pay for the cash Co-operative was giving him.

The intercontinental gimmick wasn't just for the Crees' benefit: it was an important part of a noisy campaign that Co-operative had launched, with the World Wildlife Fund, against Canada's oil sands. The bank had published a damning report on the industry, titled *Scraping the Bottom of the Barrel*,[3] stating "such investments are both environmentally and economically unsustainable and can only serve to undermine international efforts to combat climate change."[4] Then it came across the Beaver Lake Cree band, who was suing the Alberta and Canadian governments, claiming its members' hunting had been harmed by the oil sands development, and the bank realized it had found the perfect, sympathetic human face for its campaign. Funding an Indian band's lawsuit to stop the oil sands was just a flourish to drive Co-operative's point home.

The Co-operative Bank is just one of a growing number of so-called ethical investment funds. It's a mushrooming part of the financial industry that promises investors something more than just a good return on investment; it assures them that they can feel good that the money they're saving for their retirement is being put to use in ways that don't conflict with their own personal values, as long as those values fall within the boundaries set out by the contemporary left. Ethical funds – or socially responsible investments – generally steer clear of arms manufacturers, for instance, and tobacco companies. They often avoid distillers of liquor. And increasingly, as a way to attract even more money, they've been putting a major emphasis on avoiding companies with significant environmental impacts. And it's working: in Europe, the ethical investment market grew a phenomenal 60 per cent, from £1 trillion to £1.6 trillion just between 2005 and 2007. In the United States, socially responsible investments are expected to be worth $3 trillion by the end of 2011.[5] That's not an insignificant chunk of an American retirement fund market worth about $14 trillion.[6] These funds are an increasingly important player in the financial industry: they are gaining the power to move markets. And their ratings of various investments, like those of the corporate ethic ranking firms in the previous chapter, are fast becoming an official part of the narrative about which companies are "good" and which are "bad." And, perhaps just as importantly, like the Co-operative Bank, they don't always stop at boycotting certain investments: they become vocal activists against certain companies and industries, adding pressure for other investors to avoid them too. Not surprisingly, the oil sands, representing the future of a carbon-intensive economy increasingly out of fashion, have found themselves frequently on the top of the no-go list for ethical funds.

As the Co-operative Bank's Paul Monaghan – official title: head of social goals and sustainability – posted on the bank's website, the oil sands "push us closer to climate disaster." Monaghan called the oil sands a "hostile" source of energy. "The long and short of it is that it is plain and simply 'wrong,'" he said. "With the support of our customers and members we hope to help secure a safer, low-carbon future." According to the bank's website, oil sands aren't just environmentally dangerous – it uses the words "ecological disaster" – but they're a "significant investor risk." The fifty-two-page report is just as tough, and it names names, condemning companies like Shell, British Petroleum (BP), and Total in particular.

Total is a special case. It's not just a fossil fuel extractor – something Co-operative boasts it swore off more than ten years ago, with a video on its website stating that in "1998, the bank adopts a policy to end the financing of fossil fuel extraction and production."[7] And Total's not just up to its eyeballs in the oil sands – the worst sort of energy extractor, according to Co-operative's own study. But Total goes a step further: it is the largest European company doing business in the fascist regime of Burma.

Of all the ethical red lines, this one is the brightest for Co-operative. It's so adamant about its opposition to the Burmese regime that the bank even sponsored a feature film about its brutality, called *Burma VJ*, in honour of the video journalists who smuggled its footage of human rights abuses out of the country. It was nominated in 2010 for an Academy Award for Best Documentary Feature. Co-operative's website has righteousness on every page, but its indignation reaches a whole new level when the subject turns to Burma.

"The Co-operative Bank has engaged with the issue of Burma since 2000, and has declined to provide financial services to it, or any company with a significant presence there," says its annual *Sustainability Report* – its social version of a financial update, sent to all their members. And as Co-operative tends to do, it showed its support with a very public display of patting itself on the back. The bank spent "£13,000 for adverts in the national media highlighting the continued oppression of the Burmese people and promoting the Burma Campaign UK."[8]

So there you have it. By Co-operative's judgment, Burma is evil. Fossil fuel extraction is evil. Shell, BP, and Total are evil. And, of course, the oil sands are evil. And the Co-operative Bank and its investment arm were the kind of people who had enough with immorality – they'd be good with your money, and do good with it too. They'd even go so far as to fund lawsuits against the oil sands to stop the damned thing, which is certainly their prerogative.

Except one thing: Co-operative owns shares in every single one of the companies it's denounced.

That's not a typo: Co-operative's investment funds – the one where Monaghan is the head of social goals and sustainability – own tens of millions of dollars worth of stock of Total, BP, Shell, and myriad oil sands companies.

Just look at Co-operative's European Growth Trust.[9] An inspection of the company shares owned by Co-operative through this fund in the fall of 2009 shows that Total is the third-largest holding in the whole fund. It's not a mistake or an afterthought: Co-operative's Europe fund has more shares in Total than it does of any other company except two. While Co-operative was spending a few grand trumpeting its moral virtue on Burma, it was shovelling eight figures of their customers' money into Total's treasury, to finance its Burmese drilling and other fossil fuel operations.

Total also plans to make a $15 billion to $20 billion investment[10] in Alberta's oil sands, buying new leases of land, pumping the oil, and even building a massive upgrader. That's why they need Co-operative's money.

Well, surely Co-operative's most righteous fund – its Sustainable Leaders Trust[11] – would at least do better. Each of those three words is golden; the only way it could be better is if the words "seeing eye dog" or "organ donor" were added to it.

According to Co-operative's description of the fund, investments are focused on companies that will "improve the environment, human health, safety and the quality of life." The fund chooses companies making "above-average efforts to minimize environmental damage" and avoids those doing business in "countries where human rights are disregarded."

Here's how Co-operative sells the fund: "Are you one of the thousands of people becoming more and more concerned about climate change, alternative energy or nuclear power? This fund helps you invest your money in a responsible way without sacrificing the returns you can expect to achieve."[12] If you're a fair trade coffee–drinking, Prius–driving, Green Party–voting recycler who dabbles in vegetarianism, you've found your fund. And that's what you pay Co-operative its management fee for: let it do the hard work in finding the handful of companies that meet that strict moral code. After that kind of hard sell, how many of Co-operative's investors would actually bother to go through the lists of the bank's investments to see what shares they're buying?

The Sustainable Leaders Trust is not really the place you'd expect to find companies that own open-pit coal mines and coal-fired power plants – with a specialty in Third World coal plants. But that's exactly what you'd find, hidden in plain sight.

According to Co-operative's share holdings disclosure, one of the top companies in which this fund invests is International Power PLC – a global coal-burning colossus, operating some of the world's oldest and most outdated power plants.

International Power is the proud operator of a fifty-year-old coal-fired power plant in Prague, in the Czech Republic – built as part of the Communist Party's Cold War industrialization push. By one cynically literal definition perhaps, any coal-fired plant that has belched smoke for fifty years really has proven it's sustainable. International Power runs a couple of forty-five-year-old coal-fired plants in Australia, a forty-year-old coal-fired plant in the United Kingdom, and more coal-fired plants in Texas and Portugal. So much for industries of the future. And as for Co-operative's pledge that this fund would also respect human rights, International Power operates a coal-fired plant in Paiton, Indonesia, a country where, just to pick an example, homosexuality is a crime punishable by one hundred lashes[13] and adultery is a capital crime, punished by stoning.

Well, is International Power at least considering moving into new fuels? They're happy to answer the question about their future plans: "We are working on a competitive bid for Nghi Son 2 (1,200 MW), a coal-fired independent power project which has recently been announced in Vietnam."[14] In terms of human rights, Vietnam makes Indonesia look like a Boy Scout. It is a Communist dictatorship[15] where political dissidents are rounded up and imprisoned. The Communists have ruled the north half of Vietnam since 1954, and the south since they conquered it in 1975. Fifty-five years of dictatorship and counting is probably not what investors had in mind by "sustainable."

Well, surely International Power has other green plans to compensate for their coal-fired behemoths belching black smoke into the skies of dictatorships? Actually, no. "We do not have a specific target for reducing total CO_2 emissions," they concede. In a way, their honesty is refreshing: "Firstly, we are a growing business and any fossil fuel stations we add to our fleet will add to our aggregate CO_2 emissions level. Secondly, we are a demand-led industry. We are obligated to generate electricity to meet customer demand and we are committed to 'keeping the lights on.' Finally, the choice of fuel is often dependent upon client specifications (which for new-build plants are specified during the bidding process) and the most economic and secure fuel available in the local market."[16] Not a lot of wiggle room there. But give International Power credit: their investor relations team must be real crackerjacks, if they can sell shares to Co-operative.

It couldn't be any more embarrassing for Britain's most boastful "ethical investor" if its clients knew it was a leading financier of Third World coal. Or maybe it could: if those clients realized that Co-operative, while its executives are making a big show of dancing with the elders of the anti–oil sands Beaver Lake Cree, is busy investing in oil sands companies too.

The RPS Group PLC is another company that is on the top ten list for the Sustainable Leaders Trust. Like so many of their shareholdings, you wouldn't have any idea what the company did if you just looked at Co-operative's reports.[17]

Only by going to RPS's website – something few of the Che T-shirt–wearing Co-operative customers are likely to bother doing – would you discover that they are, in fact, expert consultants in oil sands engineering. If you're looking to boil tar out of the sand, RPS is your company. "RPS involvement in this key area has included well design, artificial lift studies, production optimization, reservoir simulation and development planning peer reviews," claims their site, adorned with plenty of oily photos, including a money shot of the thick, molasses-like bitumen being poured out of a beaker. Which is a more accurate image of what goes on in Co-operative's Sustainable Leaders Trust: that beaker of thick tar or a video in solidarity with Burmese monks?

To be clear, RPS isn't just about helping companies wring more oil out of the sand. They're about getting more companies into the business. Examples of their work include "assistance to a number of potential new entrants into the Alberta Oil Sands" and advising "lenders for a major . . . development in N.E. Alberta." [18]

But the one thing many "ethical funds" agree on is that they won't invest in nuclear power. Never ever.

Well, that's what they say. And if you were a trusting investor, you'd never know better. If you were a bicycle-riding, hemp-wearing investor, you'd probably trust Co-operative on that one. That's why you pay them a 5 per cent fee up front and 1.5 per cent per year. It's their central promise, right? You'd be shocked.

Co-operative's U.S. Growth Fund[19] lists among its top holdings Exelon Corp., which just happens to be the largest nuclear power operator in the United States. And one with active plans to build new reactors.[20]

Seriously.

But it gets better: Exelon operates the most famous nuclear power plant in the world, with the possible exception of Chernobyl. They own and operate a reactor in Pennsylvania called Three Mile Island Unit 1.[21] The adjacent reactor, Three Mile Island Unit 2, was the one that had a partial meltdown in 1979. That melted-down reactor still hasn't been decommissioned, and part of Exelon's business is to monitor and maintain[22] it – Unit 2 is owned by First Energy Company of Akron – courtesy of Co-operative's ethical investors.

Not that Exelon's operational reactor there is a model of safety; in November 2009, it had a radiation leak too, forcing the evacuation of 150 workers.[23] Twenty staff were exposed to radiation that day, but even more troubling, the company didn't alert the local Emergency Management Agency for five full hours after the leak was detected. Comments by the local town manager indicated that the company did not want to cause unnecessary panic by going public earlier.

What luck for the two British bankers with the perma-grins on their faces, mugging for the cameras in Northern Alberta, that no one asked them to explain why the oil sands are unethical – a "disaster" – but investing in a company that operates Three Mile Island isn't.

Owning Exelon – one of its top holdings – isn't an anomaly. Co-operative's European Growth Trust also has plenty of shares in Siemens, which builds nuclear power plants, and E.ON, a major European power producer that relies mostly on nuclear and coal.[24] And its Corporate Bond Income Trust[25] owns shares in Iberdrola, a Spanish company that also relies on coal and nuclear.[26] It's a tough call which of those two fuels are more hated by Greenpeace, but Co-operative has 'em both.

Co-operative's UK Growth Trust,[27] meanwhile, owns shares in British Petroleum, with major holdings in Canada, producing half a billion cubic feet of natural gas *each day*. And BP is investing $3 billion of its shareholders' money – thanks Co-operative! – into adjusting its U.S. refineries to better accommodate Canadian oil sands oil.[28] The UK Growth Trust has as its single largest holding a company called the BG Group[29] – a major oil and gas producer with interests in more than a quarter-million hectares in Canada's pristine north, the ancestral home of so many Aboriginals, and more than 2.3 million acres in Alaska's North Slope, which combined comprise an area almost as large as the whole of Northern Ireland. Forget Co-operative's worries about climate change melting the Arctic; its largest U.K. growth holding is busy drilling the hell out of the Arctic, and what it isn't drilling it's dynamiting in seismic tests to find new places to drill. Co-operative's BG Group makes Sarah Palin look like a tree-hugger.

To top it all off, the ethical folks round out their U.K. fund with some shares in British American Tobacco – the sixth-heaviest investment in the fund.

There is no other way to put it: Britain's noisiest ethical investment fund invests in just about everything they claim is unethical.

How can the Co-operative Group get away with this? How can it swear on a stack of Bibles that it doesn't extract fossil fuels but then buy shares in a dozen companies that do just that? How can it vilify Burma – quite rightly – but then buy shares in businesses there and in other human rights–abusing countries? Isn't it a violation of its own code of conduct?

An inquiry to Paul Monaghan went unanswered. Inquiries sent to a half-dozen other executives at Co-operative yielded a boilerplate response, from Dave Smith, Co-operative's PR manager: "As a shareholder we can exhort pressure and lobby business at every opportunity to improve their ethical and environmental performance, whilst those companies that proactively adopt commendable initiatives are publicly applauded."

Pressed for any examples of how Co-operative had tried to change oil sands practices, and whether Co-operative had ever sold its shares in an oil sands company for not changing its policies, Smith didn't respond despite saying he would do so. Nor did he respond to the more basic question of whether his ethical investors might have been misled by his website's noisy opposition to oil sands, Burma, and anything else "unethical" – while their money was doing the opposite.

Perhaps it's some fine-print sleight of hand: perhaps only certain parts of Co-operative's mega-company are bound by those ethical rules. The bank does offer a few tiny anecdotes of Co-operative turning away business – it claims that in 2007 it sacrificed all of £188,000 in "foregone" income (out of billions in holdings) by refusing to truck with some companies making oil drilling equipment. But all of them appear to be companies that wanted to do business banking with Co-operative. The multimillion-dollar deals all appear to be done through the Co-op's investment department. But both are branches of the same company, the Co-operative Group. Their websites link seamlessly to each other; and they all certainly trumpet how ethical both are. Surely a member of Co-operative could be forgiven for being confused into thinking that a no-Burma rule meant that her money wouldn't be invested in Burma. But at the end of the day, the Co-operative has to make money like any other bank. Investing in nuclear plants like Three Mile Island or oil sands operations like Shell's is about profits, pure and simple.

How the United Kingdom's Co-operative reconciles its words with its deeds is unclear, and it's obviously not eager to try to explain it, but what is clear is how successful it has become financially. It knows that anything marketed as "green" or "ethical" will attract conscientious customers. It turns a regular product or service – like banking – into a premium product. And Canadian companies haven't missed that trend either.

Canada has almost a dozen major ethical funds in the same mould. Vancouver's simply named Ethical Funds claims to be Canada's first ethical investment house. Not only do they promise to screen out unethical companies, but when they do invest, they're not passive – they press for policy reforms in the companies they own through shareholder activism.

Like their U.K. counterpart, Canada's Ethical Funds is hard on the oil sands. In October 2008, they released a twenty-page paper entitled *Unconventional Risks* – surely something that a responsible investor like Ethical Funds would want to stay away from. That report was full of scary phrases to describe the oil sands – "the world's dirtiest oil," "too much development too fast," "a heady mix of litigious, liability, regulatory, and reputational risks," "heavy impact on the environment and human health," etc. – nothing that the Brits hadn't said, except that, unlike the Brits, they didn't pay for an Aboriginal chief in full regalia to celebrate the publication of their report.

Ethical Funds goes so far as to call for an immediate freeze on any further oil sands development, a radical step that would mothball tens of billions of dollars' worth of projects – throwing tens of thousands of people out of work across the country. They pretty much come right out and say it: they're happy that the latest recession hit the oil patch hard. "Faced with rising capital costs, oil price volatility and recession many companies are re-evaluating the oil sands and some have shelved projects," they write. "While not welcoming market turmoil, this is, in some ways, a welcome breather." Perhaps that passes as "ethical" when it's being typed by someone who still has a job. The thousands of laid-off workers might have a different view.

Ethical Funds' report ends with a righteous challenge aimed at influencing other investors: "We welcome investment industry colleagues to join our efforts in asking the hard questions."[30] Fair enough. Here's a hard question: why didn't the author of the report disclose that Ethical Funds, behind all its bluster, is actually a major investor in the oil sands?

That doesn't just go to whether Ethical Funds is acting unethically by holding shares in the very industry they deem to be so "risky." Hypocrisy is one thing. But there's another level there: if the Ethical Funds solution is to maintain current oil sands operations, but simply ban new development, that's a pretty clever way for Ethical Funds to protect their own oil sands companies while trying to have the government ban competitors. It would be one thing for a neutral think-tank to make the audacious demands that Ethical Funds does. But Ethical Funds isn't a neutral think-tank. They're major share-holders, and their prescription just happens to be to keep their own holdings but ban their rivals. It's pretty clear why that little

93

detail wasn't in their report, or any of their press releases[31] on the matter: it demolishes their credibility.

Ethical Funds' holdings have so many oil and gas companies[32] that you'd think they were based in Fort McMurray, not Vancouver: Canadian Natural Resources; Canadian Oil Sands Trust; EnCana; Husky Energy; Nexen; Petro-Canada (acquired in 2009 by Suncor). After their twenty-page rant against the oil sands, how can their Ethical Growth Fund[33] own shares in the largest energy company in Canada, with 300,000 barrels per day from the oil sands alone?[34]

But Ethical Funds is an equal-opportunity hypocrite. Their Ethical Growth Fund doesn't just own oil sands stock, but also HudBay Minerals, which the 2006 National Pollutant Release Inventory lists as Canada's worst polluter.[35]

When pressed by a Vancouver reporter to explain Ethical Funds huge stake in the oil sands, Ethical Funds' vice-president for sustainability, Bob Walker, gave this laughable reply: "It's hard not to be in the oil sands, because if you're not in the oil sands you're not in oil." That's not true, of course. There are plenty of oil companies – hundreds in Canada alone – that are not active in Canada's oil sands. And plenty of international oil companies don't have oil sands stakes either. But even if Walker was right, isn't that the whole point of a so-called ethical investment – that it puts principles ahead of profits? That's certainly what the Ethical Funds website leads their customers to believe. "How do you want your investments to change the world?" asks the site, next to an image of a child holding up windmills.

Walker told the *Vancouver Sun* that Ethical Funds was "making pretty significant efforts to engage the sector in ways that they can begin to think about carbon neutrality by 2020." There sure are a lot of weasel words in there – and a generous timeframe of a good decade for Walker to reap big bucks while he waits for his "efforts" to push the companies to "consider" a different approach. What's so laughable is that, by Ethical Funds' own admission, oil sands companies like Husky refuse to even meet with Walker or his staff. It's not clear what a "pretty significant effort" to engage a company means when it won't return your phone calls. Maybe Walker sends unrequited letters to Husky each month.

Walker should have ended his interview there. He kept going. "It's not about who you own," he told the reporter, admitting that Ethical Funds really doesn't care what companies' shares it buys. "It's about . . . engaging [companies you hold] to improve their performance," he said. Give Bob Walker full marks for being forthright. By his measure, Ethical Funds will buy just about any company out there.

It's tough to top the U.K. Co-operatives jaw-dropping stake in Three Mile Island, but Ethical Funds figured out how to go one step further in stretching the boundaries of "ethical" investing: they've invested in Power Corp., the Canadian company that built the Chinese railway to Tibet.[36]

It's hard to imagine a more ethically suspect project. The railway's purpose is to ship in soldiers and ethnic colonists and to ship out Tibet's natural resources. To hell with the Dalai Lama and his Nobel Prize–winning efforts to free his country, brutally repressed by China since their illegal invasion in 1950. There's money to be made, and as Walker says, it doesn't matter what company you own, as long as you're "engaging" them.

Ethical Funds describes their attempt in 2006 to engage Power Corp. over the issue of the Tibetan railway. Their goal was to press the company to "adopt a human rights management system." That's actually quite a noble goal. It's not just a clichéd statement about human rights, but an actual plan on how the company would enforce it, who would be responsible for overseeing it, how things would work. Great idea! On May 11, 2006, Ethical Funds sent a representative to Power Corp.'s annual shareholders meeting to press for that proposal. It was rejected by nearly 90 per cent of shareholders – a massive defeat. Power Corp. was clearly not interested in some do-gooders from Vancouver interfering with their railway in Tibet. After all, if you're building a railway into Tibet for the Communist Chinese government, you've already come to terms with the fact that you're helping to brutalize Tibet and tighten Beijing's authoritarian grip on that imprisoned province. It just doesn't make sense to have a human rights management system when the whole purpose of the project is to crush human rights.

So what did Ethical Funds do after their spectacular defeat? Did they storm out of the meeting, hold a press conference to denounce Power Corp., and sell their stock? Of course not. Because remember what Walker said. It didn't matter what company you owned, as long as you were making efforts to engage the sector. As long as you had good intentions, that was licence enough to own shares in the Chinese killing machine that's aiming for the heart of Lhasa.

Ethical Funds loves their stock in Power Corp. They actually called their 10 per cent support among shareholders "substantial" and said they would "pursue a meeting with the company." How do you say "sucker" in Chinese?

Another year passed, and Ethical Funds enjoyed the profits that Power Corp. extracted from Tibet. Encouraged by their 10 per cent support in 2006, they proposed the same resolution in 2007. Perhaps they'd break through to 11 per cent support – another abject failure but enough to justify their continued profit-making from the Chinese dictatorship.

But before the 2007 shareholders meeting, Ethical Funds "reached an agreement" with Power Corp., so they withdrew their resolution. On their website, Ethical Funds even put a little bull's eye[37] – the rarely used symbol for shareholder success! How did they do it? How did Ethical Funds, which had the support of only 10 per cent of shareholders in 2006, manage to stare down mighty Power Corp. – and, really, China itself – and get them to implement a human rights management system?

Er . . . they didn't. Power Corp. didn't blink, Ethical Funds blinked. In return for Ethical Funds dropping their resolution, Power Corp. agreed to put a tiny statement on their website[38] – literally tiny, written in 7.5-point font, in English and French, not Chinese or Tibetan – that announced Power Corp.'s intentions to "comply with applicable laws" and to "conduct itself in a manner consistent with the goals" of the Universal Declaration of Human Rights.

Of course, those two things are irreconcilable. Complying with "applicable laws" in China means submitting to the laws of a dictatorship. The declaration, on the other hand, is a U.N. treaty[39] signed by governments, and its lofty language is clearly outside the power of a private company to act upon. Does Ethical Funds really think that Power Corp. will bring "freedom of thought" to China, as per Article 18 of that declaration, or maybe the right to free elections, under Article 21? Of course they don't think so, and Power Corp. doesn't either. But if it's a website page they want, they'll get it. Power Corp. wins because a nuisance is gone. Ethical Funds wins because they can justify their shareholdings for another year. What a joke.

It's not even a PR stunt – that would involve a more prominent and romantically written commitment to human rights. It's a token effort to placate a shareholder that was only looking for tokens.

Power Corp. doesn't just build railways in Tibet; it also owns a significant stake in Total, which operates in Burma. In 2008, Ethical Funds again attended Power Corp.'s annual meeting.[40] This time it didn't ask for Power Corp. to actually do anything – no human rights management system, not even a meaningless cliché on an unread website. All Ethical Funds did was to "reques[t] clarification on how they have assessed the human rights risks of their investment in Total . . . and how this investment meets their Corporate Social Responsibility Statement commitments."

Excuse me, master. Sorry to interrupt. You made a promise on your website in tiny writing. Can you please tell us if you kept that promise? Sorry to be a bother.

Seriously. Ethical Funds had long since given up on asking Power Corp. to improve its behaviour. Now they just wanted some news – any news – about what Power Corp. was doing. But even that pitiful request was thrashed at the meeting, rejected by almost precisely the same number of shareholders who had rejected their first attempts at "engagement" two years earlier.

Three years, three failures. But Ethical Funds kept their shares in companies doing business in some of the nastiest places in the world.

Other companies must have been watching because they soon figured out that the way to get Ethical Funds off their back for human rights abuses in foreign countries was simply to write a little something on their websites, in English. That's how, in 2007, the Canadian telecom firm Nortel got out of an embarrassing pickle[41] about its active involvement with the Chinese government in tracking political and religious dissidents on the Internet.[42] Like Power Corp., Nortel just made an empty, symbolic gesture. Ethical Funds withdrew their shareholder resolution "asking the company to disclose how it is developing appropriate policies and management systems that promote and protect human rights, given the company's growing involvement in countries with poor human rights records."

Got it? Nortel was actually increasing its role in human rights–abusing countries. Like Power Corp., it refused to even talk to Ethical Funds about how it dealt with human rights abuses. But as long as it swore it would salute the United Nations, and have a few more meetings with Ethical Funds, all would be forgiven. More than that, actually: Ethical Funds gave itself another bull's eye. Nice work!

Just how embarrassing does a company's rejection of an Ethical Funds idea have to be for them to actually sell stock? In 2006, Ethical Funds put forward a shareholder resolution for Loblaws groceries to label genetically modified foods (GMOs).[43] Literally 98.5 per cent of shareholders rejected the idea. Did Ethical Funds sell? Of course not. Maybe one day they'll get that number down to 95 per cent, or get a one-liner on a website, and give themselves a bull's eye for ethical awesomeness.

It's not entirely fair to single out the Co-operative funds in the United Kingdom or the Ethical Funds from Vancouver.

They're just the most self-righteous, especially when it comes to denouncing the oil sands. Every other ethical fund in Canada owns shares in companies that either operate in the oil sands or do even dirtier work.

To list them all would take a hundred pages – most if not all ethical funds have major holdings in oil sands, or Third World oil, or coal. But it's worth taking a few pages to list some of the largest oil sands holdings in Canada's other ethical funds. Do you own any of these? And if you do, are you surprised by what your fund owns?

The Investors Group – a company owned by the aforementioned Power Corp. – has ethical funds[44] itself. Its $1.4 billion SRI Fund[45] has both oil sands giant Suncor and Trinidad Drilling[46] in its top ten list of holdings. Investors Group's Global SRI Fund[47] is even bolder, owning BHP Billiton,[48] a company that specializes in massive open-pit mines in nasty places, extracting zinc, lead, coal, and uranium.

They also own shares in the Noble Group,[49] one of the world's largest traffickers in carbon. Noble boasted a 35 per cent annual increase in coal mining, helping to push their energy revenues to a record $18.2 billion. That's 60 million tons of coal, if you're counting. Noble ships coal to steel mills and ships steel to oil fields. Without carbon, there is no Noble Group. Also in the fund is Husky Energy,[50] with its massive oil sands play.[51]

Quebec has its ethical funds too. Desjardins'[52] $126 million Environment Fund[53] has a particular fondness for the oil sands: by far its largest stock – 9.3 per cent in its latest published report – is in EnCana, with fellow oil sands miner Petro-Canada accounting for 5.4 per cent of the fund. EnCana (which in 2009 split into two companies) recently announced plans[54] for a new multibillion-dollar oil sands project – with longer term plans for ten undeveloped oil sands properties.

Other resource companies in Desjardins' top ten list include Talisman Energy and the Potash Corporation of Saskatchewan, a mining firm, which together make up more than 11 per cent of the fund.

Do you really think that the thousands of Quebec clients who pour their ethical savings into Desjardins' Environment Fund know that their top picks are all fossil fuel companies?

Desjardins has a partnership[55] with Vancouver's Ethical Funds – the company that put out a report damning the oil sands as unethical and inappropriate for investment. Those funds are called SocieTerra – basically a French-Latin version of the word "Greenpeace." It holds a mix of other funds – including Ethical Fund investments that are fully stocked up on oil sands oil too.

Another Canadian ethical investment is run by Acuity Funds. Their Social Values Global Equity Fund[56] has Santos Ltd. as one of the fund's top picks. You might think, by that name, that Santos was a health-care company. It's not – it's an oil and gas extractor, specializing in Third World countries like Bangladesh, Kyrgyzstan, Vietnam, and war-ravaged Timor.[57] It pumped more than 54 million barrels of oil in 2008.[58]

Then there's Acuity's[59] holdings in Occidental Petroleum.[60] It's active in dictatorships like Yemen and Libya.[61] Oxy produces more than 600,000 barrels of oil each day.[62]

Oxy does what a number of ethical funds require of it: it has a formal, written human rights policy. Section D.1 of its human rights policy promises that Oxy's foreign contracts will respect UN standards of human rights.[63] But Section D.2 says that exceptions are allowed as the company "deems appropriate" for matters like security or even the "nature of the product or services" the company is providing. That's not a loophole – there's no loop, it's just a hole. But Oxy's good enough for Acuity's ethical funds.

And unlike many in the energy sector, Oxy is honest about its skepticism of human-caused global warming.[64] Besides expressing doubts, Oxy insists that no industrial sector or geographic area should be singled out for regulation – an objection that cuts to the heart of the Kyoto Protocol and its successors, that exempt OPEC countries and developing nations like China, India, and Brazil but put heavy burdens on North American producers.

Even though it doesn't believe in global warming, that doesn't stop Oxy from showing off how much CO_2 it injects into the ground – keeping it out of the air. Only when Oxy does it, it calls it Enhanced Oil Recovery: it pumps CO_2 into deep wells underground so that it can force the last few million barrels of oil out.

Acuity's Social Values Balance Fund[65] has an even bigger carbon footprint than other Acuity funds. The biggest chunk of its holdings – 22.4 per cent, according to its latest report – is in energy. And not solar or wind power either. Petrobank is the second-biggest investment of this fund. They're in the oil sands business in Alberta, but they've got even bigger dreams:[66] they've leased 23,000 acres across the border in Saskatchewan to explore for oil sands there too. And Petrobank is actually the single largest investment of Acuity's Clean Environment Equity Fund.[67] Call it creative writing, or science fiction, or non-linear thinking, but putting an oil company in the "Clean Energy Fund" that wants to replicate Alberta's oil sands in Saskatchewan is remarkable.

Other Acuity Social Values Balance Fund oil sands companies include EnCana, Suncor, Teck,[68] and Enbridge,[69] which
just got approval to build the Alberta Clipper – a massive pipe
from Fort McMurray to Wisconsin, with a planned capacity of
800,000 barrels of oil sands oil each day.

Mackenzie Financial (also owned by Power Corp.) lists as
its top holding in its Universal Sustainable Opportunities fund
the Brazilian company Petrobras,[70] a company with 13,000 drilling rigs including 112 at sea, 25,000 kilometres of pipelines, 16
refineries, and 2 million barrels a day of oil.[71] Petrobras is big
and plans to get even bigger, by drilling for oil in dictatorships
like Iran, Libya, and Cuba.[72]

Some ethical funds give Petrobras high marks for disclosing
its environmental track record. But shouldn't the substance of
that track record count even more than the fact that it's being
disclosed? Petrobras's emissions of nitrogen oxide – a smog-
producing pollutant that harms human health and depletes
atmospheric ozone – climbed from 205,000 tonnes to 246,000
tonnes in the past five years.[73] The number of oil spills increased
each of the last three years, from 269 in 2005, to 436 in 2008.
Water use was up four years in a row, nearly doubling from
2004 to 2008. Effluents were up every year. Greenhouse gases
were up more than 16 per cent from 2007 to 2008. Is that all it
takes to make a dirty polluter ethical – the fact that they confess
their eco-sins?

Meritas[74] – corporate motto: "socially responsible investments" – is another Canadian ethical fund that can't get
enough of the oil sands. British Petroleum,[75] Nexen,[76] EnCana,
Enbridge, Suncor, Devon Energy, Canadian Natural Resources:[77]
it would almost be quicker to make a list of oil sands companies
that *don't* get investment from Meritas.

Inhance[78] is another Canadian ethical investment house, affiliated with Vancity. Unlike most other fund managers, they give a little blurb about why they pick their top companies – which shows a lot of guts when so many of their picks are fossil fuel companies, and many of those are rooted in the oil sands. Take Enbridge, which is building the massive new oil sands pipeline down to the United States. Inhance doesn't mention this fact at all, choosing instead to focus on happier thoughts. "The company's distribution of natural gas provides opportunities to reduce emissions from more environmentally harmful fuels," they coo.[79] Reading that, you wouldn't guess that Enbridge is the same company that's going to ship 800,000 barrels of those "harmful fuels" from Fort McMurray to Wisconsin every single day.

One of the great bête noirs of climate change has been jet aircraft. Which is why it's odd to see Inhance investing in Canada's busiest airport, Toronto's Pearson International.[80] But don't worry about all those jets burning high-carbon jet fuel; according to Inhance, Pearson has "fuel efficiency targets for its vehicles." Its luggage trolleys and catering trucks – not the jets themselves.

Full marks for chutzpah to those boys.

Is there really any difference between an ethical fund and a "regular" investment fund? It's hard to see the difference. The funds listed above have it all: oil sands, Burmese oil, coal-fired power plants, the Tibetan railway, tobacco, and even Three Mile Island itself. Other than investing in a company that makes land mines or cluster bombs, there really isn't anything these ethical funds haven't bought – and as Bob Walker of Ethical Funds tells us, that's not an accident. His company – and the others that claim to be shareholder activists – have a pitiful record of reforming companies they find morally disappointing.

If the Walkers of the world could demonstrate that they are ethical turnaround artists – the moral equivalent of financial wizards who buy near-bankrupt companies and make them profitable again – then buying the world's worst companies would be righteous indeed. But the track record shows the opposite: year after year, their shareholder demands are either ignored outright or voted down overwhelmingly. Yet instead of divesting, they keep coming back for more. The few cases of "compromise" that the funds have been able to achieve are laughably impotent – such as a righteous cliché being published on a company's corporate website in tiny font, rather than actually doing anything righteous. Oh, there's ethical lobbying going on, but it's the ethical funds, not the corporations they invest in, who are being convinced to change their minds.

Has the phrase "ethical fund" become an Orwellian cover for what they truly do? By claiming to care about ethics, and giving themselves the beautiful name "ethical funds," it seems that companies have licensed themselves to be the exact opposite – to actually become unethical funds, protected by waves of propaganda, and accepted by customers who likely know no better.

This is the character of the oil sands' critics. These are the folks who loudly bash the oil sands, publish reports badmouthing them, launch campaigns against them, and even spend money on lawsuits to foil them, even as they quietly profit from them. At first, their behaviour seems awfully counterproductive: why would firms publicly denounce, and appear to actively sabotage, the very companies they hold investments in? It seems entirely illogical. But it isn't. Here's why:

The revenue that investment funds make comes from management fees they make from clients who hand over their retirement portfolios. Before the rise of conscientious investing, attracting more clients and their dollars meant achieving an impressive return on investment. Ethical funds have figured out a more clever way to do things: they can attract funds from the morally conscious investor, those trusting enough to believe that the investment managers will stay true to their own, personal values.

Just ask Warren Buffett what he thinks about managers of mutual funds. At an annual meeting a few years back for Berkshire Hathaway, the conglomerate run by Buffett, considered one of the most successful investors in history, he said this about fund managers: "One thing I can almost guarantee you is that the promotional types are very unlikely to meet any long-term tests of ability and sometimes integrity."[81] Sound familiar?

Still, ethical fund managers can't rely entirely on slick promotion. They have to keep up at least a reasonably passable performance or they won't keep those clients long: no one wants to lose money, even on an ethical investment. So they quietly sock the money into the oil sands, nuclear and coal producers – not to mention repressive regimes. In the meantime, all they need to do is keep up a reasonable facade of left-wing activism, dancing with Aboriginal chiefs, issuing damning reports about the oil sands, and making sanctimonious promises on their promotional material. In short, it's all a big show, where the average investor is played for the fool. And these are the supposed arbiters of ethics? If ethical funds are willing to play these games with their own customers, it only makes you wonder what else are they doing.

Chapter 7

THE MOST SCRUTINIZED INDUSTRY ON EARTH: ENVIRONMENTAL PROTECTION AND THE OIL SANDS

Only in Alberta's oil sands do companies not only volunteer to dig up naturally occurring petroleum that's bubbling out of the soaked ground and oozing into the rivers, they spend billions of dollars for the privilege of doing it. You might call it the largest cleanup of an oil spill in the history of the world.

Bitumen, the viscous petroleum permeating the land of Northern Alberta, naturally seeps into the water. That's how it was first discovered by European explorers hundreds of years ago. In many areas, they could see the bitumen slicking on the surface of the soil. Alberta's Aboriginals would scoop it up near riverbanks and apply it as waterproofing to their canoes.

In 1788, one early explorer named Sir Alexander Mackenzie wrote,[1] "At about 24 miles from the fork [of the Athabasca and Clearwater Rivers] are some bituminous fountains into which a pole of 20 feet long may be inserted without the least resistance. The bitumen is in a fluid state and when mixed with gum, the resinous substance collected from the spruce fir, it serves to gum the Indians' canoes. In its heated state it emits a smell like that of sea coal."

One hundred and twenty-one years later, in 1909, adventurer Agnes Deans Cameron retraced some of Mackenzie's steps by canoe, writing a book about her travels called *The New North*. She, too, couldn't help noticing the oil that saturated the land around her – and the natural but unusual effect it had on the water. "At Fort McKay, thirty miles below McMurray, a fine seam of coal is exposed on the river-bank," she wrote. "It is bituminous . . . while extensive sulphur deposits have been discovered on the east side of the river between Fort McMurray and the lake. On the Clearwater are medicinal springs whose output tastes very much like Hunyadi water."[2] (Hungary's Hunyadi Springs produce a bitter-tasting mineral water that was imported by North Americans in the nineteenth century).[3] Before any industry could be blamed for it, the land was oily and the water was bitter.

"Tar there is, too, in plenty," Cameron continued. "Out of the over-hanging banks it oozes at every fissure, and into some of the bituminous tar-wells we can poke a twenty foot pole and find no resistance. . . . Where it is possible to expose a section, as on a river-bank, the formation extends from one hundred and twenty-five to two hundred feet in depth, the bitumen being distributed through the sands.

"Twelve miles below the last exposure of the tar-sands and about two miles above the mouth of Red Earth Creek a copious saline spring bubbles up, and there is an escape of sulphurretted hydrogen whose unmistakable odour follows the boat for half a mile. Kipling was right when he said, 'Smells are surer than sounds or sights.'"[4]

Anti–oil sands groups today obsess over the weird smells and odd water quality around Fort McMurray, convinced it can only be the unnatural by-products of industrial activity. They have short, selective memories. Explorers who visited Northern Alberta a century or two ago saw all this: tar spilling into the Athabasca; the smell of sulphur wafting for miles; natural springs that tasted like bitter drinks – all decades before anyone tried boiling oil out of the sand.

Bitumen has a consistency similar to that of peanut butter, so getting that thick stuff out of the earth consumes a great deal of energy. The machines and processing equipment used to extract bitumen are frequently powered using fossil fuels, and burning those is what emits the carbon dioxide that environmentalists claim is part of the reason for global warming. When they're not rewriting history by pretending that Fort McMurray's smells and tastes are human-caused, they're fingering the oil sands as Canada's "climate criminals;"[5] their favourite environmental whipping boy.

In reality, the oil sands are more environmentally progressive and emit less waste than all sorts of other common industries in Canada and around the world. In just nineteen years, from 1990 to 2009, the intensity of greenhouse gases (GHGs) from the oil sands has plummeted by 38 per cent.[6] In other words, every barrel of oil extracted in 2009 took between one-third and one-half less GHGs to produce than a barrel extracted in 1990 – and the emissions continue to fall every year.

Of course, carbon dioxide has only been deemed to be pollution in the last couple of decades, when some scientists began theorizing about a link between greenhouse gases and global warming – before that, every elementary school student knew CO_2 simply as "plant food."

Whether you're a believer or skeptic when it comes to the theory of human-caused global warming, the fact is that Alberta is the only province in Canada that charges carbon emitters for not meeting climate-change targets – $15 for every tonne of CO_2 they emit that is over their assigned limit. It's basically a fine on companies that aren't aggressively working to cut their GHG intensities. Far from being the Wild West of unfettered carbon emissions, Alberta is actually the only province that creates negative incentives for industrial emitters to improve their carbon profile. Ontario with all its coal-fired plants doesn't do that. Quebec doesn't care how much carbon its factories send into the atmosphere.

But it's not just a tax grab: rather than pouring into the government's general revenues, as most taxes do, the money is recycled back into research funds aimed at reducing CO_2 emissions even further. Alberta isn't only making huge gains in reducing its own carbon intensity, its industries are paying to discover new carbon-cutting technology and methods that are going to help industries around the world slash their outputs too.

But if we're going to talk about threats to the environment, it would be reckless to focus only on carbon dioxide. After all, there are other pollutants that long ago were proven to have toxic effects on humans and wildlife. And while the oil sands have aggressively improved their carbon profile over the last few years, we can get an even fuller picture of the real environmental impact of the oil sands by looking at other measures.

Carbon monoxide (CO), for example, is considered a major atmospheric pollutant that can react in the air in ways that are harmful to human health. And for the last fifteen years, the Fort

McMurray/oil sands area has had *falling* CO levels and in every single year has had lower concentrations of that gas than Alberta's major cities of Edmonton and central Calgary.[7] Ozone (O_3), which even though it's a natural part of our upper atmosphere is considered a respiratory irritant when it's at lower levels, is also no more concentrated in the air around the oil sands than it is in Edmonton and Calgary.

Hydrogen sulphide (H_2S) is one of the nastier chemicals often found floating in the air around industrial installations like oil plants, pulp mills, animal feedlots, and sewage treatment facilities. In sufficiently high levels, it can be lethally toxic[8]; lower-level effects range from breathing problems, fatigue, and headaches. Every Canadian city has a little of it in the air: In 2006, in Alberta, for instance[9], Calgary's annual H_2S average was 0.9 ppb, an extremely safe level. In Fort McMurray, H_2S levels that year ranged between 0.9 ppb and 1.1 ppb – almost identical.

Nitrogen dioxide (NO_2) is a reddish-brown toxic gas that's one of the major atmospheric pollutants carefully tracked by environmental regulators. According to monitoring by Alberta's environment department, the average NO_2 concentrations in Calgary and Edmonton ranged from 13 to 24 parts per billion (ppb). But in the Fort McMurray area, and the air around the oil sands installations, the presence of NO_2 ranged between just 4 and 8 ppb – a fraction of what you'd find in Alberta's big cities. The five-year average concentration of NO_2 around the oil sands is just 30 per cent of Toronto levels, according to data provided by the Clean Air Strategic Alliance.[10] Ottawa nearly triples Fort McMurray's NO_2 levels, and even St. John's is higher. What's more, the city that thinks of itself as North America's "greenest,"[11] Vancouver, British Columbia, has NO_2

concentrations more than twice as high as around the oil sands. Want fresh air? Stop working at a Starbucks on Robson Street and go work for Syncrude.

Of course, anti–oil sands groups aren't keen to talk about the generally low level of actual pollutants around Fort McMurray, which is why they're so focused on carbon dioxide and its presumed effect on climate change. As it happens, though, carbon dioxide is only a small part of the greenhouse gas story, and the oil sands, despite all the environmental fuss about them, are really an exceedingly small part of the carbon dioxide story.

While carbon dioxide may get all the attention, it isn't really the biggest source of greenhouse gases on the planet: water vapour is. According to reporting by the Intergovernmental Panel on Climate Change, water vapour is responsible for between 60 per cent and 80 per cent of the greenhouse effect.[12] And both gases are a natural part of our ecosystem. The planet can't survive without a great deal of carbon dioxide, and a massive amount of it is naturally occurring: more than 95 per cent of all the CO_2 in the atmosphere comes from nature, including the world's oceans, decaying plants, and the exhalation of all of the earth's tens of billions of creatures.[13] Then there are all the forest fires and volcanoes. Every single year, 210 billion tonnes of CO_2 are released into the atmosphere – and CO_2 is just a small fraction compared to water vapour, which accounts for the majority of the greenhouse effect.[14]

Humans – who take all the blame for carbon emissions, with our cars, factories, power plants, oil sands operations, and everything else – emit a minuscule amount of that total. Each year Canadians emit about 600 million tonnes,[15] or roughly 2 per cent of the world's human emissions. And the oil sands? They account for approximately 5 per cent of Canada's total human emissions – which works out to 0.1 per cent of the world's human-caused emissions. Not bad for the world's biggest source of oil.

That, evidently, is enough to worry a lot of people. But that mathematical exercise is important to keep things in perspective: shutting down the oil sands, as environmentalists would have us do, would have the same effect as a worried Boeing 747 pilot unloading a few pillows as a way to save on precious fuel. While the effect of closing down this massive energy reserve on North America's economy would be devastating, the effect on the atmosphere would scarcely be noticed.

In absolute terms, the oil sands release about 29.5 million tonnes of carbon emissions annually. That's not even one of the biggest GHG sources in the country, let alone on the planet. Agriculture in Canada, for instance, emits 60 million tonnes,[16] of which "enteric fermentation" accounts for 23 million tonnes and "manure management" another 7.3 million. What's enteric fermentation? It's those animal farts again. Seriously, between their flatulence and their manure, Canadian livestock emits more greenhouse gases every year than the oil sands do.

When we look outside the country, the scale of the oil sands impact comes into even sharper focus. For instance, according to the U.S. Department of Energy's latest statistics,[17] America's coal-fired power plants, put together, were emitting 2 billion tonnes of carbon dioxide. Add in all the other fossil fuels used in the United States and you're up to just about 5.8 billion tonnes – or, about two hundred times more GHG emissions than in Alberta's oil sands. Coal actually ranks far worse than oil on the scale of GHGs released for the amount of heat it produces.[18]

On the spectrum of major fossil fuels, no other source emits as much CO_2 as coal does.

But America isn't even the biggest emitter. In 2006, China overtook the United States in terms of greenhouse gas emissions when it broke the 6 billion tonnes mark.[19] As of 2007, two-thirds of the world's CO_2 emissions growth came from that one country.[20]

The government of China estimates that within a decade, their country will have developed to the point where it will emit more than 10 billion tonnes a year,[21] nearly twice what the United States emits and 330 times more than what's coming from the Alberta oil sands. That's partly because China has its own version of the oil sands too. And they're just starting to tuck into it. They call it oil shale,[22] and in Jilin Province, there are an estimated 546 million tonnes of total proven reserves of it, 317 million of which are currently considered commercially exploitable.[23] The state-owned China Power Investment Corporation has plans to invest about U.S.$350 million to exploit the shale for facilities that will producer power, heat, and cement products. But, unlike Alberta's oil sands, Beijing and its crony industrialists don't give any thought to water quality, air quality, or other environmental impacts. Just look at how China treats the environment today – with utter disregard. There are underground coal-mine fires in that country that have burned for years that are responsible for emitting more GHGs – between 30 million tonnes and 450 million tonnes a year, according to estimates[24] – than everything emitted by the entire oil sands region put together.[25]

China plainly doesn't care about CO_2 emissions; it hasn't bothered even to take its own national "inventory" of them since 1994, leaving it to others, like the UN, to make best guesses.

And it's true it has other more pressing environmental matters: China's real pollution is so staggeringly bad that it has become the cause of widespread civil unrest – there were 87,000 riots in 2005, according to leaked Chinese government documents, "many due to environmental pollution," says a 2008 report to the U.S. Congress.[26] That's 87,000 individual *riots*, not individual *rioters*. In an authoritarian country with a history of murdering or imprisoning even peaceful demonstrators, those citizens must be pretty infuriated about what's happening to their environment. No wonder: in 2007, the World Bank estimated that the cost of the horrendous air and water pollution is $100 billion a year, or nearly 6 per cent of China's GDP.

The oil sands aren't just a vastly cleaner operation than the environmental catastrophe that is China. And they're not just a smaller GHG concern than the thousands of coal plants across North America that also represent a critical part of our energy supply. Alberta's so-called carbon footprint is actually less of an issue than many other kinds of oil being produced around the world. Relative to other sources of petroleum, the oil sands look better and better all the time.

We've all seen those photos of the oil sands that environmentalists love to hate. Hulking steam shovels tearing into vast, mucky open-pit mines; the sprawling tailings ponds stewing with residues. It's not pretty, yet it's attracted some of the world's top photographers. *National Geographic*'s Peter Essick produced a remarkable photo series of the oil sands in early 2009,[27] celebrated photographer Edward Burtynsky followed suit with a series of his own unsettling photographs.[28] They showed the world only the ugly side of the industrial disruption going on in and around Fort McMurray, the environmental disturbance.

It was a political statement aimed at the heart of the Canadian oil patch. It's not journalism; it's activism.

It's oil sands porn.

And it's a misrepresentation. The photographs capture only a tiny portion of what's happening in the oil sands, and in many ways, it's the oldest work the cameras focus on. But the audience is left to assume that more oil sands production means more of the same – more open pits, more giant machines. But that's as misleading as taking a bunch of photographs of some drab, undeveloped stretch in one of New York City's industrial areas and leaving the impression that that's what Manhattan looks like. In reality, a growing segment of oil sands exploration, and the work that represents the future of the resource, doesn't photograph nearly as well as those big, messy pits. That's because, in an increasing number of cases, you can barely tell there's any oil sands extraction going on at all.

Only 20 per cent of the oil sands is mined in those ugly open pits. And that 20 per cent takes up just 2 per cent of the oil sands total geography. The other 80 per cent of the oil, accounting for 98 per cent of the land area, is drilled out of the ground without ripping open photogenic scars. Likely *National Geographic* knew that 98 per cent of the land subjected to the relatively inconspicuous oil sands operations called SAGD (steam-assisted gravity drainage) wasn't the only issue and pictures of this wouldn't sell magazines. Pictures of SAGD oil wells are as boring as their name sounds.

The story about dump trucks and steam shovels and pits serves an important purpose over and above just trying to scare people into believing, as environmentalist groups want them to, that the entire northern part of Alberta will be turned into one big strip mine. Just as important is the fact that the whole process feels outdated – like a throwback to some earlier stage of economic evolution. It makes Canadians look primitive: the old saw about hewers of wood and drawers of water. Not the kind of thing that has a place in the post-Internet era of high-tech, a world of solar panels and fuel cells. And there's a reason that kind of technology might seem a bit behind the times: those operations are the very first created in the oil sands, when Suncor first started work there in 1967.

Today, Alberta's oil sands are easily one of the most techno-logically advanced resource operations in the world. Behind every dump-truck driver are teams of computer modellers, engi-neers, geologists, and technical operators. For every strong back working a shovel, there are a dozen M.A.s and Ph.D.s some-where working a computer. And increasingly, the ratio is getting even wider, because the newest oil sands technologies, and the ones that represent the future of the region, don't need a whole lot of dump-truck drivers and shovels. Often they're just pipes run deep underground – just like in conventional oil production – pumping in steam and pumping out bitumen.

In places like Saudi Arabia, where there's still some light, sweet crude oil sitting relatively near the surface of the earth, waiting to be easily pumped out, there isn't a great need for technological progress. But in the oil sands, oil firms are constantly having to come up with innovative ways to tap the resource. That's because the bitumen isn't always easy to get at, it isn't easy to get out, and those extra challenges mean extra costs. Making the oil sands competitive in a global energy economy means an ongoing race to reduce the use of the energy, of the water, of machinery, and of the labour required to pull the thick bitumen out of the ground and process it into usable oil. And if you're concerned about the environment, that's great news: because the more oil sands producers can cut their costs – their need for energy, water, and other resources – the better it is for the environment.

The rest of the oil in the world, in the meantime, is consistently getting worse environmentally. We already talked about how the world has begun to exhaust much of the cheap, easy-to-get-at oil that represented the first wave of exploration in the petro age. We aren't running out of oil: we're running out of a certain kind of oil. That's one reason why companies are eager to get involved in the more complicated, often more expensive work required in the oil sands. We've picked the fruit off the lower part of the tree, and we're going to need more effort and energy to get to the rest of it higher up.

That means that all around the world, more energy is being put into extracting deeper and deeper reserves of unconventional oil. A barrel of oil made from the Athabasca region puts out GHGs about 15 per cent higher, on average, than those from a barrel of oil produced from good old-fashioned conventional deposits that could be easily drilled and pumped in the past. Not a lot, but not nothing either. But the difference between the GHGs emitted to make a barrel of oil from the oil sands and the GHGs emitted to make the average barrel of oil you'll find on the market today – which could come from deep-sea deposits, or so-called heavy oil – is even narrower, and it's getting more narrow all the time.[29] The difference between the oil sands and the average barrel's cocktail of non–oil sands oil is already down to 10 per cent, according to independent studies.[30]

That's another important statistic to help keep things in perspective because it means that the anti–oil sands campaigners would have us continue to rely on oil from regimes that brutalize human rights, sponsor terrorists, and recklessly despoil the landscape, all to save a modest 10 per cent of GHGs. As that gap shrinks further, how willing will we all be to overlook the troubling ethical costs of foreign oil for a marginal difference in GHG emissions?

With a producer like Nigeria, where a corrupt, warmongering government controls all oil production without having to answer to shareholders or environmental regulations, waste simply isn't taken as seriously (never mind environmental degradation). For instance, when oil is pumped out of the ground almost anywhere, it comes accompanied by natural gas too. The Nigerians, whose "Bonny Light" crude is a fairly heavy oil to deal with, don't want to bother with the gas. They can't barrel it up and sell it as easily as oil – so they simply flare it, meaning they burn it right there at the well site, emitting huge amounts of greenhouse gases and wasting, in the process, the equivalent of up to 18 per cent of the energy potential of the oil. That's like drilling for oil with a pump that leaks out one barrel out of every six. Only, instead of spilling into the ground, it's torched and turned into carbon dioxide (and pollutants) in the air. Already, using today's methods, the oil produced from Alberta's oil sands has a 20 per cent smaller carbon footprint than the Nigerian oil that constitutes a major part of both American and British oil imports,[31] not that you'll find many environmentalists working to pressure Nigeria to clean up its act (they wouldn't get very far).

You don't even need to go to Africa to find oil projects with higher GHG emissions than the oil sands. California has a reputation as being the most eco-conscious state in America. Certainly it has the toughest auto emissions standards. And Governor Arnold Schwarzenegger has been drawing up laws banning Alberta's oil sands products for its supposed carbon dioxide issues.[32]

But here's the thing: California exempts its own oil industry from the kind of strict emissions controls they'd like to put on the oil sands. No wonder: these kinds of laws would end up forcing most of the state's oil projects out of business. The heavy oil pumped in California, with its high GHG emissions, represents a significant two-thirds of its on-shore oil production.

In Iraq, the amount of good, usable energy lost to flaring is estimated at 7 per cent of the equivalent oil energy. Flaring is prohibited in Alberta, but it probably doesn't even need to be because it's considered such a foolish thing to do: why burn all that useful gas when you can put it to good use? Instead, oil sands producers capture the natural gas they extract with their bitumen and use it for "co-generation" – meaning they use it to produce steam they pump back into the ground to soften up more bitumen for extraction. When producers find themselves with more gas than they can use for processing, they use it to generate electricity that they then upload to the provincial power grid. It's like the old legend about the Aboriginals that once roamed the area: almost nothing in the oil sands that can be used is allowed to go to waste. Sure, the end result of exploiting, rather than wasting, natural gas is good environmental practice: it reduces waste, reuses resources, and recycles by-products. But all of these improvements happen because it's also smart business to conserve as much as possible.

All those efficiencies only shrink the difference between the oil sands carbon footprint and that of its competitors even further. The co-generation decreases the need for heavy-carbon-emitting coal-fired power. Credit that in the oil sands' CO_2 ledger, as we rightly should, and the difference between the emissions from oil sands petroleum and the conventional stuff coming out of even the lightest deposits shrivels further.[33] With carbon credit for co-generation taken into account, oil sands mining does better on GHG emissions than California's heavy oil and about the same carbon footprint as Venezuela's oil. An analysis by the research firm Energy Probe found that if the United States replaced all the California heavy oil and Nigerian oil that it consumes with the lowest-emitting oil sands oil on the market, the global GHGs associated with American gasoline consumption would immediately fall approximately 2 per cent to 3 per cent or more.[34] In other words, America could actually cut its carbon emissions by relying more on the oil sands.

In oil sands projects that use the newer SAGD Dilbit technology, emissions levels are even better than oil from Saudi Arabia.[35] That's right: new oil sands plants are actually greener than Saudi oil, the easiest oil in the world to pump. So, now how willing are we to turn away Alberta's oil so we can buy more from human rights–abusing, terrorist-sponsoring countries?

Next-generation oil sands technologies will only make oil sands production more attractive from a GHG perspective. Take expanding solvent–steam-assisted gravity drainage (ES-SAGD), which adds solvents to the steam to make the bitumen even easier to pipe out of underground reservoirs. ES-SAGD is already being used in advanced field tests and uses less than half the energy, and 45 per cent fewer GHG emissions, than current SAGD technology. Pilot trials with Electric Heating technology, used to get at deposits that are too deep to mine but too shallow for steam, is being shown to cut CO_2 emissions in half, or even less (down to zero if it can tap into an existing power grid).[36] Another new process, high-temperature froth treatment, can reduce carbon dioxide emissions by 10 per cent to 15 per cent. "This means less production of the heaviest, dirtiest part of the crude steam and less pollution," according to Brad Komishke, a Shell chemist leading a team of fifty scientists developing new methods for the company at the University of Calgary. "It's about more efficient use of energy."[37]

Yet groups claiming to care about the environment could find nothing but bad things to say about Shell's pioneering technology. "Major cuts to emissions would still not make every oil sands operation in the province cleaner than more traditional, conventional operations around the world," Simon Mui, a representative of the Natural Resources Defense Council, told reporters. And the oil sands could never keep up with the constantly changing emissions-reduction targets being put out by pro–Kyoto groups. "Right now, Alberta is just trying to get back to where the conventional crude oils are," Mui said. "The challenge is, how much further can you go when we need much further reductions from a climate standpoint from the status quo? The baseline is moving." In other words, no matter how much you slash your emissions, or how clean you make your operations, it will never be enough. You can't call our bluff. We'll just keep changing the rules of the game so that no matter how much oil sands producers improve their environmental profile, they will always be guaranteed to fail our tests.

There are remarkable improvements that oil sands operators have made in just the last few years on their rates of water usage too. A new method called Zero Liquid Discharge allows Suncor to recycle 90 per cent of the water it uses at its Mackay River operation[38]; the process means it takes only one-sixth of a barrel of water to produce a barrel of bitumen, and all the water comes from underground salty sources rather than freshwater rivers.[39] Imperial Oil's *in situ* operation at Cold Lake reuses 95 per cent of its water. And when it can't recycle water, the company uses brackish water from deep saline aquifers when it needs more. The total amount of fresh water used there now is miniscule: it's gone from about 3.5 barrels of water per barrel of bitumen when it first started there in 1985 to a mere half a barrel of water today. Companies including ConocoPhillips, Nexen, and Devon aren't using any fresh water for their SAGD operations, but instead use non-potable water with recycling rates at 90 per cent.

Nonetheless, environmentalist groups are peddling the myth that the oil sands are draining Northern Alberta's rivers dry.[40] But it's just not true. An immense 131 billion cubic metres of water flows out of Alberta every year; that's 131 trillion litres, or 35 trillion gallons. In fact, whatever fresh water oil sands producers use is drawn from the enormous Athabasca River – which actually has one of the lowest allocation levels in the province. The Athabasca, where the oil sands get their water, represents 23 billion cubic metres of that, or about 17 per cent. Only 3.9 per cent of the river's natural flow is available to all users, including municipalities in the area and other industries, and just 2.2 per cent of the Athabasca's water is allocated for use to the oil industry. And the operators don't use even half of that: they use about 1 per cent, and even less in the winter, when flows are lower (the river isn't dammed). Forecasts show that, even when all approved projects are active, that will rise to just 2 per cent. That kind of conservation level must sound like a watery Utopia to Americans, especially those living in the Southwest, where various U.S. states have signed contracts dividing up literally 100 per cent – every last drop – of the natural flow of key rivers, including the mighty Colorado.[41] If environmental NGOs like the Natural Resources Defense Council are looking to fight water overuse, they should relocate from their headquarters in Washington, D.C., to Fort McMurray. After all, it's not unusual for 85 per cent of Washington's Potomac River's flow to be drained for human use – about forty times more than what oil sands operators are allowed to take from their fresh watershed.

Meanwhile, technological advances are making the unphotogenic tailings ponds in the oil sands disappear too. The majority of oil sands operations are already using processes like SAGD that don't require any tailings ponds. Where there are ponds, Suncor has developed a new technology for its existing ponds that will speed up their elimination. Using "tailings reduction operations," the company has come up with a way to separate water from other residue in a matter of weeks, not the years it used to take.

That should be great news for anyone who claims to want to be rid of the ponds. But when Suncor announced its new breakthrough technology, the Pembina Institute put as dour a spin on it as it could manage. "It shows that tailings management is a significant challenge facing the industry and the fact they've made the decision to move away from [older technologies] shows that the industry's current approach to tailings management is not sustainable," said Simon Dyer, oil sands program director for the institute. The fact that the company is making dramatic improvements shows that it was doing something it shouldn't have in the first place. It's like criticizing Kellogg's for adding more raisins to every box of Raisin Bran cereal because it proves that before, Raisin Bran was a terrible product. By that logic, no company should be working to make anything it does any better – unless it's willing to admit failure.

Suncor has found a new and better technology that could collapse tailings timeframes by as much as a hundredfold – the technological equivalent of leaping straight from a World War One bi-plane to a passenger jet – and all the Pembina

Institute can do is grumble about it? What's more important to the institute – improving the environment or being able to bad-mouth oil companies? Its negative reaction is almost enough to make a skeptic wonder if Pembina secretly doesn't want the big tailings ponds to be made obsolete. If those disappear, what is it going to use for its oil sands horror photos in all those fundraising pamphlets?

Getting into the intricate details of how oil is made, rather than relying on the spin from environmental groups, is hard work. But it's a much smarter way to weigh the environmental impacts and to create government policy. For instance, when it comes to measuring the carbon footprint of fuel used just in transportation, the United States uses a sophisticated measuring standard called GREET – as in Greenhouse gases, Regulated Emissions, and Energy use in Transportation. It was developed by Argonne National Laboratory, and it's the most informative model because it measures all the emissions that go into the gasoline production process – everything from the wasted, flared gas that some countries burn off as they're pumping oil to the fuel burned by the tanker ships required to haul oil from Arabia to U.S. ports. Past studies that claimed Alberta's oil sands have much larger GHGs compared to other sources didn't take the full carbon life-cycle into account like GREET does. But they should – they're a part of the fuel production and delivery process and they emit CO_2. Why shouldn't the environmental effects of Saudi tankers be taken into consideration?

And most any kind of oil tends to come out of the ground along with water, so deep-sea oil drilling, such as what goes on in the Gulf of Mexico, means pumping five barrels of water for every barrel of oil. That's a relatively common ratio, by world standards, but producers there have to pump all that extra water up from depths of more than fifteen thousand feet. Water is heavy, so that, too, wastes a whole lot of energy. Meanwhile, Mexican Mayan crude is produced by injecting nitrogen produced from the world's largest air-separation plant. All of a sudden, when the GREET standard is used, and all of these other energy requirements are taken into account, the oil sands don't look like an environmental problem. They become the environmental solution.

All of these little wrinkles – flaring natural gas; pumping from very deep depths; injecting nitrogen – add to the energy required and GHG footprint of producing a barrel of oil. That's why these sources are comparable to oil sands oil. But there's a difference: oil sands companies are working aggressively to cut their GHG emissions; we've already seen GHG intensity in the oil sands drop by 38 per cent in less than twenty years. But that's simply not a priority in Nigeria, where they can't even be bothered to sell the natural gas they flare.

Alberta, on the other hand, is the most environmentally obsessive jurisdiction there is. It doesn't have much choice: unlike the corrupt warlords running Nigeria, the politicians in Alberta's legislature know that voters consider the environment a priority, according to surveys,[42] and polls show they aren't ready to leave the responsibility for it entirely in the hands of industry.[43] Environmental carelessness has the potential to harm Alberta's government. And not just at the ballot box. Revenues from the energy industry are the single biggest contributor to the province's bottom line,[44] with the tax collected from all the jobs and businesses the industry spins off adding billions more. And the most worrisome threat the province faces, by far, is the disruption that could come from international boycott or taxes over its environmental practices. Far from corrupting Alberta, the reliance on oil wealth has actually motivated it to keep its reputation as clean as it can – which is why the Alberta government last year announced it would spend $2 billion on the largest effort in history to capture carbon emissions.[45]

One of the most dramatic measures the Alberta government insists oil sands operators undertake is the reclamation process. It's part of the deal: if you want a licence to mine the oil sands, you have to agree to return the land back to the natural state you found it in when you're done – minus all the unsightly bitumen, of course. The oil sands is a young industry, so most of the first installations are still in the middle of their work. But already, while 530 square kilometres of land had been disturbed by the oil sands, as of 2008, more than 12 per cent of it, 65 square kilometres, has been reclaimed – replanted with the native grasses and trees and habitable by wildlife. Only a portion of it has been so far "certified" by the province as reclaimed. But already the huge reclamation processes being pioneered in Alberta have garnered an extraordinary amount of attention. It's probably the most studied environmental phenomenon in Canada: literally thousands of research papers, reports, and university theses have been devoted to studying reclamation. At any one time, you're likely to find academics from ten universities and dozens more researchers from other interests in the field studying the fascinating way in which Alberta's oil companies erase the traces of their work.

Mitigating and monitoring the oil industry's environmental impact is also why the province spends yet more on a whole suite of agencies it has established to constantly measure and track the quality of Alberta's air, water, and land quality, especially in and around the Wood Buffalo oil sands region. The Wood Buffalo Environmental Association (WBEA) is one. It has fourteen continuous air-monitoring stations across Northern Alberta, and thirteen more passive stations, measuring air quality data that are constantly streamed onto its website so that anyone can see, at any time, how clean the air is across the 70,000 square kilometres the WBEA measures.[46] Five more air quality associations monitor other vast areas of the province. It takes a lot of confidence to stream your environmental data directly to the Internet for the world to see; but after fifteen years of monitoring, the WBEA has yet to find any significant acid or nitrogen effects. And Alberta's Regional Aquatics Monitoring Program (RAMP) has been monitoring water in Alberta's industrial areas for twelve years. It monitors the Athabasca River, eleven tributaries, and fifty lakes. Though RAMP is a government initiative, any oil sands company whose work might have an impact on Alberta's water is required to be a member.

RAMP has also never noted any significant changes in water quality. It's not just the water itself that's checked; more than 2,500 fish are caught by environmental officials every year and tested for signs of environmental toxins. The agency has found no deterioration in key measures such as arsenic, sulphates, and organic carbon compounds. In fact, what the studies have found, peculiarly, is that by some pollution measures, the water in the Athabasca is actually cleaner downriver from Alberta's major oil sands operations than it is upriver. The PAH concentration in a naturally occurring bitumen seep measured in 2002 was about ten times the amount measured downriver from the oil sands plants.

That puzzling phenomenon can be explained by nature; there are places upstream on the river where there is a natural seepage of bitumen into the water that's been going on for millennia. All those early explorers noticed it happening more than a century ago.

North American oil companies, like pretty well every industrial business on the planet, have their tangles with nature that don't always turn out well. In 2009, oil sands giant Syncrude was charged in the drowning deaths of sixteen hundred ducks that had landed on one of its tailings ponds, a pool where residues like clay, bitumen, sand, and other materials are left to settle out from water used in the oil sands mining process before being cleaned up.

Nothing like this had happened to Syncrude in at least twenty years of oil sands operations[47]: the phalanx of bird-repelling devices, including noise cannons, Syncrude explained, hadn't been properly activated in time for the birds' spring migration because of stormy weather in the region.[48] Had Syncrude been an airport, the failure of the bird cannons might have downed a jetliner, killing hundreds of passengers. The failure at the tailing pond meant that the only casualties were the birds themselves.

Since the 1970s, Syncrude has become pretty good at using scarecrows and noise makers to keep birds off their tailings ponds; it certainly had strong incentives to do whatever it had to do. In addition to the PR disaster that followed, the maximum legal penalty for "depositing or permitting the deposit of a substance harmful to migratory birds in waters or an area frequented by birds" could see company executives jailed for six months,[49] in addition to nearly $1 million in federal and provincial fines.[50] Of course, that wasn't good enough for environmental groups: a Greenpeace spokesperson called the penalties "very weak."[51]

While Syncrude executives had every reason to want to save the ducks, the incident has turned into a bonanza for environmentalist groups, which finally– for the first time in decades of safe, victimless oil sands operation – had some genuine evidence to back up their claims that the operations were harmful. International media suddenly wanted to hear their warnings of the coming calamities; the ecological apocalypse of which this was just a first sign. MSNBC even dutifully published photographs handed to them directly by the anti–oil sands campaigners at Greenpeace, which still had the Greenpeace logos printed on them.[52]

Never had anti–oil sands groups been given a PR gift like this, and they intended to milk it for all they could. The Pembina Institute, in league with a list of foreign lobby groups, issued a press release, screaming that "more than 160 million" birds from Canada's boreal forests would die from oil sands development, according to a new study they had just prepared.[53] All that was missing was the *Austin Powers* character Dr. Evil raising his pinky while saying the word "million."

That's quite a statistic, and if you heard it on the news, as many people did, without any examination of how that figure was arrived at, you could be forgiven for being worried.[54] How many people hearing about the looming bird Armageddon took the time to read that report in full? How many journalists did? Because, if you did, you'd see that Pembina's "report" on the future of the oil sands was a report in the same way *Star Trek* is a report on the future of space travel.

Pembina pulled out every trick they could to make headlines with that number, and make headlines they did. If oil companies reported their finances, their oil reserves, or their environmental impacts using methods even resembling the exaggerated techniques applied by Pembina in this report, they would face fraud charges. But who in the media, or government, bothers to scrutinize environmental groups?

Here's how the Pembina Institute, considered one of the most respected environmental groups in the country, pulled off that trick.

If you waded through the thirty-nine-page Pembina document – as you can be sure very few people reading, and probably writing, the news about the 160 million dead birds projection actually did – you'd discover that the group acknowledges that if you count all the tailings pond in all the oil sands in all of Canada combined, there might be one thousand birds a year in the oil sands region that meet a fate like that of the ducks that drowned at Syncrude's pond. Or roughly, over the course of twelve months, the same scale of calamity caused by a single Sunday's dim sum crowd in any big city's Chinatown. "It is difficult to estimate the number of birds that may be killed annually at tar sands tailings ponds, but one recent paper noted that hundreds of birds are typically known to be oiled every year at each of 10 or more tailings ponds in the region. Little public information is released about bird deaths, making it difficult to know the true number, but such an estimate could place the number of birds killed annually at a thousand or more."

So, even Pembina can only come up with a report showing hundreds of birds ending up getting "oiled" at tailings ponds every year (though oilings are not always fatal). But from that, the lobbyists at Pembina begin inflating the number with gusto. First, they multiply it by ten, just because it seems like something worth doing. "Conservative projections using recently published landing rates of birds on tailings ponds with deterrent systems show that annual bird mortality on current tar sands tailings ponds could range from more than 8,000 birds to well over 100,000, depending on mortality rates."[55] From there, the report loses all grip on reality, ending with a flourish – a "projection" of 300,000 birds killed per year. The report takes it for granted that every single mining project will be active, and running at full capacity for fifty years, which plainly isn't true: some projects end before others are begun, while earlier projects are shut down and returned to wilderness; some won't begin for another twenty-five years, but their impact is counted as if they had been running at full tilt all along. Imagine a car company booking sales on its income statement this year for models that won't even be developed till 2030 and you start to get an idea of the kind of accounting that's going on here.

But the environmentalists are clearly worried that even 300,000 dead birds per year – which is basically the arbitrary multiplying of one estimate by 300 – may not be enough to sufficiently scare people into believing the oil sands is one giant bird death trap. So instead of just counting (and then "projecting") the number of birds oiled, the study switches vocabulary about halfway through. You have to be on guard to see it: they stop talking about dead birds and start talking about "lost" birds – or, to use more accurate terms, birds that simply go elsewhere.

The Pembina Institute can't just keep on about oiled birds because it won't get them far enough. That's because the kind of oil sands work that creates tailings ponds, and thus creates the potential for what happened to Syncrude, is actually a small and shrinking portion of the total oil sands program. Most oil sands operations just don't have tailings ponds.

Environmentalists estimate that Canada's boreal forest – which reaches from the Alaskan border to Newfoundland – covers 2.3 million miles (6 million square kilometres).[56] That's

1.4 billion acres. And 35 million acres[57] of that is set to be developed for oil sands – about 2.3 per cent of the total forest. Anti–oil sands campaigns conjure up images of massive patches of clear-cut to make way for Brobdingnagian earth movers to churn up the soil in search of bitumen in every one of those acres. But it's a trick: open-pit oil sands mining – the kind that actually requires opening up ground, the kind whose pictures adorn every environmental lobby's website – actually represents only a tiny fraction of even that marginal land area. Most oil sands work is *in situ*, meaning in the site, underground – the oil being buried too deep below the surface to shovel it out. Instead, producers drill a low-profile hole into the ground, much like conventional oil drillers, and then use technologies like steam to suck up the bitumen. That's what happens, or will happen, to tap 98 per cent of the oil sands. Of the 1.4 billion acre boreal forest, about 160,000 acres, or 1 per cent of 1 per cent, is set aside for old-fashioned strip mining. That's so small it needs a little propaganda help, now doesn't it?

After all, it's awfully tough to blame underground, *in situ* oil sands for the loss of birds. But the Pembina report was co-written by a woman named Susan Casey-Lefkowitz, one of America's most prominent anti-oil lobbyists.[58] If anyone could figure out a way to make Big Oil's small hole in the forest sound like an unprecedented environmental catastrophe, you can bet it's her.

And so she does, claiming that the compressors placed next to those holes – the machines used to produce the steam injected into the ground – bother the birds. The word she uses is "displaces" – meaning, presumably, the birds move a few trees to the left to get a bit farther away from the machinery. That, Pembina assumes, means fewer nests and, hence, fewer hatchlings – evidently good enough to consider a vast number of birds "lost," as in never born. Add in a healthy dose of the same kind of extra-polation magic used in calculating tailings ponds effects, multi-ply it over fifty years, and the lobbyists' report tots it all up to a total of "425,000 fewer birds."

Once the Pembina report has spun every last statistic it could rally beyond all recognition, it adds them all up to get the hair-raising numbers dutifully reported by the press. Yet even the report itself can't fully avoid acknowledging how statisti-cally conjectural the entire exercise is. Boreal forest breeding habitats are estimated to be between 0.64 and 4.86 breeding individuals per acre – an astounding gap that could produce results that are off the mark by no less than 750 per cent. And so, not surprisingly, the final tally comes up with an impact on birds ranging from "6 to 166 million." Their margin of error, in other words, could be as high as 2,600 per cent. In the process, Pembina spends a lot of its time citing other "studies" – few of which have been peer-reviewed, many of which were written by other environmental lobby groups and, in some cases, rigged up by PR firms.[59]

And if mere numbers like that still can't tell a scary enough story, blatant appeals to emotion and to the mysticism of earth-worship would close the deal. The bird study – purporting to be a work of science – actually claimed that Aboriginal "Elders in a community could listen to the loons talk and they would tell them what was happening around the water." That's Pembina's idea of a sound basis for public policy: Dr. Doolittle says the birds told him to stop the drilling!

There's a fudge factor to the numbers even beyond the extrapolations and multiplications. In reality, oil sands opera-tions, especially the open-pit mines, are not worked all at once. As new areas are mined, old areas are reclaimed – the land is returned back to its original state once the oil work is done. Reclamation isn't optional; a reclamation plan is a required element of any oil sands operation's licensing application before work can begin. Syncrude, one of the pioneers in the oil sands, had its first reclaimed area certified by the Alberta government in 2008.[60] Its thirty-year-old Mildred Lake site is now a quarter reclaimed. Its newer projects don't wait nearly as long: Syncrude's new Aurora site started land reclamation just three years into operations.

And underground operations can begin reclamation much sooner than open mines. Imperial Oil's Cold Lake project has 65 per cent of its affected land area under reclamation. One-fifth of the land is already reclaimed, including the planting of more than seven hundred thousand trees and shrubs indigenous to the region.

The lobbyists' bird Armageddon horror story didn't account for reclamation; it simply dismisses it by outright denying that it works – even though, in the very same document, they grudgingly acknowledge that Syncrude has already had its first reclamation efforts officially certified by the government. Their report just declares that there will be "no production of young birds from mined tar sands areas for at least 20 to 40 generations." None at all – though anyone who strolls through Syncrude's reforested hiking trails can tell by the chirps that that doomsday prediction has already proved false. In its zeal to inflate the case against Alberta, the report even finds a way to somehow throw the environmental impact of refineries in Chicago and Louisiana onto the shoulders of the oil sands, as if those refineries didn't exist long before the oil sands were developed, and as if they wouldn't be processing oil from other countries if the oil sands simply disappeared.

As it happens, Syncrude isn't the only oil company to have found itself brought up on charges for committing crimes against the avian community. ExxonMobil pleaded guilty in federal court in August 2009 to killing eighty-five birds that had accidentally come into contact with chemicals on its U.S. properties and agreed to pay U.S.$600,000 in fines and costs. A month earlier, PacifiCorp, an electric utility in Oregon, paid nearly U.S.$1.5 million after more than two hundred birds were electrocuted by its power lines. Over the past twenty years, hundreds of similar cases have been brought against American energy firms.[61]

Of course, some companies actually make it their business to kill birds: Colonel Sanders and Tyson Foods became American business legends for dispatching millions of them every year. The difference seems to boil down to which kinds of birds you kill and whether it was by accident or on purpose. Paradoxically, accidents are punished, while deliberate bird-killing isn't.

Or, to be more accurate, accidents are punished only when they happen to the kind of companies that environmentalists hate. Because birds die all the time, accidentally, in our industrialized landscape. Even office buildings, as benign as those are, are responsible for millions of deaths every year, from birds flying into their windows.[62] The law only gets involved when there's an energy executive to blame for it.

Take a look at one of the environmentalists' favourite kind of "green" power: wind. There's a sizeable wind farm at Altamont Pass in California. All those turbines spinning in the breeze are the kind of environmentally friendly energy sources Greenpeace goes ga-ga over. Mind you, if you're a bird, they probably don't look quite so friendly; more like giant shredders in the middle of your migratory flight path.

A 2008 study of the Altamont farm, conducted by the Alameda County Community Development Agency, calculated that the turbines kill an average of eighty golden eagles every single year. That's just one unlucky species, though. In total, the study estimated that about ten thousand other birds are killed annually at the Altamont blender farm. Nearly all of them, it turns out, are protected by the Migratory Bird Act. It would take six Syncrudes, with their bird-warning noisemakers malfunctioning constantly, or one hundred Exxon chemical incidents to keep up with the avian bloodbath at Altamont's earth-friendly energy facility. Perhaps authorities haven't been pressing charges against Big Wind because they simply don't have the labour force to keep up.

After all, that's just one wind farm. In total, the number of birds mutilated by environmentally approved energy across America are many times larger. According to estimates from the American Bird Conservancy, wind turbines across the United States butcher between 75,000 and 275,000 birds every year. And things are just getting started: since wind energy enjoys the blessing of the earth-first crowd, they're putting pressure on policy makers in Washington to ramp up wind power until it provides 20 per cent of American electricity by 2030 – or about 300,000 megawatts. That's about twelve times the amount of wind energy that was being produced at the end of 2008. The American Wind Energy Association itself figures that every one of those megawatts will doom between one and six birds a year to a grisly fate. Twenty years from now, spinning blades may well be felling 150,000 birds a month, or nearly 2 million every year.

Of course, in fairness to the folks at Big Green, birds die all the time, for all kinds of reasons. That's a reality the American Wind Energy Association is understandably quite eager to remind us of. They point out that housecats alone kill an "estimated one billion birds annually."[63] Then they list all the human-caused ways birds meet their maker: Some 130 million to 174 million birds get zapped in the United States every year when they fly into electricity transmission lines – many of which are birds with large wingspans, including raptors and waterfowl. Another 60 million to 80 million birds are hit by cars or trucks. Communications towers, they point out, take out another 40 million or 50 million birds a year (one tower in Wisconsin was the site of thirty thousand bird fatalities in a single night). And loads more are victims of agricultural pesticides, jet engines, smokestacks, and bridges – the list goes on and on.[64] That's the wind industry trying its hardest to put things into context: pointing out that a few dozen, hundred, or even thousand birds killed by their machinery isn't all that much in the grand scheme of things. Hey, that's how it goes for birds, right? What's a few more?

Syncrude hasn't yet tried excusing its duck accident by using that kind of cold calculus (the company instead offered "a heartfelt and sincere apology" and promised changes to "ensure a sad event like this never happens again"[65]). Maybe it should give it a try. After all, it's not entirely untrue: cats kill birds, meat factories kill birds, office buildings kill birds, and turbines kill birds. Only energy executives, it seems, face fines and prison time for killing birds.

Whether it comes to the impact on waterfowl, water usage, air pollution, water pollution, and even carbon emissions, the numbers tell the real story: the environmental impact of Alberta's oil sands is actually as good as or often better than many other energy producers. It seems surreal, given how widely vilified the oil sands have become. But the reality is that the oil sands aren't really hated for their environmental impact: any objective observer looking at the hard, factual data can see how unexceptional the environmental impact really is when stacked up against other industries and jurisdictions. The oil sands aren't hated for that. They're hated for the fact that they represent a seemingly bottomless supply of oil – the lifeblood of industrial growth. It's a nightmare vision of the future for those who despise commercial expansion and urban development. And it's clear they'll pull out any stop – no matter how spurious and unethical – to prevent it.

Chapter 8

GREENPEACE'S BEST FUNDRAISER EVER

The oil sands are not perfect, and criticizing them is fair game. But why has criticism of the oil sands been so disproportionately loud compared to criticism of other, larger, more disturbing sources of oil?

Does it make sense to call the peaceful oil sands "blood oil" and yet not even apply that term to describe oil from dictatorships that actually have the blood of tortured and murdered innocents on their hands? Does it make sense to focus on an unfortunate, one-time accident that killed sixteen hundred ducks but to ignore the hundreds of millions of birds killed every single year by other industries?

Why do the world's most prominent anti-oil groups focus on Canada's oil sands but virtually ignore polluting dictatorships that are worse by any conceivable measure? Why is peaceful, clean Canada the target of such a political assault, but dirty, authoritarian countries get a nod and a wink?

These are critical questions. The media eagerly reports

every anti–oil sands campaign, and treats every energy company's executives with doubt. Is it too much to ask that they
apply the same journalistic independence and skepticism
towards the lobbyists and corporations who have turned fighting the oil sands into an industry itself? Major environmentalist
groups are multimillion-dollar enterprises, dependent on generating publicity and raising vast amounts of cash. It's naive to
think that given these vested and urgent interests that they act
always and only out of benevolence and altruism: we've
already seen the way that certain groups select undeserving
targets for the wrong reasons and distort statistics to deceive
their unsuspecting donors. If just a fraction of the skepticism
that reporters have for Big Oil were applied to Big Green,
we'd have a much clearer picture of these groups' true
motives. If reporters covering these groups won't ask the hard
questions like the ones listed here, we'll have to do it for them.
And an examination into the internal politics at a leading
environmental group like Greenpeace will give us a pretty
good idea of the answers.

Let's look at an example of an environmental issue that
doesn't even involve the oil sands: nuclear power. Greenpeace
says it hates nuclear power. Its annual report describes it as
"dangerous," a "dead end," "dirty," and a "threat to everybody's
security." That's pretty unambiguous. And Greenpeace describes
at length its street activism on the subject, including its trade-
mark protests at a new nuclear reactor being built in Finland.
The word "nuclear" appears more than forty times in its
annual report. It hates the stuff.

So you can only imagine what Greenpeace might have to say
about the world's largest nuclear power plant builder: China.[1]
China has eleven nuclear power plants in commercial operation

now, but it's on a building spree, with 51 new plants under construction or in the planning stage. Another 110 plants are proposed after that. And China isn't just building nuclear plants for itself – it's exporting plants to other countries too, like Pakistan. By 2030 – just twenty years from now – China is expected to produce up to 160 gigawatts of electricity through nuclear power, which is more than the United States, United Kingdom, or Russia produce now – combined.

And it's not just the plants; China has five major mines for uranium, a primary fuel for nuclear reactors, including two open-pit mines, and two nuclear waste disposal sites.

So what does Greenpeace have to say about this nuclear monstrosity? Greenpeace China has a lot of criticism of nuclear power – at least when it's talking about nuclear power in Holland, Russia, Spain, and France. It condemns those countries for expanding their reliance on nuclear. But it's never uttered a word of criticism about China's nuclear program. In fact, in one bizarre press release on the subject, it positively engages in PR spin for China's nuclear industry.[2]

Take the massive China Guangdong Nuclear Power Group (CGNPG), which produces four thousand megawatts of nuclear power a year and has another ten thousand under construction[3] and more planned.[4] That one company alone produces more nuclear power than all of Canada or all of the United Kingdom. And it's going to build even more.

But, as a PR gesture, CGNPG announced its intention to build some windmills – fifty megawatts' worth,[5] compared to the fourteen thousand megawatts of nukes it runs. That's 0.36 per cent of the power it'll be putting out. That's not even a rounding error. But that was enough to earn Greenpeace's praise. "Every player in China is actively devoted to wind energy," gushed

Greenpeace in a 2005 press release. That's a laugh, given the 300:1 ratio of nukes to wind, and an even higher ratio of coal to wind. But then the Greenpeace press release does something downright bizarre: instead of quoting a Greenpeace activist calling for more wind or solar power, it hands the pen over to the Chinese government's power industry spokesperson – Li Junfeng, director of the Chinese Renewable Energy Industry Association (CREIA) – who fills in the rest.

> Every player in China is actively devoted to wind energy, including the Big Five Power Companies, some private companies and some provincial energy investment companies. Even companies like China Guangdong Nuclear Power, which has been investing in nuclear power, is paying attention to wind power.[6]

Just to be clear, that's from the official Greenpeace press release, put out on Greenpeace letterhead. And it's giving a propaganda platform to the Chinese government.

Because, in reality, despite its deceptive name, that's what the Chinese Renewable Energy Industry Association[7] is: it's a front group for the Chinese Communist Party. "Front group" is probably unfair because the CREIA doesn't try to hide who it is. It publishes its list of officers and directors, all of whom work for the government or government-owned power companies, all of which are dominated by coal or nuclear power. They even list which government ministries the directors hail from, like Director Liu Wenqiang of the State Economic and Trade Commission Resource Department. There's no possible way that Greenpeace didn't know these were government bureaucrats and spin doctors.

It's unthinkable that Greenpeace would give its seal of approval to some PR flack from the U.S. coal or nuclear industry or the Canadian oil sands, let alone the Canadian or U.S. government. But when it comes to government-owned China Guangdong Nuclear, Greenpeace won't lift a finger – other than to let the Chinese government boast about "paying attention" to wind power. The Greenpeace release even explicitly advertises the fact that this new corporate hero is investing in more nuclear plants – and yet Greenpeace still applauds them.

What's that all about? Why is Greenpeace so tough on a single nuclear power plant in Finland but cheers on Chinese nuclear companies and even quotes them approvingly in its press releases? And is the explanation any help to understanding why lobby groups like Greenpeace are so hard on Canada's oil sands but so meek on the oil coming from the world's worst dictatorships?

Patrick Moore, one of the founders of Greenpeace, might have an answer. Moore was on Greenpeace's very first project, when the group was formed in Vancouver in 1971. Along with a half-dozen other founding members, he set sail on a rented ship to protest the U.S. military's plans to detonate a hydrogen bomb off the Alaskan coast. Moore has a Ph.D. in ecology and was the only environmental scientist in the group. He personally put the green in Greenpeace.

Moore went on to become Greenpeace Canada's president for nine years and a director of Greenpeace International for six years. He was on the front lines of some of Greenpeace's most audacious adventures, including a run-in with a Soviet whaling ship that fired a harpoon over one of Greenpeace's little boats, and he was even aboard the Greenpeace ship *Rainbow Warrior* just hours before French commandos bombed it in New Zealand. Moore was the embodiment of Greenpeace in its first decade, lobbying everyone from the United Nations to the pope.

As Moore describes it, he and the other founders had a pretty simple mission: "opposition to nuclear testing and protection of whales." Moore helped expand Greenpeace's mandate to other scientifically based environmental issues. But after fifteen years, Moore quit the group he loved so dearly. "None of my fellow directors had any formal science education," he explained. "They were either political activists or environmental entrepreneurs. Ultimately, a trend toward abandoning scientific objectivity in favor of political agendas forced me to leave Greenpeace in 1986."

"Sadly," Moore says, "Greenpeace has evolved into an organization of extremism and politically motivated agendas . . . stewardship requires that science, not political agendas, drive our public policy."[8]

Pity the honest scientist who dares to point out how a small group of volunteers has morphed into an unrecognizable multinational lobby group run by professional agitators. Greenpeace still grudgingly acknowledges that Moore is one of its founders[9] – its official history page lists him as one of the passengers on that first Greenpeace voyage. But it has deleted any mention of his scientific credentials or his fifteen years of service. He's like the uncle whom no one in the family wants to talk about. Other founders are given whole pages on Greenpeace's website, as a sort of secular shrine. Moore's contributions are thrown down the memory hole.

Well, not completely. While Moore's role in building Greenpeace has been sanitized from the official record, a search of the Greenpeace website reveals an enormous amount of effort spent trying to destroy Moore's reputation. Moore "misrepresents himself in the media as an environmental expert or even an environmentalist," states one angry Greenpeace rant. Given Moore's Ph.D. in ecology and his central role in the first decade of Greenpeace, it's Greenpeace's press release, not Moore, that misrepresents the facts. And then Greenpeace gets nasty, claiming, without substantiation in a press release, that Moore's motive for leaving was "an opportunity for financial gain."[10]

Moore's criticism that Greenpeace is an uninformed gang of mercenaries might sound harsh, but even Greenpeace's bosses don't exactly deny that they're more about propaganda than science. Their outgoing executive director, Gerd Leipold, was asked about this point by the BBC, one of Greenpeace's most supportive media outlets. Leipold was honest: if Greenpeace didn't exaggerate, no one would pay them any attention – or any money. "We were confronted with a world that unfortunately only recently has woken up," he told the BBC. "We, as a pressure group, have to emotionalize issues."[11]

Note that Leipold didn't call his organization a scientific group or a think-tank. It's a pressure group – but the emotional pressure he described wasn't pressure on politicians but pressure on the public, whom he blamed for not caring enough.

Actually, stripped of Moore's negative adjectives and Leipold's positive ones, the two men say pretty much the same thing: Greenpeace isn't a scientific organization. Both men agree that Greenpeace is a lobby group that uses hype and emotion, not facts and research, to make arguments.

A truly scientific approach to nuclear power would consider China's massive building spree a considerably bigger issue than a lone reactor in Finland, just as China's out-of-control greenhouse gas emissions dwarfs the oil sands' small GHG footprint. But as Moore and Leipold both say, it's about money and PR, not the environment.

Sometimes Greenpeace lets the mask that covers its actual agenda slip even more. In 2006, when U.S. president George W. Bush was visiting Pennsylvania to promote his plans for more nuclear power, Greenpeace did what it did best: it went into protest mode, looking to capitalize on the media presence that a president naturally brings with him. Greenpeace issued a "fact sheet" denouncing nuclear power. But the release was sent out prematurely, without being proofread, and it contained this whopper: "In the twenty years since the Chernobyl tragedy, the world's worst nuclear accident, there have been nearly [FILL IN ALARMIST AND ARMAGEDDONIST FACTOID HERE]."[12]

The press release actually arrived on the desks of hundreds of newsrooms exactly that way – unfinished, with the author of the release writing a note in capital letters to remind himself to rack his brains for the right scare-mongering phrase for that perfect Greenpeace touch.

It was a rare glimpse behind the PR facade of Greenpeace, the $340 million per year[13] lobbying powerhouse, and a chance to see what is really on the minds of their spin doctors.

Had the unfinished release said something else, likely it would have been perceived as nothing more than a typo – a Greenpeace staffer just reminding himself to do some research. But it wasn't research or facts this lobbyist was after – it was "factoids," rhetoric pretending to be facts but is really just spin. And the spin Greenpeace was looking for was supposed to be as jam-packed with fear and loathing as possible.

Greenpeace wasn't looking for truth. It was looking for "alarmism" and "Armageddonist" language. It called the press release a "fact sheet," but clearly that was just an Orwellian flourish. It was the opposite. It wasn't selling the truth or even facts. It was selling fear – and always with an eye to fundraising. When your global lobbying company has to raise $1 million a day to keep operations going, you've got to constantly be scaring the hell out of anyone who cares about the environment – college kids, moms, retirees, whoever: just get the dough. Never mind that you're using alarmism to upset innocent people; there's money to be made. They're like unethical tel-evangelists milking their congregants – right down to the warnings about Armageddon.

So why the Chinese exemption? If it's Armageddon you're after, surely China is every bit the compelling story that the oil sands is. Entire lakes in China are covered over with algae blooms caused by excessive pollution. Multicoloured smoke belches from industrial smokestacks right in the heart of China's overcrowded cities. The skies are permanently opaque from pollution. It's like a scene in a Charles Dickens novel, except for a hundred times the population and with a host of chemicals that hadn't been invented 150 years ago.

Greenpeace isn't particularly proud of its double standard. Which is why it's lucky that most Greenpeace members speak English or other Western languages while Greenpeace China publishes its most appalling work in Chinese. It literally carries on two different dialogues: one for people in China and one for the rest of us.

For example, Greenpeace China has an English-language Twitter account, twitter.com/GreenpeaceCn. And it has a Facebook page, both in Chinese and in English. But neither

Twitter nor Facebook work in China – both are kept out by China's censorship technology, dubbed the Great Firewall of China.

Those Facebook and Twitter accounts are tailor-made for Westerners – Greenpeace members and journalists – who think they're getting a real look at what Greenpeace China is up to. It's propaganda to cover up their other propaganda. One of the strangest "tweets" on their Twitter page reads simply, "China apparently blocks Twitter! Sorry all our mainland tweaters! [sic]"[14] As it turned out, they had been pretending all along that they were broadcasting their online comments from Beijing, even going so far as to report the air quality index in that city, as if they were sitting right in the heart of it. I asked Fanny Lee, a spokesperson for Greenpeace China, about it, and while she claims that Greenpeace has the technology to get around China's Twitter censorship, she admitted that many Twitter posts claiming to be from Beijing are actually written in Hong Kong or Taiwan.

And Greenpeace China has a Facebook page, in English[15] and Chinese, again giving the impression that their activists are working hard right in the belly of the most polluting beast on the planet.[16] Anyone care to track them down, wherever they really are, and tell them Facebook is banned in China too?[17]

It's a fascinating game: pretending to get tough with China – but doing so only safely outside the country, for the consumption of foreigners (but not too strenuously, mind you). Behind the Great Firewall, where the rest of us cannot see them, Greenpeace's actual Chinese branch spends its PR efforts demonizing the West and praising China's environmental achievements. It even suggests that China's headlong rush to industrialization is not the cause of its pollution – but that rapacious Western companies are to blame. In other words, it acts as a mouthpiece for all the nationalist propaganda the Chinese Communist Party requires of an activist group as the price of maintaining a footprint in its country. Of course there's no such thing as real activist groups in China; they're simply banned. Any group that operates in that authoritarian state is, in fact, just a client of the Communists.

Does Greenpeace play along because, as Patrick Moore claims, "the values of the organization have been corrupted and influenced by liberal and leftist agendas?"[18] Is China being given a free pass because it's the world's last, great remaining Communist dictatorship? Is it political correctness – because it's a Third World country? Why would Greenpeace accept the terms that political NGOs must accept in order to do business in China – that it submit to the will of the Chinese government?

The answer may lie in the great transformation from the Greenpeace volunteers who sailed to Alaska back in 1971 to the international mega-corporation that Greenpeace is today. Greenpeace isn't idealistic. It's a corporation, with a large staff, a fleet of ships thirstily guzzling fuel, and a nine-figure annual budget. It sells idealism – that's the commodity it offers its members – but it is structured similarly to any multi-national, answerable to a board of directors, a chief financial officer, auditors, and other money-men. And, like almost every other corporation in the world, it likely sees China as its next great market.

Greenpeace claims 3 million members worldwide. But if only 1 per cent of the people in China were to join, that would instantly add 12 million members to Greenpeace. Most Chinese are still quite poor and could never afford such a luxury. But for the couple of hundred million people in the burgeoning middle class, for whom anything Western is a sign of affluence and class, joining Greenpeace is like wearing a brand-name Lacoste or Polo shirt: it's a sign of success and prestige and international fashion. And if 12 million new Chinese members could be convinced to give just five yuan a month – less than a buck – to such a good cause, why that's an extra $100 million a year for Greenpeace.

In North America and Europe, Greenpeace has to compete with hundreds of other charities and non-profit causes – including countless other environmental movements, many of which have a more sober reputation. But that would be the upside of doing a deal with China's censors: there simply are no other environmental NGOs that are given Greenpeace's free access to the 1.2 billion potential donors there. As a result of singing from the Communist Party songbook, Beijing lets Greenpeace sign up members.

Grassroots political organizing is normally a very dangerous thing in China – it's the sort of illegal democratic activity that gets average Chinese citizens sent to political re-education camps, or even crushed by tanks. But with Greenpeace effectively acting as a propaganda arm of the Chinese Communist Party – greenwashing China's record and smearing its Western competitors – why wouldn't Beijing allow Greenpeace to have the run of the place? It looks as if Greenpeace's hard-earned reputation for ideological ferocity and independence – the very qualities that Moore himself helped build – is being rented out to the Chinese government in return for a few bucks. Greenpeace gets exclusive access to China's citizens, and the Chinese government is given a powerful Western apologist.

Could it be that Moore was right – that Greenpeace put politics ahead of science, or even ahead of its own principles? A look through the rest of Greenpeace's work in China shows the same pattern: the lobby group that is so tough on Western industry is a teddy bear when it comes to Chinese pollution.

Sometimes it's hard to tell where Greenpeace China ends and the Chinese government begins, they're in such lockstep. Take this hilarious Greenpeace description of rooftop hot water heaters[19] in a Chinese town called Dezhou, featured in a Greenpeace China promotional video:

> China is often branded a climate killer. Well, with 70 percent of its energy needs coming from coal this vast country is indeed one of the key culprits. But what's little reported is the nation is making some giant strides in green innovation. Don't believe us? Take a trip to Dezhou, a city in east China where the sun always shines.

Of course in the Greenpeace video of Dezhou, as with all Chinese cities, the sun isn't visible in the sky – it's too smoggy to see the sun or even clouds. It's just light or dark out; the sky is always a muddy shade of grey. Welcome to Greenpeace's green innovation utopia.

To be fair, the video does highlight a gadget that works: a factory in Dezhou makes rooftop hot water heaters. Water from a tank coils through a glass tube, and the sun warms it. But it's hardly cutting-edge environmentalism. The technology is nearly a century old, and has been used extensively in other countries, like Israel, where rooftop solar heaters have been a building code requirement for thirty years.[20] In fact, it's not even technically solar power. Congratulations to the Chinese for picking up on a good, tried-and-true idea. But really, how does that tiny experiment, in one Chinese town, make up for China's massive pollution and greenhouse gases?

And yet that's exactly what the Greenpeace announcement does: it forgives China its coal-fired power plants in return for a trinkety, old-fashioned water heater. Greenpeace says China is "often branded a climate killer" – a reference to China's new status as the world's largest emitter of greenhouse gases. But "climate killer" is actually Greenpeace's own catchphrase, the one it uses to smear Canada and other Western democracies. In reality, it never uses that insult against China. It's too busy pointing to a few rooftop water heaters to take on China's coal industry. It's too busy pointing out China Guangdong Nuclear's 0.3 per cent wind efforts to talk about its 99.7 per cent nuclear power.

Not that Greenpeace China doesn't ever talk tough about greenhouse gases and climate change. But when it does, it's always to denounce Western countries and companies, never China itself. Greenpeace's Chinese-language propaganda videos always manage to demonize foreigners, never local culprits. And unlike Greenpeace's American or European propaganda, when Chinese government officials or industry tycoons are caught on tape, it's to give their canned propaganda messages. In the Dezhou solar video, Greenpeace actually hands its own microphone over to a member of the Dezhou People's Congress, and the Communist founder of the solar factory, and a government commissioner, and a model employee of the factory, and a factory sales rep. There wasn't a single Greenpeace spokesperson in the video; only handpicked government and industry shills. In its thirty-nine years, has Greenpeace ever not had an activist, or even its own logo, in one of its campaign films? Greenpeace is not a particularly modest organization; everything it does is with an eye to publicity. Was this film – featuring Communist Party bosses and shilling for a particular company – even made by Greenpeace?

Gerd Leipold says that Greenpeace uses emotions to press for change. What emotions did its Dezhou propaganda touch, other than blind loyalty to the Chinese government and one of its favoured state-capitalist tycoons?

You have to look very hard on Greenpeace China's website to find the speak-truth-to-power call for revolution that is Greenpeace's hallmark in the West. For example, you might think that, in its report from Tibet, it'd mention the suppression of human rights and the exile of the Dalai Lama, or Beijing's full-speed-ahead resource exploitation there. But you'd be wrong.[21] In fact, the most common theme of Greenpeace China's videos has nothing to do with China. It's Arctic polar bears, and Arctic ice – a safe topic of discussion that won't rankle Beijing's political censors. Topics like China's Three Gorges Dam, the world's largest, are ignored, along with their environmental and social costs – except to praise the dam's lack of GHG emissions. And yet, after the Three Gorges Dam was finished in 2008, after 1,350 villages were submerged, and 1.3 million people displaced from their homes, it increased droughts, pushed species like rare river dolphins and sturgeons toward extinction, and polluted nearby waters. Even government officials recently had the honesty to admit the dam risked setting off "an environmental collapse."[22]

Greenpeace China does mock the president – but not China's president. It built a whole campaign attacking Barack Obama in the lead-up to his state visit to China. And – you can probably guess by now – while Greenpeace China officially called Obama the worst leader in the world when it came to climate change, it cheerfully gave China "top points."[23] Pay no attention to the kaleidoscope-coloured fumes belching out of every chimney; ignore the dead fish floating in the river. Who are you going to believe about China being "tops" in the environment: Greenpeace or your lying eyes?

Obama is the "most failed leader," declared Greenpeace China. And as to China's official position that it is not willing to reduce its carbon emissions under the Kyoto Treaty, Copenhagen Treaty, or any other treaty? Why that's just *Obama* "trying to weaken the international agreement." By pointing out China's intransigence regarding GHG emissions, Americans, the group argued, are merely trying to "cover their own inadequacies."

China, on the other hand, has made "great strides." Really? Who writes Greenpeace China's stuff – the same folks who came up with Mao's famous slogan for his own human-caused disaster, the "Great Leap Forward"? And, just in case Greenpeace China didn't make its loyalties clear, it flew in an Obama impersonator to Beijing and had him dress up like Michael Jackson, doing the moonwalk in white socks and black shoes. The Chinese teens laughed hilariously at Greenpeace's bigoted antics. After all, that's what all black people, even Obama, do, right – sing and dance?

Greenpeace China doesn't really hate Obama. It just makes fun of him so it can tell its Chinese members that China is doing so much more for its environment than America is. But

a Greenpeace campaign without a target to hate is like a war
without an enemy. So if Obama himself is merely the jester,
who plays the evildoer for Greenpeace China?

The answer is an enemy that everyone from the People's
Liberation Army to the Chinese Politburo could agree on: evil
Western capitalists.[24] They're the reason Chinese citizens are
awash in filthy water and breath foul air.

> Developed countries export their e-waste to poor developing
> nations including China where impoverished workers recycle
> it. The e-waste though is mostly toxic and these workers, many
> of them children, are exposed to hazardous chemicals that can
> harm nervous, respiratory and digestive systems.

Just a reminder: that's Greenpeace talking, not a Communist
Party editorial in the official *People's Daily*. Wang Jue,
Greenpeace China's director of public projects, actually has
foreign recycled cell phones as the number-one public project
on her list of pressing issues. Not Chinese cell phones, mind
you, although with more than 700 million cell phones in use,[25]
China is far and away the largest phone consumer in the world,
with nearly triple the number in use in the United States. Just
foreign ones, from capitalist countries. And what's her second
highest priority? Opposition to disposable chopsticks.[26] These
are the campaigns approved by the Communist Party.

The World Bank has a rather different list of environmental
concerns in China.[27] It notes that Chinese industry uses 20
per cent to 100 per cent more energy to do the same processes
that Western industry does – it's flagrantly wasteful. It has poor
emissions standards, lagging ten years behind the West when

it comes to auto emissions. And of the world's thirty most polluted cities, twenty are in China. But Greenpeace wants to talk about reusing chopsticks.

What Greenpeace is doing in China isn't illegal. It's just contrary to everything the group says it stands for, sacrificing what were once its principles for money. It's proof that, as Moore says, Greenpeace is just "looking to enrich themselves."[28]

So when that same Greenpeace comes around to Canada and shouts and screams at the oil sands, it's worth remembering just who Greenpeace really is. After all, China isn't just an enormous consumer of oil. It's now one of the world's largest producers of oil, both at home and around the world – from Sudan to Burma to the oil sands itself. And it has its own heavy shale oil operations. Whether you're concerned about fossil fuels and greenhouse gases, or you're concerned about human rights, China has among the world's worst records on both: it's not big on green, and it's not big on peace. You'd think a company calling itself Greenpeace would give a damn.

Now, Greenpeace is a corporation – that's its legal status – and there's nothing wrong with operating in such a way that maximizes revenues. Lots of corporations operate that way. The trouble is that Greenpeace is tricking its supporters. We're under no illusions when we buy a tube of toothpaste or a DVD that we're fattening the bottom line of some faceless consumer goods manufacturer or movie studio. But Greenpeace actually tells its donors their money will be "put to work" in "campaigns from Beijing to Brazil" to "stop climate change" and "end the nuclear threat" among other things. But, really, Greenpeace isn't working to stop climate change in Beijing or curtail Chinese investment in nuclear power. And it's enabling China's pollution problems.

Any donor who gives part of their paycheque thinking it's to help fight pollution, nuclear power, and carbon emissions would be justified in feeling ripped off if they discovered their money, instead, was being used to promote one of the worst polluters on the planet.

But environmental groups are lucky: everyone presumes their motives are always pure and that they operate always in good faith. And few journalists have the interest in investigating or even critically analyzing organizations that have such a powerful public reputation. As a result, green groups get away with all kinds of behaviour that would be scandalous if it were perpetrated by for-profit companies. And it's not just Greenpeace.

In fact, if Greenpeace is the shock jock of the environmentalist movement – always pulling outrageous stunts just to get noticed – the Pembina Foundation for Environmental Research and Education, another one of the oil sands' loudest, highest-profile critics, tries to be a bit more buttoned down and credible. Pembina staff work as environmental consultants to some of Canada's most powerful corporations, including Alberta's biggest energy firms. They work in partnership with the University of Calgary's internationally regarded Institute for Sustainable Energy, Environment and Economy and the Toronto Dominion Bank's economists. Pembina publishes textbooks for schools and economic analysis for governments; it issues wonkish reports like "Hydraulic Submersible Pump Technology Assessment: A Global Energy Services Limited Technology"[29] and "The Canadian Teacher's Guide to Accompany World Military and Social Expenditures."[30] It's the mainstream face of environmentalism; a "think-tank"[31] rather than an activist group. And like Greenpeace, Pembina has to raise an enormous amount of money every week just to meet its payroll. Money is a big part of its mindset.

On the Pembina Foundation's website, you'll find a copy of something called the Association of Fundraising Professionals' Donor Bill of Rights. It's a one-page document, created by a bunch of different charity associations, that spells out for people who give to charities like theirs that they are guaranteed certain things: the right to know who works for the charity, the right to see their annual financial statements, to have their name deleted from mailing lists, and probably, most importantly, "To be informed of the organization's mission, of the way the organization intends to use donated resources, and of its capacity to use donations effectively for their intended purposes."[32]

But how much do donors of the Pembina Foundation really know about its mission and what it does with all their money? The foundation's website offers this rather harmless explanation: the foundation's mission, it says, "supports innovative environmental research and education initiatives to increase understanding within society of the way we produce and consume energy, the impact on the environment and the consequences for communities, as well as options for the more sustainable use of energy natural resources."

When donors exercise their "right" to ask about what the foundation is doing with the millions it raises every year from donors, that kind of explanation probably makes most of them feel pretty good about giving. "Education." "Environmental." "Communities." "Options." Who'd object to a stew of feel-good words like that? And given that, unlike Greenpeace, the Pembina Foundation is a registered charity in Canada, every donation is tax-deductible and, so, gets a financial boost thanks to help from every Canadian taxpayer. It's perfectly natural for donors to the Pembina Foundation to expect that their money is going to a fair-minded, non-partisan group aimed at making everyone's life a little better.

But they'd be wrong.

The Pembina Foundation isn't like the United Way, a registered charity that takes no partisan political positions and uses the money it gets to help support poor people – goals that no reasonable person could object to. The Pembina Foundation is what almost anyone who took a cursory look at its activities would recognize immediately as a political activist group. In fact, it's a rebranded, reconstituted version of a group originally called the Gaia Foundation[33] – as in Gaia, the pagan earth goddess that environmentalists usually now call Mother Earth.[34]

That's pretty bizarre stuff, and a heck of a way to pursue the "innovative environmental research" and study the "way we produce and consume energy, the impact on the environment and the consequences for communities" that the foundation says are its goals. A good deal of this politics goes unnoticed because instead of lobbying the voters of today, the Pembina Foundation focuses a lot of its efforts on lobbying the voters of tomorrow – our children.

One of the foundation's major campaigns is called "GreenLearning" and it's being sent out to teachers in classrooms across the country.[35] Lots of groups do that; the producers of Al Gore's movie, *An Inconvenient Truth*, are trying to get DVDs of their movie to make their way into schools.[36] But they don't have the benefit of being a registered Canadian charity and they don't get tax subsidies to do it. One of the things that

GreenLearning does is to have schoolchildren send "e-cards" – emailable postcards – to Canadian politicians demanding action on climate change, and urging Canada to sign international cap-and-trade treaties like the Kyoto and Copenhagen accords. Pembina even somehow got Alberta oil giants Shell Canada, ConocoPhillips, and Transcanada Pipelines to sponsor the program.[37]

Of course, since the foundation's primary purpose isn't to get involved in politics, those firms may not know what they've been paying for. But they should. Take this note from Hailey R., featured on the Pembina's GreenLearning website: writing to Canadian prime minister Stephen Harper, she tells him his policies should not "be blinded by economics alone. In the international community, Canada has become a laughing stock on the issue of climate change. This fact is shameful at best."[38]

Sure, we all want our kids to learn to be active citizens. But how many of us want them learning civics from an activist group with a blatant anti-economic agenda? Pembina is explicitly anti-business. In one example that Karl Marx himself would approve of, Pembina calls the money that the oil sands companies make, after paying all of their costs and taxes, "excess profits captured by companies."[39] There are no "profits" in the oil sands, according to Pembina – just "excess profits."

That indoctrination is Pembina's calling card. As one teacher featured on the GreenLearning website gushes, the organization's pro-Kyoto "educational" package is "good for teachers because they will not have to spend time searching for stats and info about climate change in a bunch of different places."[40] Sure. Why spend all that time and effort seeking out broader contexts and different viewpoints when the Pembina

Foundation will tell your kids all they should know? Or at least all that Pembina thinks they should know.

The Pembina Foundation's political, overtly anti–oil sands activities aren't just limited to the schoolroom. Almost all the money the foundation raises ends up transferred directly to an even more aggressive anti–oil sands lobbying group: the Pembina Institute. Of the $2.17 million the Pembina Foundation received from donors in 2008,[41] $2.05 million – 95 per cent of it – was handed right over to the Pembina Institute. Other donations to the institute added up to all of $73,245.[42]

The Pembina Institute can take the Foundation's money and use it for activities that are far more nakedly political than what its patrons might expect. In fact, the Office of the Commissioner of Lobbying of Canada reports that the Pembina Institute lobbied the Conservative government on no less than thirty occasions between October 2008 and July 2009.[43] It's all about politics. It criticizes federal and provincial governments for not meeting emission-reduction targets set by the Kyoto Accord; encourages voters to reject Alberta's plans to cut emissions by storing carbon emissions underground; calls for more input from Canada's Aboriginals in the oil sands; and insists that the effectiveness of regulations in the oil sands for tailings ponds, water usage, and reclamation is all a "myth."[44] It would seem that pretty well anything short of shutting down oil sands operations would be insufficient for the Pembina Institute.

The oil sands are "a nasty and dirty business," according to Dan Woynillowicz, the Pembina Institute's director of external and strategic relations. That kind of talk is likely what Alberta's deputy premier had in mind when he complained about "misrepresentations" made by the environmental groups in his province and announced a $25 million promotional campaign designed to counter the kind of anti–oil sands propaganda coming out of groups like Pembina.[45] Amazingly, some of the very companies the Pembina Institute is intent on putting out of business are the same ones that pay the institute for "advice": companies including ConocoPhillips and Suncor Energy.[46] In 2009, the Toronto Dominion Bank hired the Pembina Institute, along with another anti–oil sands group, the David Suzuki Foundation, to author a report that would determine how Canada's federal government could meet the kind of climate change targets advocated by . . . the Pembina Institute and the David Suzuki Foundation. Their answer? By hobbling Alberta's economy, penalizing the province 8.5 per cent of its GDP, largely by shutting down oil sands production.[47]

Woynillowicz has also said groups like his are dedicated to getting North America's economy off fossil fuels and toward energy sources like wind and solar, the kind of thing, he argues, that "[President Barack] Obama has put forward."[48] It's hard to get more outright political than an endorsement of the U.S. Democratic Party's environmental policies.

Of course the people and groups that are fighting to shut down the oil sands have every right to their opinions, no matter how bizarre they may be, and they have every right to operate however they see fit, no matter how mercenary. But the efforts of anti–oil sands lobby have consequences: every attack on Alberta's industry further risks people's jobs, their retirement portfolios, and their peace of mind. And, more to the point, every barrel of oil not produced in the oil sands means one more, less ethical barrel produced in some OPEC dictatorship. These are considerable stakes. If we can't trust the biggest environmental groups out there to take them seriously enough to operate ethically, then we certainly shouldn't be taking any guidance from them on how to measure ethics in the oil sands.

Chapter 9

THE CANCER SCARE THAT WASN'T

Not long ago, an American documentary film crew arrived in the largely Aboriginal community of Fort Chipewyan, Alberta. Leslie Iwerks, the Academy Award–nominated director, whose films include documentaries about the Third World and surfing, came to tell the world about a sensational story. As the promotional material for the movie, *Downstream,* released in 2009, described it: "At the heart of the multi-billion dollar oilsands industry in Alberta, Canada, a doctor's career is jeopardized as he fights for the lives of the aboriginal people living and dying of rare cancers downstream from one of the most polluting oil operations in the world."[1]

The hero in the movie is an unassuming doctor named John O'Connor. A transplant from Nova Scotia, he flew into Fort Chipewyan a few times every month to minister to the twelve hundred people in town, a place so remote it has no permanent roads leading to it. O'Connor was a general practitioner – a regular family doctor, but he'd read up on various kinds of rare cancers. That's because one of them, a cancer of the bile ducts called cholangiocarcinoma, had killed his father in Ireland. By astonishing coincidence, he began diagnosing rare cancers in his small Fort Chipewyan practice – specifically that very same exceedingly rare type, cholangiocarcinoma.

And he was diagnosing it at an astounding rate. And he began to publicize his diagnoses. "Statistically, I'm not supposed to see any more than one to two per hundred thousand population, and I've diagnosed five in a population of twelve hundred in the last three years," he told one radio show. "That's extraordinary."[2] He would later diagnose another case, bringing the total to six.[3]

It was indeed extraordinary. And O'Connor began spreading alarm across the province to everyone who would listen. Fort Chipewyan happens to be located downstream from oil sands facilities along the Athabasca River. That, plus the rare cancers, was all that was needed to transform an obscure doctor's story into international news.

Fawning reports appeared in the media, some of which said O'Connor's findings supported what anti–oil sands groups had been insisting all along[4]: that the oil sands were toxic. They never had the evidence before; now John O'Connor had given them the proof they had been sorely lacking. He became a hero to the countless anti–oil sands websites that ran with their story of the Aboriginals of Fort Chipewyan being killed by callous, capitalist oil sands barons. Aboriginal groups accused the province of sanctioning "genocide."[5] Reporters and television and documentary producers poured into tiny Fort Chipewyan to report on the abominable tale.

Then things took an even more dramatic turn: physicians at Health Canada filed an ethics complaint against O'Connor with the Alberta College of Physicians and Surgeons, the board that licenses doctors. Among their complaints was that O'Connor was "causing undue alarm" about cancer rates in the community. For the anti–oil sands crowd, the complaints only intensified their suspicions: great forces were trying to silence the brave doctor.[6] O'Connor was a hero for blowing the whistle on behalf of the oppressed. And now he himself had become a martyr. He became a folk hero, in no small part due to the loving hagiographies written about him by his fellow anti–oil sands activist, journalist, and Greenpeace publicist Andrew Nikiforuk.

Except the truth was that the Health Canada physicians were the ones in the right. All the alarm really was "undue."

The reality is that most of Fort Chipewyan's population is Aboriginal, and with that racial difference comes not only cultural differences but different health issues too, none of which has anything to do with the oil sands. Take, for example, breast cancer. Statistically, Aboriginals are significantly less at risk than Caucasians: 24 per cent less likely, according to the Alberta Cancer Board. Leukemia is even more striking: whereas 13.0 out of 100,000 non-Aboriginal Albertans develop that cancer, only 9.2 out of 100,000 Aboriginals do – a rate almost 30 per cent lower than the rest of the population.[7]

But there are also some diseases, including some rare cancers, that Aboriginals develop at a greater rate than the rest of the population. Like cholangiocarcinoma. It occurs just 1.8 times for every 100,000 Albertans – but 4.7 times for every 100,000 Aboriginals in Alberta, or almost three times as often. That's still rare, but it's one of those cancers that just happens to occur more in Aboriginals, just like black people are more likely to develop sickle-cell anemia, or Jews are more likely to have Tay-Sachs disease. We call that genetics.

Fort Chipewyan doesn't have 100,000 people. It has a fraction of that. That doesn't mean there can't ever be a case of a rare disease like cholangiocarcinoma: the statistics don't have to do with 100,000 people in a given city or town. They refer to a statistical average across 100,000 Albertans. But if a case or two, or three, does turn up in Fort Chipewyan over the course of a few years, it's going to look awfully fishy, even if it is, as is often the case, entirely random.

But six cases of cholangiocarcinoma in a town of twelve hundred people? O'Connor's reports looked outright bizarre, and so it's little wonder that so many people started jumping to conclusions. O'Connor isn't an oncologist, so we don't know how he diagnosed those six cases. But when he did, it was enough to concern the Alberta Cancer Board. While O'Connor enjoyed the media spotlight, telling any journalist who would listen about his rash of cancer cases, the Cancer Board began a thorough, months-long investigation to get to the bottom of things in Fort Chipewyan. They were incredibly meticulous, even going so far as to track down Fort Chip residents who had moved to other cities. After spending a fortune, and consulting cancer experts from around the world, the Cancer Board concluded that, "Of six suspected cases [of cholangiocarcinoma] reported by O'Connor, two were confirmed."[8] That was "within the expected range," the authors concluded. Not six; two. Sort of hard to pitch movie-goers on that. But then, the documentaries had already been made, so no use in correcting things.

According to toxicity experts, cancer in children, since it occurs so rarely in natural circumstances, is considered a leading indicator of environmental health. But, the report's authors noted, not a single case of cancer – of any type – was found in children or teenagers in Fort Chip. It was a resounding repudiation of O'Connor's hype. And the study was as credible as could be: independently peer-reviewed by six scientists around the world, including one handpicked by the Fort Chip community itself.

Dr. Kenneth Cantor, senior investigator of cancer epidemiology for the National Cancer Institute in Bethesda, Maryland, called the study "excellent and comprehensive"; Martin Tobias, public health physician for New Zealand's ministry of health, called the research "superb." In fact, he was stunned to see how healthy Fort Chipewyan's residents actually were. Never before in the world had he heard of "any other indigenous population . . . who show lower cancer incidence rates overall and for most cancer types" than their non-indigenous peers. Fort Chipewyan's Aboriginals didn't have higher cancer rates than those of us not living near the oil sands – they had *lower* cancer rates. It took a while, but the truth – and half a dozen of the world's finest cancer experts – had finally caught up to a small-town doctor's error.

In the meantime, after O'Connor's explosive media declarations, Health Canada had taken an interest in the doctor's claims and wanted to investigate the cancer claims too. But something else strange happened: he refused to hand over his files to health officials, as required by law. The whistle-blower became the one who was blocking access to information about the cancer cases according to a report by the Alberta College of Physicians and Surgeons. All of a sudden it was O'Connor who was engaged in a cover-up – but in private. In public, he continued to pretend to demand the government investigate what was happening in Fort Chip. He bellowed for transparency. When Health Canada's physicians, stonewalled and increasingly suspicious, filed their ethics complaints, O'Connor claimed that he was the one being muzzled.

So what happened to all those alarming cases of cholangio-carcinoma that O'Connor had made such a fuss about? Three were entirely different kinds of cancer. One wasn't cancer at all. That's a 66 per cent misdiagnosis rate. Would you trust your doctor if his diagnoses were wrong two-thirds of the time? O'Connor isn't a hero whistle-blower. Laughably, after the Cancer Board study came out, O'Connor told the *Canadian Medical Association Journal* that he had been "vindicated."[9] And why not? His bogus tales of cancer epidemics had been swallowed whole and uncritically. He was lionized by anti–oil sands activists. He got to star in a documentary about his noble struggle. Why not try another whopper?

Then, in 2009, Alberta's College of Physicians and Surgeons completed its investigation into the ethic complaints lodged against O'Connor. The report was finished in February, but the college's own rules said it couldn't release the report without Dr. O'Connor's consent – and he refused to give it.[10] He continued to talk about the ethics complaints against him, but he refused to allow the college to do so and according to the *Globe and Mail* and *National Post* even vetoed a proposed public statement that would have given important information about the case to the worried citizens of Fort Chip.

Instead, in November, he told reporters that the ethics complaints against him had been "closed" and he was now "in good standing with the college." Based on that meagre information, subsequent news stories in more than one outlet reported O'Connor had been "cleared" by the college.[11,12] What he evidently didn't tell reporters – and what turned up when the report was finally leaked to the media – was that the college had indeed concluded that the doctor had committed serious ethical breaches in stirring up hysteria over rampant rare cancers in Fort Chipewyan.[13] He hadn't been cleared.

Someone – whether it was one of the Health Canada complainants or someone at the college – couldn't stand to stay silent anymore while O'Connor kept spinning things. The college's report into O'Connor's conduct was leaked to reporters. Canadians, and the people of Fort Chipewyan, saw, for the first time, the staggering inaccuracies in O'Connor's public statements – and the lengths he went to cover up the truth.

The law requires that all cancer cases be reported to public health officials so they can be tracked. It's a vital epidemiological tool in fighting cancer. But the thirteen-page ethics report[14] found that when Health Canada asked Dr. O'Connor for the records of all those patients allegedly suffering from rare cancers, he wouldn't produce them. For two years, as officials sent him email after email, even resorting to registered mail, he didn't respond or he outright refused to co-operate. These were patients that he said were sick; this was the community he said was in danger. Yet he was making things difficult for the public health doctors to get involved. The head nurse at Fort Chipewyan at the time was frantic. "I believe that we need this study," she wrote in an email to Health Canada. But Dr. O'Connor was "adamant that we not allow an outside agency access to the files." She couldn't understand it; "at this point I am just ready to quit."

And no wonder. When Alberta's Chief Medical Officer of Health intervened and finally managed to compel Dr. O'Connor to release his files, it turned out that he was simply mistaken. All those confirmed cases of rare cancers he had created a panic over simply didn't exist. He had told tragic tales:

colon cancers were everywhere. But of the twelve cases he claimed he had diagnosed, only three were confirmed in Fort Chipewyan over the period he had claimed (three more were found in the cancer registry). He had told reporters about a thirty-three-year-old patient who had died of colon cancer. The college's investigation found that "No patient died at age 33 from colon cancer as reported by Dr. O'Connor."

The doctor had "trumpeted to the world that he'd seen a worrisome number of cases of cancers of various types," the regulatory body's investigators wrote. He had "been quoted extensively in the media," saying things replete with "mistruths, inaccuracies and unconfirmed information." He "persisted in exaggerating his claims." He had "obstructed" efforts by doctors at Health Canada and the Alberta Cancer Board to investigate his alarmist complaints by flouting the law and ignoring repeated requests to provide critical public health data in a "timely manner" to the government with any evidence of his findings, and when the college discovered his errors, and tried to issue a statement of its findings to "provide the public with a clarification of the issues raised" to put at ease all those frightened people in Fort Chipewyan, convinced by the doctor that they were all being poisoned to death, the doctor tried his best to prevent it, even leading gullible journalists, who hadn't been able yet to see the report, that he had been cleared; that all the complaints against him were baseless. The alarming facts giving rise to the scare were simply not true; the citizens of Fort Chip didn't need his help. Dr. O'Connor, media darling, hero of the silver screen, was thoroughly discredited.

It's hard to believe that, after all that, the fake cancer scare wouldn't be the last time the media would fall for a tall tale from Fort Chipewyan. In August 2008, some kids who had been playing along the banks of the Athabasca River ran home with a strange-looking fish they'd found.[15] It was a goldeye, and it appeared to have something sticking out from its mouth that resembled a second jaw. Fort Chip's environmental activists trotted out the "mutant" fish at a Keepers of the Water Conference, which was discussing water quality issues down-stream from the oil sands, and suggested it had been deformed by unhealthy water. The "freakish," "two-jawed" creature made international news; it was compared to Blinky, the fictional three-eyed fish that swam in the water around Springfield's nuclear plant in *The Simpsons* cartoon.[16] "For us here, it's not that uncommon anymore," sighed Alice Rigney, the Fort Chipewyan resident who arranged the conference.[17] "What happens to the wildlife and the fish is eventually what is going to happen to us," said George Poitras, another anti–oil sands activist from the community.[18]

But that's only possible if Poitras and his neighbours suddenly grow bony tongues, like the goldeye has. Because scientists who later examined the fish proved that there was nothing mutant about it at all: the goldeye has a bony tongue – in fact, that's its formal Latin name – with little teethlike protrusions. When a goldeye dies, the tissue on its lower jaw decomposes, they pointed out, and the strong ligaments pull the tongue through the floor of the mandible, making the fish look like it's got two jaws. It's very common, said Joseph Nelson, a University of Alberta ichthyologist, when he finally got to examine the speci-men, months after the fish tale had gone global.[19] "This isn't an abnormal fish," Nelson said. "What's going on here is quite natural." It was another bogus story about poison from the oil sands, just like John O'Connor's. In each case, it only took somebody's unscientific, irresponsible claim about oil sands "poisonings" to bring the media pack running and to start the environmentalists spinning wildly – with their fundraising appeals close behind. By the time real science caught up to set the record straight, the fake stories had been out there for months. As Mark Twain said, A lie can travel halfway around the world while the truth is still putting on its boots.

And then there was the sad story of Maryanne Wanderingspirit, formerly of Fort Chipewyan. At the very same Keepers of the Water Conference where attendees witnessed the freakish fish, organizers from Fort Chipewyan's anti–oil sands groups delivered to the conference a casket containing Wanderingspirit's expired body. "A pall was cast over the last day of the conference," reported the *Fort McMurray Today* newspaper. She had died of cancer, undoubtedly the product of the poisonous oil sands they had all come together to bemoan. "Lionel Lepine of the Athabasca Chipewyan First Nation said her death shouldn't have happened," the paper reported. That's a strange thing to say. But what the paper didn't say in that article was that Maryanne Wanderingspirit had been taken at the tender young age of . . . ninety-three years old.

But the craven exploitation of this little community on the river doesn't even end there. With John O'Connor discredited, and the story of the two-jawed fish proved to be a natural phenomenon, the work of Kevin Timoney has become more important to the oil sands movement than ever. Timoney, an Edmonton-area scientist, has a Ph.D., something that, for journalists, understandably means credibility. And he has devoted himself to studying the water quality in the Athabasca River around Fort Chipewyan. And he doesn't like what he sees.

Timoney's reports, which invariably find heightened levels of some chemical or another in the water, get serious treatment in the press. "NEW REPORT FINDS ELEVATED ARSENIC RISK IN FORT CHIPEWYAN"[20] and "HIGH LEVELS OF POISONS FOUND IN WATER DOWNSTREAM OF OIL SANDS"[21] are the kind of headlines Timoney's work gets. He's authored studies reporting water contamination around Fort Chipewyan and that there are "contaminants" in the food supply, from fish to moose and muskrats.

But Timoney isn't your typical scientist. He doesn't work for a university. He runs his own "ecological research" business. There's nothing wrong with that. But he's part of a fringe group of deep-green ecological philosophers – or "ecosophers." He believes the earth is sacred. Humans? To Timoney, we're a blight.

"Humans have spread across the entire planet, some would say like a metastasized cancer, destroying not only organisms, but the Earth's ability to create and support life," Timoney wrote some years ago in an "ecosophy" journal called *The Trumpeter.*

"There are those of us, in the great minority, who believe that the Earth is sacred, who believe humans are one with nature, not above it, and who limit our reproduction." To Timoney, having too many children is immoral since it hurts Mother Nature. Can someone with such a passionate, even religious, attachment to the environment truly be a dispassionate scientist?

And still Timoney has more to say. "We who love nature feel the ecosphere has an inherent right to carry on its evolutionary destiny. We feel that the Earth should not be degraded, landscapes and life forms not destroyed; that we should love the planet, its trees, oceans, soil, and birds, frogs, everything.

We place the ecosphere above ourselves." Did you catch the phrase "inherent right"? Of the "ecosphere"? People have rights, not inanimate objects like rocks and plants. Except to radical ecosophers like Timoney.

The planet, he continues, is a "supraorganic entity that created and sustains people and all other forms of life" and "It is time for us, like the Mbuti pygmies, to sing songs to awaken our mothers and fathers the forests, grasslands, and oceans for we, their children, are in trouble."[22]

Clearly Timoney has some pretty passionate feelings about the supraorganic entity, blessed be it. Good for him. But in real scientific work, scientists tend not to have spiritual feelings about the things they study. And if they happen to, it becomes all the more important that we insist, if we're to take their work seriously, that they stick to consistent scientific standards: having their work peer-reviewed, for instance, and published in legitimate scientific journals – not just "ecosophy" digests or at poetry readings. If a researcher is a big believer in Scientology – a group that considers psychiatry to be evil – then we wouldn't want her issuing reports about psychiatric practices without verifying that there were scientifically rigorous checks and balances on her work. We wouldn't want to give too much weight to a study into the safety of marijuana smoke written by a Rastafarian – whose religion promotes the sacredness of marijuana – until we could be sure it had been seriously reviewed. But Kevin Timoney, fundamentalist believer in the church of Mother Earth, sometimes operates without such standard scientific diligence like peer review. And sometimes his methods are unorthodox to say the least.

Just take a look at one of Timoney's latest studies, an examination of "fish deformities" – like the freak goldeye that wasn't – around Fort Chipewyan.[23]

One of Timoney's research methods, for instance, involved eating fish he'd caught in the Athabasca and using his gourmet palate to determine whether there was something wrong with them. "We ate this lake trout," he writes of one specimen. "The flesh was softer, less tasty, and more watery than normal. The fillets curled strongly when boiled, indicative of excessive water in the meat prior to cooking." Determining that a fish was "less tasty" is an unusual comment to make in a report on fish deformities. Did Timoney cleanse his palate properly with a sorbet before sampling the filet? Did he use the right amount of salt and butter? We simply don't know. Timoney told me his fish study was "not a scientific paper," and merely done "to provide advice to those wishing to gather data in the future." But RAMP's enormous, scientifically rigorous studies of the water already does that – and not based on any taste tests.

About a whitefish, Timoney reports finding a "reddish growth." He asks, "Perhaps a rare cancer?" In fact, he asks that same question – "Perhaps a rare cancer?" – about three different specimens. Those are questions, not conclusions, and awfully speculative ones at that. Presuming a growth that you can't identify might be a rare cancer? Maybe Timoney should have called John O'Connor: at least the doctor's not afraid to make a firm diagnosis of rare cancers, even if they happen to be wrong.

Having a spiritual ecosopher at the ready to make provocative statements about the safety of Fort Chip's fish is not a convincing way to counter the exhaustive scientific research conducted by the Regional Aquatics Monitoring Program (RAMP) that was discussed in Chapter 7. I asked Timoney about his scientific methods, including peer review of his projects. He told me that the identity of the scientists who had reviewed his work was a secret – "privileged" is what he told me. That's a legal term, not a scientific one.

Timoney didn't seem to like my questions much and, like Andrew Nikiforuk, he demanded to know who was paying me to write my book and ask these questions. I told him – a literary publisher called McClelland & Stewart. But when I returned the favour and asked him if, like Nikiforuk, he had ever been paid by Greenpeace – after all, Timoney appears in one of Greenpeace's promotional videos – he refused to answer me.

So much for transparency.

RAMP's been measuring the health of rivers and lakes around the oil sands region since 1997, routinely testing water for contaminants and acid levels, sediment for quality, and fish and other life forms for toxins. Its work is periodically peer-reviewed to ensure accuracy. It's a massive undertaking – both RAMP and Timoney knew that it's not nearly as easy as sitting down to eat a filet of trout. But that's the difficult, meticulous nature of proper scientific research.

And in its latest report, issued in 2008, RAMP found the variance between a baseline measurement and the hydrology, water quality, the sediment quality, and the health of invertebrates in the Lower Athabasca and the Athabasca River Delta to be, in every case, "Negligible to Low."[24] In other words, there was no substantial difference between a natural, uncontaminated body of water and the rivers and lakes around the oil sands. RAMP's study of fish in the Athabasca found robust populations, which while showing, in a few cases, slightly elevated levels of mercury – something common to all seafood[25] – posed "a Negligible-Low risk to human health." It defied in the starkest, most rigorously scientific way all of Timoney's conclusions.

Chapter 10

PROPAGANDA WARS

T he first thing Third World revolutionaries seize in a coup is the local television station: when you're battling for hearts and minds, propaganda is the most powerful weapon. Same thing in the political revolt against the world's oil-based economy. Groups like Greenpeace aren't scholarly think-tanks or even really political lobby groups targeting politicians. They're mass-media campaigners, fighting in the court of public opinion.

But while Greenpeace and its copycats are increasingly sophisticated in their propaganda tactics, the media-consuming public has, given Greenpeace's increasingly radicalized behaviour in recent years, become understandably skeptical, and even cynical, of their message. Greenpeace's stunts might be entertaining, but few people cast their political ballots based on stunts – let alone agree to change the entire basis of an economy.

Groups like Greenpeace need allies inside the media. Which is why Andrew Nikiforuk is so indispensable to the revolution.

Nikiforuk is a business journalist. He's been published widely in Canada, including the *Globe and Mail*, the *Toronto Star*, and *Canadian Business*. Nikiforuk has created a cottage industry out of reporting on the oil sands. He was the official environmental commentator for CBC Radio in Alberta and wrote a book on the subject, *Tar Sands: Dirty Oil and the Future of a Continent*, which won an award in 2009 from the Society of Environmental Journalists. He's a regular on the environmentalist speaking circuit, and in 2009 he was even invited to testify before a parliamentary committee on the subject.

Nikiforuk can go places no Greenpeacenik can because of his reputation as an independent journalist. Greenpeace – or, for that matter, oil sands companies – is a partisan in this battle for public opinion. If members of Greenpeace or oil sands executives are going to make headlines, it's for their opinions – their facts are treated more skeptically. As a reporter who displays an award for "excellence in journalism" on the home page of his own website, Nikiforuk treasures his reputation of neutrality.

No wonder Nikiforuk is the darling of the anti–oil sands movement, invited to sit on conference panels and contribute to research reports castigating the sector. He is what anti–oil sands campaigners have yearned for: someone with a reputation for objectivity and credibility, and a gift for persuasion, who happens to be on their side. His standing in the established media has given the anti–oil sands cause more power than a hundred Greenpeace stunts; he may well be the single most important individual in the campaign opposing the oil sands.

So it's no wonder that Nikiforuk bristles at the mere suggestion that he's a partisan. When the *National Post* referred to him on September 12, 2009, as an "environmental lobbyist and author," he wrote a letter to the editor insisting he was no such thing: "individuals who hold a point of view and write about it are called journalists, authors or concerned citizens," he said. "Those who are paid to have a point of view and work to influence elected officials are lobbyists." How dare the *Post* put him in the same category as Greenpeace!

Except, the *Post*'s description may have been accurate. Nikiforuk was commissioned by Greenpeace to write a report called "Dirty Oil" that was published on September 13, 2009 – literally the day after the *National Post* characterized him as a lobbyist. He described that report in an email to me as being "an update on his book and a fully referenced piece of journalism." But unlike a book publisher or a newspaper, Greenpeace isn't in the journalism business. It's in the political persuasion business.

That's not all. In 2009, Nikiforuk had his travel expenses to Scandinavia paid for by Greenpeace, when he travelled with their delegation, which was on its way to lobby a Scandinavian company to divest from the oil sands. (I asked Nikiforuk about accepting free travel from an organization that he writes about; he said it is "common for authors to have an organization pay their travel expenses.")

The problem with this is that most people have no idea Nikiforuk was paid to write a booklet for one of the groups he reports on. Without such a disclosure, they would reasonably assume that he was at arms length from the groups he wrote about – not part of their team. In fact, while Nikiforuk, unlike many lobbyists, personally believes in his cause, it appears that met the very definition of a lobbyist that he wrote in the *Post*: Greenpeace paid him to write a report based on his book.

While in Norway, Nikiforuk lobbied the state-owned energy giant Statoil to divest from the oil sands. But that's not how the CBC introduced him on their Alberta-wide radio show that week. "Our environmental commentator, Andrew Nikiforuk, has travelled to Norway to talk to people about this," was how he was introduced – with no mention that his travel expenses were paid for by Greenpeace. For nine full minutes – an eternity in radio time – Nikiforuk criticized the oil sands. He wasn't speaking as an activist; he was presented as the CBC's commentator, there to sort the truth from the spin. "It's great that you took the time for us today," concluded the interviewer.

Nikiforuk wasn't just a one-time guest on the show. He had been a regular commentator, for years. Yet you'd have to do a lot of digging to learn that Nikiforuk had his trip paid for by Greenpeace. The CBC has a very strict corporate rule against accepting free travel. "CBC programs must be protected from improper external influence or the suspicion of such influence," reads CBC Policy 1.1.12.1.[1] The only exception allowed is if there is an announcement at the end of the program, disclosing that promotional consideration had been granted by someone. Imagine the peals of laughter if, after a nine-minute interview with Nikiforuk, the CBC had followed the rule and properly thanked Greenpeace for covering the travel costs of the segment!

Paragraph 2.4.1 of the CBC's book of Journalistic Standards requires that journalists disclose conflict of interest. I asked Nikiforuk if he disclosed his conflict of interest. He replied, saying that "he went as a concerned citizen, not as a member of Greenpeace, and Greenpeace never told him what to say." Also that he "went on the condition that he could maintain his own intellectual autonomy" and that "I have no relationship with Greenpeace" and has at times "openly criticized the group." But later in our exchange of a half-dozen emails – which felt more like a lawyer's cross-examination than a media interview – Nikiforuk acknowledged that he had been paid to write for Greenpeace and had his trip to Scandinavia paid by them – quite an important clarification of his statement that he had "no relationship."

CBC's rulebook clearly states that "The hiring of persons identified with political parties or pressure groups may only be authorized if the person concerned has resigned his or her functions within the political party or pressure group and has refrained from public activity in the party or group or in a related capacity for at least two years."[2]

I asked Terri Campbell, the CBC producer, about Nikiforuk's relationship with Greenpeace. Campbell said that Nikiforuk "did disclose that his trip was paid for by Greenpeace" – but Campbell did not answer subsequent questions about to whom Nikiforuk made that disclosure, whether it was approved by a CBC vice-president as per their ethics guidelines, and why the radio program only said he had been "invited" by Greenpeace – not subsidized by them. Campbell also repeated one of Nikiforuk's responses, that "we cannot control who else pays him and for what" – despite the ethics rules applying to both in-house staff and freelancers alike.

The last thing she wrote to me was that Nikiforuk had "won a number of journalism awards" and "has a distinct point of view." That is all quite true, but it seemed to evade my question about why listeners weren't alerted to the fact that his point of view on Greenpeace's delegation might be coloured by having his travel to Scandinavia paid by Greenpeace and having worked for Greenpeace at about the same time. It's inconceivable that the CBC would allow someone who did work for and accepted free travel from an oil sands company to appear as a commentator without disclosing these details.

After her first response, Campbell stopped answering any more of my questions, ignoring my follow-up e-mails and voice messages.

Nikiforuk gave interviews to other news media about the Statoil lobbying campaign, speaking about Greenpeace's activities as if he hadn't himself lobbied the energy giant. "There's no doubt in my mind that Greenpeace has identified those [Scandinavian] companies as the most vulnerable link in the tar sands," he told a Canwest News reporter, who innocently described him as a "Calgary journalist who has written extensively about the issue."[3] He indeed was that. But much more relevant – but not disclosed in the story – was Nikiforuk's own lobbying. As Nikiforuk adamantly told me: "I don't believe in junkets." But what was the free trip to Scandinavia, if not one?

I asked Nikiforuk how much Greenpeace paid him to write for them; he replied "Not much." Fair enough – that's his private business. But when he gives public interviews, that isn't his private business – it's him becoming a participant in a political debate.

Nikiforuk wasn't the only anti-oil sands voice who travelled with Greenpeace to Scandinavia. So did John O'Connor, the doctor we met in Chapter 9. It was Nikiforuk who transformed O'Connor into a hero. In his book *Tar Sands*, Nikiforuk said O'Connor "earned a reputation as a straight-shooter" in the North.

It was Nikiforuk who reported on O'Connor's original, erroneous claims that Fort Chip had an epidemic of cholangiocarcinoma cancers. It was Nikiforuk who blamed "years of denials and delays" on what he reported O'Connor implied was a politically corrupted Cancer Board rather than O'Connor's refusal to hand over his patient records. It was Nikiforuk who declared that John O'Connor and not Health Canada or Alberta Health is the one who "believes the people of Fort Chip deserve a proper health study" – a 180-degree inversion of what actually happened. According to the Alberta College of Physicians and

Surgeons' ethics report, the government agencies repeatedly tried to conduct a proper study of the doctor's claims: he stonewalled them at every turn. More than anyone else, Nikiforuk created the myth of John O'Connor – a myth that a thousand websites and a documentary continue to propagate.

By the time the Alberta College of Physicians and Surgeons' ethics report came out, showing O'Connor to be the very opposite of a straight shooter, the man's heroism was already well set in ink. Even the ethics complaint itself was an opportunity for Nikiforuk to wax about O'Connor's heroism. "It was the first time in Canada that government agencies had used a patient complaint process to silence and character-assassinate a physician," he wrote when Health Canada doctors reported their difficulties with O'Connor's methods. That's a powerful line, but the College of Physicians and Surgeons isn't a censorship body – it's a professional standards body and that is what they were enforcing; professional standards.

And it's downright wrong to say the Health Canada complaints were character assassination: the complaints process is completely private. If it weren't for O'Connor and Nikiforuk ceaselessly mentioning the complaint, no one would even have known about it – hardly an attempt to assassinate his character.

In fact, the confidential nature of the College of Physicians and Surgeons' report meant just the opposite: O'Connor and Nikiforuk could say whatever they wanted to about the complaint and no one at the college was permitted to fight back. Later, Nikiforuk claimed that the college had "absolved him [O'Connor] of all charges except for that of causing 'undue alarm.'" And yet the college's final report was anything but absolution – it was a long list of his obstruction of medical investigations.

Pitching a romanticized fiction about John O'Connor is Nikiforuk's greatest contribution to the war against the oil sands. His absurd hyperbole also aids the anti-oil sands movement. In *Tar Sands*, he claims that oil has "turned Alberta into a petrotyranny, while Canada has adopted all the trappings of an impervious oil kingdom" where "Canadian leaders behave and talk more and more like careless Saudi princes." In Nikiforuk's words, Canada is "nothing more than a Third World energy supermarket."

And that's just him getting warmed up. When Nikiforuk appeared before a parliamentary committee, he was asked critical questions by some MPs. Afterward, he wrote a report on the episode for the *Toronto Star*[4] about his meeting that can only be described as hysterical.

The article was headlined "A public tarring in Saudi Canada." Besides comparing Canada's liberal, egalitarian government to Saudi Arabia, which any well-informed reader would know is a fascist, misogynist, anti-Semitic theocratic monarchy, Nikiforuk also managed to call Canada a "dysfunctional petro-state" run by a "strange Communist gang" that attacks "basic freedoms."

It's one thing to be shocking and entertaining just to get some attention The trouble with this, though, is that there really is a Saudi Arabia, and to compare Canada's democratic culture to Saudi Arabia's totalitarianism isn't just a baseless insult to Canada, it's also a whitewash of just how bad things are over there. If Canada is no better than Saudi Arabia, then Saudi Arabia is no worse than Canada – so the country with one of the worst human rights records on the planet really can't be that bad, can it?

Same thing with the "Communist gang" comment. Some

countries really are run by Communist gangs; the People's Republic of China comes to mind, and it's one of the world's most aggressive acquirers of oil properties. Calling Canada a "dysfunctional petro-state" conjures up images of places like Nigeria or Venezuela, countries that would be economic basket cases without oil. In fact, all oil and gas and all other mining activity in Canada combined only accounts for about 5 per cent of the country's GDP. It's another accusation that just doesn't make any sense. And disparaging Canada's commitment to civil rights? That's an absurd charge for a country with the strongest commitment to political free speech in the world, next to the U.S. Constitution's First Amendment. The fact that Nikiforuk was writing his criticism in the pages of the country's largest newspaper, and has received awards for his reporting – instead of being jailed, Chinese or Saudi-style, was a sign that his anti-Canadian allegations were just plain false.

There's nothing wrong with a little hyperbole in the business of political action. But Nikiforuk says he a journalist, first and foremost. And if you're calling Canada a Saudi Arabia, what words are left to describe Saudi Arabia? If you call Canada's social democratic Parliament a Communist gang, what adjectives can you use to describe actual Communist gangs – like the Chinese troops who are buttressing Sudan's oil fields and aiding in the genocide at Darfur? Once in a while, Nikiforuk admits that his criticism of the oil sands is over the top. "I would expect in Russia or Nigeria, someone like me would just disappear," he told a reporter. "Thank God I live in Alberta. Where they just send letters to the editor."[5]

The most effective media publicist the anti-oil sands lobby ever had tells it like it is. Of course Canada isn't the Third World. It's not run by some Communist gang. You won't find any dysfunctional petro-state attacking basic freedoms here. Despite his bluster, Nikiforuk knows that Alberta is nothing like Saudi Arabia. Maybe the anti-oil sands proponents will get around to criticizing Saudi Arabia one day.

Chapter 11

SAUDI ARABIA'S WAR AGAINST THE OIL SANDS

I t's obvious by now that many groups claiming the authority to pass ethical judgment over the oil sands are hardly in any position to be taken seriously. But the fact is that while hypocritical environmental and spiritual activists are the very public face of the Alberta-bashing crusade that we see in North America and Europe, they are hardly the most troubling element lurking inside the anti–oil sands movement. If we wanted to pinpoint who benefits most when customers boycott and investors steer clear of the oil sands, the most obvious answer is the energy producer that stands to lose the most from the oil sands' growth: Saudi Arabia.

As recently as 2003, the Middle Eastern kingdom was far and away the largest dealer of crude oil to the American market, selling 630 million barrels a year to U.S. consumers – 12 per cent more than the 560 million barrels piped in from Canada.[1] The Saudis, as any Washington insider will tell you, had the American political system in their back pocket: president after president made it a top priority to burnish Washington's friend-ship with the Arabs who controlled their industrial lifeblood. But over the last decade, Alberta's oil sands have become a serious competitor to the easy crude pumped out by the world's oil dictatorships.[2]

Up against increasingly innovative Canadian competition, Saudi Arabia has seen its market share slip drastically while Canada's only grows. In 2004, Canada unseated Saudi Arabia to become the number-one supplier of oil to the U.S. market-place. As of 2008, the United States was importing 715 million barrels from Canada, far more than it was importing from the Saudis just five years earlier. In the meantime, Saudi imports were down by 80 million barrels. Canadian oil had, in just five short years, gone from trailing the Saudis by 12 per cent in the U.S. marketplace to beating the Saudis by 30 per cent.[3] The power, the influence, and the money the House of Saud once enjoyed by being a lifeline for the most powerful and wealthiest country in the world is being challenged by a non-OPEC com-petitor. And they are not at all happy about it. Not one bit.

And so they're taking action. The medieval, human rights–abusing Saudis, amazingly, have settled in on the same anti-Alberta team as the purportedly progressive NGOs in Europe and North America – the guys who hug trees have joined forces with the guys who stone gays. Right alongside Greenpeace, the Saudis have begun to campaign against the oil sands. They've begun telling the world's oil investors not to bother putting their money into Alberta: it's not as economical as Saudi Arabia, they claim, and the long-term price of oil will never justify spending dollars in a high-cost jurisdiction like Western Canada.[4] "They're playing hardball," one Canadian analyst pointed out after hearing Saudi oil minister Ali al-Naimi take what he called "a swipe at the oil sands" at a 2007 OPEC confer-ence.[5] Of course they're playing hardball: 80 million barrels a year lost to Canada is $5 billion to $10 billion, depending on market prices – that's a lot of money the Saudi princes could use to buy more palaces in the desert or gold-plated yachts.

The Saudi smear campaign is part of the same strategy envi-ronmental groups are using to attack against Alberta's oil patch. The World Wildlife Fund, among other activist groups, is pres-suring Western governments to change investment regulations to require companies to start accounting, on their financial statements, for something these groups are calling "carbon liability."[6] The idea is that companies that produce carbon dioxide will have to measure it all up and call it a liability on their balance sheet – like a debt they owe or a bill that will eventually come due.

It makes no sense from a financial point of view; how much CO_2 any particular firm produces doesn't change whether it's a financially sound company or an insolvent one. It would be like your banker considering how much exhaust your car emits every year in order to determine whether your family qualifies for a car loan. But when you look at what the Saudis are saying about the oil sands, you begin to see why it makes sense for the anti–oil sands campaign: the more liabilities – even made-up "carbon liabilities" – a company faces when making an invest-ment, the more risky the investment becomes. And if govern-ment regulators, like the Securities and Exchange Commission, can be convinced to buy into it – as anti–oil sands groups are hoping they will – it would become a very big anti–oil sands weapon indeed.

What the Saudis and environmentalists have going is a bril-liant symbiosis. While the Saudis warn investors, as al-Naimi did, that the oil sands will be uneconomical, their allies in the environmental groups are helping in their own way to make that prediction true, by working to ensure that oil sands expansion becomes more and more costly through regulations and taxes.

But, after decades of being the United States' number-one oil dealer, the Saudis' influence goes well beyond the World Wildlife Fund. And with the oil sands in their sights, they're no doubt prepared to use their high-powered connections to hurt Alberta, to ensure that the United States remains forever dependent on Arab oil.

In 2008, a last-minute, largely unnoticed change was quietly slipped into a U.S. energy bill, making it illegal for the U.S. Department of Defense to use any oil sands products in its vehicles, purportedly as an environmental measure. It didn't take long for Paul Wihby, president of the Global Water and Energy Strategy Team – a blue-chip firm providing strategic resource analysis to industry – to figure out what was happening behind the scenes. The legislation, Wihby said, had the Saudi lobby's fingerprints all over it. "The Saudis . . . know how to play the game, and they spend the money to do it," he told a reporter with the *Fort McMurray Today* newspaper. "They do what they have to do to protect their interests."[7]

And arguably no other country has penetrated Washington as deeply and powerfully as has the Saudi lobby.[8] Joseph Lieberman, the widely respected Connecticut senator and former vice-presidential candidate, has complained that when it comes to Saudi links to terrorists and other American enemies "the FBI and maybe other parts of our government have seemed to want to almost defend the Saudis, or not be as aggressive as they should be about the Saudis" when it comes to their role in helping America's enemies.

According to a 2004 report by the Centre for Public Integrity (CPI), Saudi Arabia was spending more money lobbying Washington that any other OPEC nation: the Islamic oil kingdom had eleven different lobbying firms and public relations companies all aimed at keeping the White House and Congress friendly to America's biggest Arab energy supplier. It wasn't just Saudi sheikhs who were hobnobbing with American legislators; an army of slick lobbyists was ensuring that the oil flowed without interruption from distractions like terrorism, human rights abuses, or anything else. Just one of the Saudi's lobby firms – Patton Boggs – had met with congressional staffers to promote Saudi interests sixty-two times within just a six-month period, the CPI found. In a single year, the Saudis had spent an astonishing $6.6 million to polish their image in Washington.[9] That's a lot of money for boozy lunches on Capitol Hill, but it's a drop in the barrel to the Saudis.

Saudi money can buy a lot more than just meetings with congressmen and senators. The Saudi royal family was the biggest single foreign donor to Bill Clinton's presidential library, writing a generous $10 million cheque.[10] They donated another undisclosed amount to the Clinton Foundation – all helping to ensure that the former president enjoyed a comfortable landing after leaving the White House.[11] And they donated another $10 million to the presidential library of George H.W. Bush.[12] That pales to the tens of millions of dollars from Saudi princes raked in by Jimmy Carter, who has, in return, turned his Carter Center into a mouthpiece for Arab foreign policy.[13]

Creating a predictable pattern like that is a smart move by the Saudis. It's a way of sending a clear message to anyone who occupies the White House, even for one term, as George Bush Sr. did, that they can count on generous post-presidential donations; that the Saudis are there to make their retirement richer and help enhance their place in history. It's all there for the taking for any president who wants it – as long as he keeps up the United States–Saudi friendship.

Vice-presidents have felt Riyadh's generosity too. After all, you certainly wouldn't expect that a petroleum-producing nation like Saudi Arabia would be big fans of the global-warming activists who demand the world end its reliance on fossil fuels. But in 2006, Al Gore – the man behind the doomsday climate-change film *An Inconvenient Truth* and the individual who has arguably done more to demonize oil than almost anyone else in history – was a keynote speaker at Saudi Arabia's Jeddah Economic Forum. It might have seemed strange that a man who has made millions hustling for the Kyoto Accord would be welcomed by an audience that included the secretary general of the Arab League, past president of the Islamic Development Bank, the mayor of Jeddah, and the director of Dubai's Department of Economy, among others. But Arab countries, using their powerful influence, have arranged things so that they'll be exempt from global environmental schemes that will ravage their competitors like Canada, even though Canada is a smaller exporter of the fossil fuels that are purportedly harming the planet.

Saudi Arabia, for instance, though it is one of the biggest emitters among all so-called developing countries when it comes to CO_2 [14] and it operates significant refining operations,[15] is exempt from having to make any emissions cuts under the Kyoto Accord.[16] So are Kuwait, Iran, and the United Arab Emirates. And when the UN began planning for the successor to Kyoto, the Copenhagen Climate Treaty, Saudi Arabia's billionaire sheikhs went to the UN and pleaded an astonishingly nervy case: since any effort to cap greenhouse gas emissions would mean cutting back on Middle East oil, they said, Persian Gulf nations deserved special compensation from Western nations.

"Many politicians in the Western world think these climate change negotiations and the new agreement will provide them with a golden opportunity to reduce their dependence on imported oil," Saudi Arabian UN delegate Mohammad al-Sabban said. "That means you will transfer the burden to developing countries, especially to those highly dependent on the exploitation of oil."[17] Think about that: for decades, the Saudis have been getting rich off of America's dependence on their oil; their country has been protected by American military aid; their exports channelled to the United States at the expense of American taxpayers paying to keep the oil flowing. And the moment it looks as though there might be a disruption to all that, the Saudis demand Americans and other Western nations pay them foreign aid to make up for the slight loss in business. Is there a word in Arabic for chutzpah?

So it makes sense that, as it turns out, Al Gore didn't come to Jeddah to lecture the Saudis about being the largest pusher of fossil fuels to a world grown addicted to oil. He had come to lecture Americans about their bigotry toward Arabs. The United States had committed "terrible abuses" against Muslims since 9/11, he said; implemented "thoughtless" visa restrictions against Arab nations; and "indiscriminately rounded up" Muslim Americans and held them in conditions "that were just unforgivable." Al Gore went to a fascist regime to lecture America about human rights.

It was exactly the kind of anti-American agitprop you'd expect to see in a state-run Arab newspaper or from a fire-breathing

Wahabbist imam – other propaganda efforts so frequently funded
by the Saudi kingdom.[18]

Why was it coming from a former U.S. vice-president and
environmental campaigner? Perhaps it had a little something
to do with the fact that the sponsor of the economic forum that
had invited and welcomed Gore was none other than the
Binladin Group[19] – the Saudi construction giant with high-level
connections in Riyadh and owned by the family of the world's
most deadly terrorist, Osama bin Laden (whom they had previously disowned). And what was the Saudi interest in hiring
Gore to come to the Middle East? We can only guess. But a
report by FirstEnergy Capital, one of Alberta's top oil-patch
investment banks, figured that Gore perceived a "political
benefit" in becoming a Saudi booster that, in his mind, out-
weighed what was a great deal of negative fallout over his criticisms of America in one of the world's most backward,
terror-sponsoring regimes.

If the suspicions were true, the report (a collaboration with
the Global Water and Energy Strategy Team) predicted that we
could "expect Mr. Gore to continue his attack on unconventional oil production as a concept and a practice," and "to
broaden the scope of [his environmental] attack"[20] against
North American, unconventional energy resources representing threats to the Saudis' oil hegemony. That report was issued
in 2006. Over the next few years, the prediction would turn
out to be true.[21,22]

A few years ago, Sara Bongiorni's family in Baton Rouge,
Louisiana, tried an experiment: she wanted to avoid, for a full
year, any product that was made in China. She had good
reasons. It was a "boycott," she said. As an American newspaper

reporter, she knew full well China's troubling record of human rights. And of course there were the millions of American jobs Bongiorni knew had been lost to the polluting factories of China's Pearl River Delta, some of which even use slave labourers. But it took one edifying Christmas with her family – as the tree drooped with Chinese-made decorations, the lights twinkled with Chinese-made bulbs on Chinese-made wires, and the house was strewn with unwrapped Chinese-made toys and Chinese-made clothes – for Bongiorni to realize, to her revulsion, that the People's Republic had quietly colonized every aspect of her life. "China was taking over the place," she wrote. "Suddenly, I'd had enough. I wanted China out."[23]

It wasn't easy: broken appliances went unrepaired for lack of non-Chinese parts, there were simply no non-Chinese candles to be found for her husband's birthday cake. For a year, her son was stuck entertaining himself almost exclusively with Danish-made Lego. But the Bongiornis mostly managed to pull it off by reading labels carefully: they could do a pretty good job of ensuring that their house remained a Chinese products–free zone. It's a benefit of laws applied widely in the United States called Country of Origin Labeling (COOL). Almost everything you buy in the United States and Canada includes information on where the product comes from. Your furniture, toys, food, clothes, tools, appliances – they all must say somewhere on them where they originally came from. Virtually everything, that is, except the one product Americans buy in vast quantities every year and is one of the most vital ingredients in their lives: oil.

If you're in the market for a tank of gas, you may end up buying fuel from Venezuela, Saudi Arabia, America, the United Arab Emirates, Canada, Mexico, Nigeria, or somewhere else.

You might end up buying some cocktail of petroleum from a bunch of those different countries that has been mixed together somewhere along the refining chain. What you cannot do, no matter how much you might want to, is use your power as a consumer to decide which oil-producing country you'd like to patronize. When shelling out $60 for a tank of gas every week, you can bet that a whole lot of Americans, given the option, would almost certainly rather see their money go to support American oil wells, creating American jobs. And probably a large number of Americans would be all right, too, with their money going to producers in Canada, their number-one trading partner, neighbour, and close ally.

But what about Saudi Arabia? Or Nigeria? Or Venezuela? These are oil producers you can be guaranteed that a significant number of consumers would avoid if they could. How many Americans would volunteer to send their money to the Kingdom of Saudi Arabia or the sharia states of the United Arab Emirates – where women are treated like livestock and oil money is used to train radical Islamists like the murderers of 9/11 – if they had the ability and the choice, through COOL, like Bongiorni did with her household purchases? How many would want to buy from persecuting, autocratic regimes, and how many would prefer friendly, peace-loving, and democratic oil producers?

Wesley Clark thinks that a lot of Americans would. Given the same consumer choice that Bongiorni had, and knowing that oil – whether it comes from Tehran or Texas – sells for the same price, Clark thinks that Americans should be given the option of which energy producers they would rather patronize.

Clark knows a thing or two about promoting America's interests: He's a four-star army general. He was the Supreme

Allied Commander of NATO. And in 2004, he took a run at the nomination to be the Democratic Party's candidate for U.S. president.[24] Today, he leads a political action committee called WesPAC, designed to "provide leadership on U.S. national security issues and develop new, innovative solutions to the challenges facing America at home and abroad."[25] When it comes to understanding the value of supporting allies, and the dangers of well-funded enemies, it's pretty safe to say that, whatever his party affiliation, Wesley Clark has a pretty solid grasp of matters.

And one thing he's certain would advance America's interests is Country of Origin Labeling on oil products. That's why he's joined forces with Growth Energy – a group promoting American-made biofuels (like ethanol, which is made from U.S.-grown corn) – to argue in favour of what the group calls its Label My Fuel initiative. The campaign is asking for rules that will make it possible for consumers to make their own decisions about whose energy they'd rather buy. "The American people deserve to know more about the gasoline they purchase every day – where it comes from and where their hard-earned dollars ultimately go every time they fill up their cars and trucks," Clark explains. "Most Americans don't want their paychecks going to Venezuela and other regimes that don't agree with and support the U.S. Requiring country of origin labeling of our fuel supply will empower consumers with the knowledge and ability to make informed decisions."[26]

That's an idea that's pretty hard to argue with in principle, even if the complexities of implementing something like that defy easy solutions. In fact, many Americans have already shown their enthusiasm for withdrawing support for their enemies' oil products by launching boycotts against Citgo, the retail gasoline chain owned and operated by Hugo Chávez's hostile, Marxist Venezuelan regime.[27]

But Clark doesn't just argue that Americans should buy friendly, preferably American-sourced energy for purely patriotic purposes – though he believes that too. He points out, convincingly, that gasoline from hostile regions actually costs Americans far more than they know. Saudi and Kuwaiti oil may sell for roughly the same world-market-price per barrel as West Texas crude. But there's a hidden price in Arab oil that isn't part of the energy produced in Texas, California, Alaska, Mexico, or Alberta's oil sands. It takes a lot of U.S. taxpayers' dollars to keep Arab oil flowing to United States' – and for that matter, the world's – gas pumps.

Over the last thirty years, the U.S. Department of Energy estimates that America's dependence on foreign oil has cost U.S. citizens an additional $7 trillion over and above the normal price of energy. The U.S.–based Center for Forensic Economic Studies estimates that for every dollar Americans spend on foreign crude, U.S. taxpayers spend another $1.55 in military costs.[28] There is a reason American foreign policy tends to pay relatively little attention, and devotes scant military or financial resources, to the massacres in Africa or the long-running civil war of Sri Lanka. It's a cold calculation, but it's true: those places don't have all the oil.

It's not something we likely think about that often when we fill up our tanks, but all that petroleum we're pouring out is the result of a great deal of American effort at keeping the Middle East stable. The Middle East is one of the most volatile, dangerous regions in the world, filled with violent, imperialistic regimes – Syria, Iran, and, until recently, Saddam Hussein's Iraq – whose goals are often precisely to destabilize the world economy. After all, when oil supplies are disrupted, the price of oil only goes up, much to the delight of regimes like Mahmoud Ahmadinejad's Iranian theocracy. Threats of war by Iran and Saddam Hussein's Iraq against Israel and, more to the point, oil-producing nations like Kuwait and Saudi Arabia have left Washington with little choice but to secure the region by filling it with thousands of U.S. troops and warships.

There are, or have in recent years been, American bases, *matériel*, and troops in Saudi Arabia,[29] Kuwait,[30] Iraq,[31] Qatar, Bahrain,[32] and Jordan.[33, 34] Americans have helped to arm – by way of military aid – those countries it allies itself with in the Middle East.[35] And U.S. battleships and aircraft carriers have for decades patrolled the Persian Gulf[36] and the Straits of Hormuz. The reason is no secret. As the website for the U.S. Navy's Historical Center makes clear: "Maintaining political stability and the free flow of oil to the global economy have been the overarching objectives of U.S. foreign policy in the Persian Gulf for almost half a century."[37] And though it may be in American interests to keep the Middle East stable, it doesn't always end up that way, and all those peacetime bases and battleships are a trifle compared to the money the United States has spend fighting a number of wars in the region.

The total tab is staggering. American taxpayers spend approximately $50 billion a year, according to research by the Institute for the Analysis of Global Security, patrolling Middle Eastern waters and supplying military aid to Gulf states; the First Gulf War cost Americans more than $80 billion; the final bill for the latest Gulf War hasn't yet been fully tallied, but estimates go as high as $1 trillion, when all the military, security, and reconstruction costs have been accounted for.[38] A key rationale for all that money, remember, is to keep Arab oil flowing to the world, not just America, which means that U.S. citizens aren't just supporting Arab regimes every time they fill up – they're supporting them every hour of their working day. They're handing subsidies to the Saudis so they can sell oil to the Chinese.

Just to get a conservative sense of how rich a subsidy we're talking about, let's forget the wars and take the $50 billion Washington spends every year keeping the shipping lanes of the Middle East open for all those tankers of Arab crude.

That money is almost all aimed at protecting the Middle Eastern oil supply in one way or another. In 2008, the United States imported more than 550 million barrels of crude from Saudi Arabia.[39] If we divide that $50 billion over all those barrels, it works out to a $90.86 subsidy for every barrel of oil the United States imports from the Saudis.

To be fair, let's throw in all the oil from not just Saudi Arabia but from the other big suppliers in the Gulf region, including Iraq, Kuwait, Qatar, and the United Arab Emirates. In total, in 2008, the United States imported 856 million barrels of oil from all those countries put together.[40] That $50 billion U.S. taxpayers spent on getting it? It still works out to $58 a barrel. The average price of a barrel of oil, adjusted for inflation, over the last decade was just more than $46.[41] That means American taxpayers have been, on average, spending more to get their oil to their shores than the oil itself actually costs.

That's an amazing statistic. Spending more to get oil than oil actually costs makes as much sense as sending a Brinks truck to pick up $100 in quarters. It's just not worth it. It's not worth the billions America spends to protect Arabian oil. And it certainly isn't worth all the blood American troops have shed in the Middle East.

What's telling is that in all their meticulous accounting for the impact of the oil sands on every bird egg and minnow in Alberta, the West's feverish conservationists haven't seen fit to run the numbers on the vast amount of resources, including all the battleships and bombs and battalions unloosed over decades, to lubricate the flow of Middle Eastern oil. But this loose coalition between environmentalists and Saudi Arabia to protect America from the rise of a more convenient, secure, (and far less shady) Canadian source isn't just about the predictable double-standard. It's a vivid example of precisely how tilted the playing field is against ethical, transparent, and democratic oil suppliers. There are some pretty big advantages that come with being an unaccountable, corrupt monarchy: you don't have to answer for your lobbying efforts, for one thing. When Alberta's government spends money on public relations, environmentalists accuse them of perpetrating a "cover up"[42]; when the province announced in 2009 that it would spend $25 million on a public relations campaign, the Sierra Club denounced it as a cynical "apologia for unsustainable dirty oil"[43]; and when Alberta officials visit Washington, they're dogged by protestors demanding America boycott their oil.[44]

But the Saudis can throw bags of money at U.S. politicians without any political consequences back home, since without democracy, their subjects' opinions don't count for beans. Because they have never bothered to build a proper, functioning economy with all their oil riches, they can call themselves developing nations, exempt themselves from climate change agreements like Kyoto and Copenhagen, and then turn around and nervily demand reparations for the loss of oil sales those treaties would bring. They can be as manipulative and underhanded as they care to, hiding behind a hundred skulking lobbyists, because no one expects more from such a poor global citizen than the most unseemly behaviour. It's depressingly ironic: the very transparent and ethical rules by which Canada must play is precisely what keeps it in the spotlight, enabling its critics to brand it as an "unethical" oil source. Meanwhile the Saudis very impunity, their freedom to operate unethically, is what ensures that their morally dubious oil stays well below the radar. Canada trying to win a PR war against the Saudis? It's like a Boy Scout trying to win a fight against a biker gang.

Chapter 12

GREEN JOBS: THE ENRON OF ENVIRONMENTALISM

I n the great public debate about the future of energy, the oil sands aren't just compared against other oil producers; they're compared against potential future energy sources too (even if they're still in their infancy and largely untested on the scale required to displace oil). This is why when environmentalists promote their vision for a new economy based on renewable fuels, like wind and solar, they put tremendous emphasis on their promise that building more turbines and solar cells will only increase our prosperity, creating millions of "green jobs" in those industries, while improving the environment, with no additional costs to any of us. If they can convince citizens, and policy makers, that switching off resources like the oil sands isn't just ethical but will deliver even bigger economic payoffs and a lighter moral burden than more investment in fossil fuels, then they'll have won a crucial battle to soften the public's inevitable skepticism about their grand new schemes.

"Millions of new jobs are among the many silver-, if not indeed gold-plated, linings on the cloud of climate change," Achim Steiner, head of the UN's environmental program, announced at a world climate-change conference in 2007. "These jobs are not for just the middle classes – the so-called 'green collar' jobs – but also for workers in construction, sustainable forestry and agriculture, engineering and transportation." Spain and Germany, where governments have led the rush into subsidizing wind and solar power, he said, have "already created several hundred thousand jobs."[1]

Jim Harris, past leader of Canada's Green Party and a best-selling business author, is warning Canadian politicians that they are missing the boat on a great job-creating opportunity in failing to keep up with European levels of renewable energy subsidies. "Spain has just committed to creating a million green energy jobs over the next decade," he wrote in an October 2009 article called "Green Jobs Will Pay for Themselves."[2] Visiting a Bedford Heights, Ohio–based plant that manufactures components for wind turbines in January 2009, Barack Obama gushed about all the great things happening in Spain, and other countries, thanks to large government investment in – and laws favouring – wind and solar power.[3] "They're surging ahead of us, poised to take the lead in these new industries," he said. If Washington didn't hurry and get Americans caught up, he warned, "think about all the businesses that wouldn't come to be, all the jobs that wouldn't be created, all the clean energy we wouldn't produce." Visiting the Edison Electric Vehicle Technical Center in Los Angeles two months later, Obama again held up the Spanish example as one that Americans should be hastening to follow. "Spain generates almost 30 percent of its power by harnessing the wind, while we manage less than 1 percent," the U.S. president complained. "The problem is that for decades we've avoided doing what we must do as a nation to turn challenge into opportunity."[4]

As luck would have it, Spain is a pretty instructive country for Canadians to look to as a comparison to our own situation, since it has a population that's similar in size (Canada population is 33 million; Spain's is 40 million) and in 2008 had a roughly similar-sized economy (Canada's GDP is $1.3 trillion; Spain's is $1.4 trillion).[5] And Spain has truly been a leader in throwing all its policy muscle behind the green-economy effort. Environmental groups that had argued for decades that if we would only try switching from our fossil fuel habit, we would discover how achievable it is to create a flourishing economy without them, finally had in Spain the pilot project they had been asking for.

But, although you wouldn't know it from the cheerleading of environmentalists in Canada, the United States, and the UN, the reality is that back in Spain, the country supposedly leading the way on renewable energy, the truth was that that entire experiment has turned out to be an unmitigated disaster.

In March 2009, economic researchers at Spain's King Juan Carlos University, after hearing so much of this international praise for their country's renewable energy policies, and sensing something quite different going on around them, decided to finally examine the benefits and costs to Spain of this massive "green jobs" creation strategy, which has been underway for more than a decade. After all, no one else, not even the Spanish government, had actually bothered to measure whether the initiative was actually working. The report, the authors noted, was the "first time a critical analysis of the actual impact [of the 'green jobs' initiative] has been made."[6]

Now that the critical analysis has finally been done, it's plain to see why the government avoided doing it all along. It's much easier, after all, for Madrid to baldly claim – as Obama and the UN have been doing – that everything is working wonderfully, and to enjoy the global fawning over their government's brilliant management, than to make the effort to see whether the Spanish people were actually benefiting from their ambitious experiment. Or maybe they really had checked and decided it was best to keep the findings under wraps. Because what the thorough university study discovered is definitely nothing that any "green jobs" promoter would want publicized.

The net effect of Spain's green policy, the authors found, was that it actually "destroys jobs." Lots of them. The report found a "surprisingly low number" of green jobs created in Spain overall – about fifty thousand – and most of them were only short-term work, such as building and installing facilities: just one out of every ten jobs created was considered "at the more permanent level of actual operation and maintenance of the renewable sources of electricity."

But, whether permanent or short-term, for every single so-called green job created in Spain since the government first embarked on the initiative in 1997, the policy killed 2.2 jobs elsewhere in the economy. For every green megawatt of electrical capacity installed, five jobs were wiped out from the economy, often as a result of higher power prices. "These costs do not appear to be unique to Spain's approach," the researchers concluded, "but instead are largely inherent in schemes to promote renewable energy sources," whether they're implemented in Japan, Canada, or the United States. In fact, according to the study's analysis, were the United States to adopt the same policies as Spain has – just like Obama has said he hopes

ETHICAL OIL

to – it could expect to create 3 million to 5 million jobs, but it will likely eliminate, based on Spain's experience, as many as 11 million other jobs in the process.

But that only represents a portion of the economic damage that has befallen Spain as a direct result of the policy. Because the few "green jobs" that were created didn't just appear out of thin air: they only happened because the government poured billions of taxpayer dollars into the renewable energy sector. All those green jobs were purchased by taxpayers; that doesn't take any kind of brilliant environmental leadership. Any government can funnel taxpayer money into make-work plans, whether it's digging holes or building windmills. The question is whether the jobs created are worth the money spent.

In Spain's case, the answer is obvious: every green job created cost the government €571,138, or about $850,000 (all figures using exchange rates as of late 2009). Every wind-industry job created cost, on average, more than €1 million to create, according to the report – roughly a staggering $1.5 million. Of course, all that government money has to come from taxpayers, and you don't need an economist to tell you that higher taxes means less prosperity – and fewer jobs – somewhere else in the economy.[7]

Spain's green jobs initiative has absorbed an "enormous" portion of the country's tax resources, notes the report: the average amount being spent each year to keep renewable energy viable in Spain "is equivalent to 4.35% of all VAT [Value Added Tax] collected, 3.45% of the household income tax, or 5.6% of the corporate income tax for 2007." That's a massive burden on Spain's tax base. And how many other jobs were destroyed, or never created, due to the crushing tax load required to sustain an otherwise unsustainable industry?

And Spaniards are paying over and over again. After all those extra taxes, they're being walloped again by higher electricity rates. Wind and solar power simply can't compete with the low price of traditional power plants, unless the government dramatically tilts the playing field either through subsidies or, often, by forcing utilities to buy renewable power at unrealistic prices. Spain has implemented nearly every kind of market-distorting policy to keep its renewable power industry functional. And between 2000 and 2008, the total "over-cost" to Spain for renewable energy – that is, the premium electricity rate the government guarantees the power plants get versus the real market price – was a budget-busting €8 billion. That's about $12 billion in unnecessary surcharges for electricity. And that's on top of the €29 billion ($43 billion) the renewable plants received in subsidies or subsidy commitments. Spain's energy regulator, the report notes, has calculated that electricity rates to consumers would have to rise 31 per cent to repay "the historic debt" accumulated under all the money-losing giveaways to the renewable power industry.

Spanish businesses aren't safe from the hammering the soaring energy bills have delivered, and in 2004, Spanish stainless-steel manufacturing giant Acerinox, whose executives had been warning for years about higher electricity rates turning Spain into an uncompetitive place to do business, announced it was expanding – into Kentucky and South Africa. It would freeze any operations growth in Spain, due to the unaffordability of electricity there. "We are going to have the highest prices in Europe," then CEO Victoriano Muñoz had warned of the green policies. As the policy picked up momentum, he said, "We are afraid that the worst is yet to come."

But at least the Spanish people can feel great about

redesigning their economy around the environment even as they reel from the massive job losses, higher taxes, and soaring electricity rates, right? At least they know that their energy is now "clean" and "renewable" and they never need to burn fossil fuels for electricity again, right? Not so fast. For all their damage to Spain's economy, renewables have a long way to go before replacing the country's coal plants. According to the report, solar power "failed even to reach 1% of Spain's total electricity production in 2008." They're still burning coal in Spain. Now they're just burning a lot more money too.

Spain is a living example of the risks a country faces when it tinkers with a sector as vital as its energy economy: solar power and wind initiatives affect only a small fraction of the country's power grid, and yet within just a few years the country has lost the equivalent of 5 per cent of all the taxes paid by every company in the nation and its consumers face a 30 per cent jump in power costs.

But the effect of the oil sands on a historically impoverished part of Northern Alberta is evidence of how the very same economic factors – the immense demand in the world for abundant, affordable energy – can deliver phenomenal economic benefits and opportunities to people who would otherwise have virtually none.

Canada's Aboriginals are, on a national level, unquestionably the most economically disadvantaged segment of the population in the country. Unemployment rates among Aboriginals are three times the national average. Those that are employed are more likely to earn less, and poverty among First Nations and on reserves is rampant, occurring at rates far higher than among non-Aboriginals. About half of all Aboriginals subsist on an income less than $10,000 a year.[8] But in Northern Alberta, since the development of the oil sands industry, it's safe to say that Aboriginals have never had it so good.

Where there was for decades little for Aboriginals relegated to the remote northern muskeg to do beyond hunting, trapping, and fishing, the oil sands industry has created in just a matter of years a huge, thriving, and prosperous network of Aboriginal-owned businesses and thousands of jobs for any Aboriginal who wants one.

In 2008, Aboriginal-run firms in the Wood Buffalo region around Fort McMurray were hired by oil sands operators to perform more than $575 million in contract work. In the last ten years, Aboriginal companies earned more than $3 billion from contracts from companies working in the oil sands. Suncor Energy alone – just one single operator – has paid more than $1 billion to Aboriginal firms for services since 1992. Syncrude, another oil sands operator, has spent more than $1.5 billion on contracts with Aboriginal firms since 1993.

That's obviously an impressive amount. But the impact is even more staggering when we put it in perspective with the number of Aboriginals benefiting. The Fort McKay First Nation, located in the heart of the oil sands region, for instance, consists of all of 648 people. It's really the size of a village. Yet its oil sands contracting operations – the Fort McKay Group of Companies – which is owned entirely by the First Nation, rakes in more than $100 million in revenue every single year. That's more than $150,000 a year for every man, woman, and child in the community, or close to $1 million every year per family. In total, there are just 6,400 First Nations people living on reserves in the Wood Buffalo area. More than half-a-billion dollars every single year flows mostly to just a few thousand people – allowing families to make six-figure incomes in a part of the world where, not long ago, there was almost nothing for them. In fact, the oil sands region is the biggest single area of employment for Aboriginals in the entire country; roughly 1,500 Aboriginals worked for oil sands industries in full-time, permanent positions in 2008.

Still more Aboriginals work in something called an Industry Relations Corporation (IRC). Every First Nations community in the Fort McMurray area has one. The IRCs, heavily funded by the oil sands industry, are set up to act as agencies that make it easier for the Aboriginal bands to respond to any impact from the industrial activity near their reserve land and to consult with the companies and the government – a key part of the outreach to Aboriginal groups being made by industry and the province. They're like permanent town hall meetings about the oil sands.

IRCs are involved in helping with air quality monitoring, water quality monitoring, and monitoring the environmental impact on the landscape. In 2008, oil sands firms and governments paid out $7 million to the IRCs to hire staff and technical consultants, an important step to ensure that Aboriginals are part of the decision-making process in evaluating any industrial work that could effect them. Just as importantly, however, it creates jobs and expertise among Aboriginals that can only help them get further ahead, to take advantage of the multiplying opportunities in the region.

Of course, oil sands firms are careful to make sure they stay on good terms with Aboriginals in the area, even if a few noisy malcontents like Beaver Lake Cree chief Al Lameman figure they'd rather sue the industry. These companies aren't foolish: they know that all this employment and prosperity among the area's Aboriginals is good public relations; it keeps militant

Aboriginals from blockading their roads and facilities, as happens elsewhere in Canada when Aboriginal groups are convinced they're being taken advantage of; and it helps make their lives easier with politicians, who aren't anxious to start needlessly interfering with the country's best Aboriginal assistance program just for the sake of quieting some urban environmentalists demanding the oil sands be stopped. But there's another, critical motive too. For years, oil sands operators have been running ever-larger labour shortages, and, as they expand, it will only get more intense.[9]

Alberta's oil executives know that with Aboriginals they have a largely untapped talent pool right at their doorstep, and they're as anxious to help get Aboriginals working as Aboriginal leaders are to see their people employed. That's why oil sands operators have spent a fortune on all kinds of education initiatives. Suncor[10] has rolled out literacy program for young Aboriginal kids; it funds an outreach program that enhances classroom science, technology, and engineering lessons for Aboriginal students; it has set up scholarships for Aboriginals in college who want to study engineering, science, or business; and it funds the National Aboriginal Achievement Awards, an annual ceremony that celebrates successes among First Nations people and connects young Aboriginals with role models and mentors. Do you think oil producers in Sudan or Mexico offer anything like those programs to ethnic minorities in those countries?

But a lawsuit like Al Lameman's would put a stop to all that. He, with his allies in the environmental movement and the phony ethical fund industry, are asking the court to put a stop to thousands of projects, existing and planned,[11] bringing the oil sands region's industry to a grinding halt. His statement of claim filed in court is a brief twelve pages – with an additional

690 pages attached, listing every single business, structure, or permit that has been issued within hundreds of miles of their tiny village.[12] They've unilaterally declared themselves to be the sole "keepers" of an enormous swath of land that crosses the border between Saskatchewan and Alberta.[13] But Lameman and his reserve are not keepers of that massive swath of land in any meaningful way; they don't tend to it; they don't look after it or protect it; they don't improve it or develop it, and they certainly don't work it. They just claim it for themselves. Keepers is right. If Al Lameman has his way, he'll end up keeping thousands of Aboriginals from improving their lives, getting an education, escaping poverty. All of those jobs, all that education, all those opportunities ended, all for one band. A band that totals 379 people, including children.[14]

But then, it's easy for a bunch of middle-class European environmentalists to put their irrational anti–oil sands campaign ahead of an explosion of new opportunities for thousands of Aboriginals. They don't live here. The Aboriginals and their tragic levels of poverty and social ills are of no consequence to British green groups. And they certainly don't have to worry about the $10 billion a year the Canadian government spends on First Nations support programs. They like the fact that they can put Chief Lameman, in his headdress, in the middle of London's financial district and draw a crowd of curious onlookers. Once the environmentalists have won their oil sands boycott, they won't have any more use for Alberta's Aboriginals, who would return, without the oil sands, to a hopeless life of high unemployment, grinding poverty, and epidemic alcohol and drug addiction and violence.[15]

An oil sands–blocking lawsuit is a lot easier for Al Lameman too. He has a secure job: he's been chief of the Beaver Lake

Cree for more than twenty years.[16] Before that, he was a band councillor. He can afford to take a shot on a long, arduous lawsuit in hopes of winning some kind of moral victory or multimillion-dollar cash settlement for his office, while spoiling so much opportunity for so many others.

For a career chief like Lameman, the jobs and education brought by the oil sands can be a threat too. The chief, after all, presides over a petty kingdom. In his tiny little nation of 379 people, there is a huge government in place: there's the chief himself, three members of council; and no less than nine bureaucrats,[17,18] including three people on their "intergovernmental affairs" team. There are 98 private dwellings[19] on the whole reserve. So that's one bureaucrat for every nine houses – on top of the provincial and federal politicians that represent them in the two legislatures, and all the federal bureaucrats that work in the community at Indian Affairs. If Calgary operated its government using that kind of ratio, it would have to employ fifty thousand politicians and bureaucrats – the size of a small city.

Having a government-centred economy is the way things are; and it's the way things always will be, if Lameman gets his way. The oil sands would replace Lameman's government, and his personal power, by giving his band members another way to earn a living, and another lifestyle off the reserve. Blocking oil sands development isn't in the best economic interests of Northern Alberta Aboriginal families.

The problem for those who, like Lameman, want the oil sands shut down for their own misguided reasons is that the economic benefits the industry has brought to Northern Alberta, and to hundreds of thousands of Canadians, complicates their argument. No one likes the idea of sixteen hundred ducks drowning in an oil slick, and we can be virtually guaranteed that given the bad optics of it, Syncrude will take every measure to ensure that it never happens again. And if they died in the middle of some operation that had scant economic benefits, the decision to close a pond like that would be easy. But when millions of people prosper from the oil sands, the lives of some ducks inevitably becomes worth a lot less. If I told you that we could feed one hundred starving people every month, but to do so we'd have to kill one hundred ducks, most people would probably accept that as an unpleasant but worthwhile bargain. After all, that's exactly what we do all the time: we kill animals, we impose ourselves on the environment, in the name of putting food on our own tables. The only thing up for debate is how much of an imposition we're comfortable making to do it.

Which is why it's also so important for anti–oil sands crusaders not only to publicize fantastic scenarios about the economic blessings that will come from solar farms and windmills, but they must also undermine the economic benefits the oil sands has delivered to the world. It's awfully hard to argue with the number of people working, and one of the lowest unemployment rates on the continent.[20] So, instead, the oil sands haters emphasize the downside of prosperity; for Fort McMurray, they have painted for the world a portrait of a town corrupted by wealth. There are dumptrucks full of money there, they admit, but this has made everyone's life worse, they claim, not better.

"Life here is intolerable," complained John O'Connor, the doctor whose erroneous reports created a cancer scare that vilified the oil sands. Back before his errors were exposed, when he was still seen as a brave whistle-blower willing to speak truth to power, he wrote a stunning anti–Fort McMurray statement in a letter to a newspaper back in his home province of Nova Scotia. Few people out there would know any better, and if he was wrong about statistics as gravely serious as cancer risks downstream from the oil sands, why not suspect his accuracy when he tries his hand at the reputation of the prosperity of Fort McMurray too?

And yet, strangely, this man who called life there "intolerable" managed to tolerate it just fine, working there for fourteen years. Still, he wrote: "No one can afford housing here – where the average cost of a house in 2007 will be $550,000 – and there is nothing to do for teens and children, heightening the risk of drug involvement. . . . Quality of life here is extremely low. Oilsands expansion carries on at an unstoppable pace, despite the objections of citizens, native communities (who stand to gain the most from employment opportunities), health-care providers – who have been categorized as 'special interest groups' – and the local municipality and mayor."[21]

It's not likely O'Connor would have gotten his bitter diatribe in an Alberta newspaper: too many people in the province are familiar with the reality of Fort McMurray, and know people there, to believe his horror story. But, 4,800 kilometres away, in the paper of his hometown of Halifax, Nova Scotia, his account got play. Of course, he made it likelier he'd get published there when he pandered to the home team: "Nova Scotia, in my estimation, is the best place in the world for quality of life." He ended with a warning: "As a physician, and a husband/father/concerned human, I urge anyone thinking of making the move here to inform yourself fully of the consequences of such a move."

That's smart advice, even if it did come from an unreliable, embittered doctor facing ethical complaints for stonewalling health officials. But, as with the unnecessary cancer scare, anyone able to check the doctor's data for accuracy would find it sorely wanting. According to an actual study on the area's quality of life co-sponsored by the regional government and produced by independent consultants, Fort McMurray is far from intolerable.[22] About those houses no one can supposedly afford? According to the statistics, housing for the average earner in Fort McMurray is easier to afford than for the average earner in comparable cities or towns, like the nearby capital city of Edmonton.

In 2003, for example, the average couple in Fort McMurray earned $116,600, compared to $67,300 in nearby Edmonton. And the 73 per cent increase in income you get in Fort McMurray is more than enough to cover the increase in real estate prices you'll face. Using an affordability index for houses – income compared to housing prices – if Edmonton's benchmark was 100, the study calculated, Fort McMurray's affordability came out to 152. In plain language, the average family in Fort McMurray could afford 52 per cent more house than the average family in Edmonton, the nearest major city.

Families in Fort McMurray earning a "modest" income – meaning they earn less than 75 per cent of people in town – were far better off than those with a modest income in Edmonton: the affordability index for the lowest quartile of income earners was 177. That is, they could buy 77 per cent more things in Fort McMurray than they could in Edmonton. Even when the higher real estate prices are taken into account, it's still better to be working poor in Fort McMurray than anywhere else in Alberta.

In fact, more people are buying homes in Fort McMurray today than ever; home ownership was 82 per cent[23] in the area in

2008, up from 65 per cent in 1999, before the boom began in earnest. No wonder *Canadian Business* magazine recently ranked Fort McMurray as the best place to live in the whole country, from an economic point of view, with an average household income more than $40,000 higher than in Toronto.[24]

But it's not just money. It's the environment too. Air quality is better than in Edmonton, Red Deer, or Calgary, according to monitoring stations: in the four years studied by the Ministry of the Environment, Fort McMurray had air quality rated as "good" about 99 per cent of the time. Even the rate of traffic collisions in and around Fort McMurray were lower than in other major centres, such as Edmonton.

O'Connor isn't completely wrong in noticing that there are strains on a boom town: Fort McMurray doesn't have as many doctors per capita as other, more established regions of the province. That may have as much to do with a government-mandated fee structure for doctors that makes it impossible for Fort McMurray to pay premiums to recruit doctors in the way it has recruited every other type of professional. Nevertheless, health statistics show that emergency room waits are "substantially shorter" than in other cities in Alberta.

It's also true that community cohesion is always tough in boom towns where nearly everyone is a newcomer. But Fort McMurray seems to be making the best of it; their donations to the United Way charity are the highest in the province – more than twice as giving as in Edmonton. In 2007, 2008, and 2009, the United Way named Fort McMurray "the most generous, caring community in Canada,"[25] and Albertans as a whole give the highest dollar amount in the country to charity each year.[26] Volunteerism probably isn't as high as it ought to be. But that's not really surprising in a city with virtually no unemployment: jobs offering $100,000 a year have had trouble finding people too.

A hard-working boom town like Fort McMurray is going to attract a lot of young men, and demographically that means crime is likely to be higher than, say, retirement communities such as Victoria. But as Fort McMurray has grown, its crime rate has actually fallen, including for violent crimes. From 2001 to 2004, Statistics Canada's Centre for Justice Statistics shows that crimes per 100,000 residents – the crime rate – actually fell 15 per cent, and violent crimes fell even faster. The crime rate for sexual assaults was down 59 per cent in that same period, drunk driving was down 51 per cent and drug crimes were down 36 per cent.

And what about all those kids with supposedly nothing to do? You might find them at the 380,000-square-foot, $170-million leisure centre – the largest in Western Canada – which opened in 2009.[27] It includes an NHL-sized hockey arena, two other ice rinks, eight curling sheets, two field houses, a running track, a state-of-the-art fitness centre, a children's playground, and a babysitting area. The aquatics centre, when complete, will include an Olympic-sized swimming pool, an additional four-lane pool, and two water slides. The facility was paid for, in large part, by oil sands giant Suncor.

And even before that mega-centre opened, O'Connor was just plain wrong about Fort McMurray being a desert for young people. A growing city is always playing catch-up, but, for example, Fort Mac had as many indoor swimming pools and almost as many skating and curling rinks as Edmonton had per capita – and almost twice as many playgrounds.[28] The city hosts an array of summer festivals from Yoga in the Park[29] to Battle of the Bands. Fort McMurray is home to the most northerly mosque in the world,[30] along with a bevy of other multicultural organizations. There's the 52,000-square-foot central library,[31] which is bigger, relative to population, than metro Vancouver's. More than 10 per cent of the city – 8,000 residents – join in the community cleanup twice each year.[32]

What's astonishing about the oil sands, when you begin to seriously consider its potential, is how much prosperity is sitting there waiting, if we have the will, to be tapped: not just enough to elevate whole generations of Aboriginal communities out of poverty; not just enough for thousands of Atlantic Canadians, suffering the collapse of their own local industries, to find plenty of lucrative jobs (with air shuttles to and from Newfoundland every few weeks provided by their oil sands employers); and not just enough to give opportunity to the thousands of workers from poor nations who have come to work in Alberta. After all that, there is still billions more in economic benefits to come to millions of people.

In July 2009, the Canadian Energy Research Institute (CERI),[33] an independent think-tank based at the University of Calgary, published a study projecting the national economic impact of the oil sands.[34] Given that the oil sands account for 53 per cent[35] of all "accessible" oil in the world – that is, oil not owned by state-run entities like Saudi Aramco – it's not surprising that the value of the resource exceeded $1 trillion.

What was surprising is how much of that benefit accrued to other parts of Canada, not only in direct oil sands–related work across the country but through massive tax revenues the oil sands are projected to pay for decades to come.

Obviously, it's important for Alberta: capital investments are projected to run to $190 billion, with 1,889,000 person-years of employment. That's just to build the thing. Operating the oil sands for 25 years is expected to yield $1.5 trillion in GDP, and 9,530,000 person-years of employment. Put another way, if someone starts work at 20 and works till they're 65, that's 45 person-years of employment. Building the oil sands and then running it for 25 years is the equivalent of a lifetime's work for more than 250,000 people. And it's likely that the oil sands will continue for a lot longer than that.

The bulk of the work will be in Alberta, but a project of that size has enormous impacts across the country. According to the CERI study, constructing the oil sands means $11.4 billion spent in Ontario, and then operating the oil sands means another $43.4 billion for Ontario – or 812,000 person-years of work. Again, based on a 45-year career, that's the equivalent of 18,000 Ontarians starting oil sands work after high school and continuing until they retire. But that understates the impact, since the CERI study is only for a 25-year period – or about half a career. It didn't project out ahead a full 45 years. So 812,000 person-years of work in a 25-year period is the same as 32,500 full-time permanent jobs. And still it's bigger than it sounds; in the fall of 2009, the total number of Ontarians employed full-time was 5.2 million, with an unemployment rate of 9.2 per cent.[36] Without those 32,500 full-time, permanent jobs in Ontario, unemployment would be nearly half a percent higher.

Just for a comparison, in 2008 there were only about 29,000 Canadian Auto Workers union members still working for the Big Three automakers,[37] a number that shrank by 16,000[38] even before those companies were reorganized. And the kind of oil sands work that makes its way to Ontario tends to be high-value jobs, ranging from building mining equipment to operating Ontario refineries, to working in the financial sector.

Other provinces do well too: British Columbia will reap $45.5 billion in GDP from the oil sands and 713,000 person-years of work. Even the farther regions geographically will do handsomely: Atlantic Canada will benefit with $8 billion in GDP and 158,000 person-years of work. And that's on top of the thousands of Atlantic Canadians who commute to work in Fort McMurray directly.

That's all the private sector benefit. But, not surprisingly, the biggest winner in the oil sands boom is the tax collector – all fourteen of them, from the federal government to each province and territory. Total federal taxes paid in both the construction and operation of the oil sands is projected to be a whopping $188 billion over the 25-year term. Total provincial taxes paid over the same period are another $118 billion, with five provinces other than Alberta joining the billionaires club. And none of these huge numbers include the royalty payments – technically not a tax but the fee the oil companies pay for actually taking the oil: that works out to another $184 billion.

So between federal and provincial taxes and oil royalties, the oil sands are projected to pump $690 billion into government coffers across the country. For a country of 34 million people,[39] that's like handing $21,000 worth of government services to every man, woman, and child – or more than $80,000 for a family of four. That's a lot of hospital visits, library books, and pothole repairs, courtesy of a small patch of oily land in Northern Alberta.[40]

That's an economic story, and it's a story of the success of capitalism, and of the success of science too, which finally solved the puzzle of how to extract the oil in an economically viable manner. But it's also a story of social justice – the kind of equitable sharing of the wealth that many anti-capitalists talk about.

Most other oil-exporting countries are a tale of woe, poverty, and strife. It could fairly be said that oil has cursed, not blessed, the people of Saudi Arabia, Iran, Nigeria, Sudan, and most of the other godforsaken places where oil happens to be found. In no other country, in no other industry, do semi-skilled labourers make $100,000 for driving a truck or $150,000 for working on a rig.

This is the kind of magnificent prosperity that a vast resource deposit can bring to a country. It's the kind of wealth that Saudi Arabia has enjoyed for a generation. Of course, Saudi's oil money isn't shared with that country's poorest souls through government social programs or even with the people who toil to get the oil out of the ground— especially foreign temporary labourers from Third World countries. The vast majority of it is skimmed by the Saudi royal family, with its thousands of "princes" for most of whom their sole talent is their conspicuous consumption. If the Saudis have proven the dramatic consequences of abusing energy, and Spain has proven the drastic consequences of misusing energy, then the oil sands are proof of the great good fortune that a huge amount of energy, in the right hands, can deliver to a staggering number of people.

Conclusion

So now that we know so much more about the facts behind the oil sands, and the motives behind those who criticize them, the big question is: what should we do about the oil sands?

We know what the oil companies want to do: they want to develop them, full tilt. Of course they do – the vast majority of the world's oil reserves are controlled by state-owned companies like Saudi Aramco. Literally 53 per cent of the world's accessible oil is now thought to be in Alberta – which just happens to be one of the safest places to do business that an oil company could find. It's hardly surprising that investors would rather put their money in Canada, one of the most stable investment climates in the world, than to set up shop in a country like Russia, where the Kremlin literally forced Royal Dutch Shell to hand over half of Sakhalin-2, the world's largest oil and gas export project, to its own state-owned Gazprom,[1] and impudently imprisons capitalists for daring to hold political views.[2] Or Venezuela, where the socialist tinpot revolutionary Hugo Chávez steals entire plants out from underneath their rightful owners.[3] The world needs energy: unable to put their efforts into Alberta, however, investors will have no choice but to take risks with more erratic regimes, which, until the oil sands came along, hadn't done much to make those countries any more stable.

We know what Canadian governments want too. They want the half-a-trillion dollars of taxes that come from oil sands development to shore up the health care, education, and other social services for their citizens. They also want the hundreds of thousands of high-paying jobs the oil sands have been creating across the country, driving down unemployment numbers and spinning off countless economic benefits. They certainly want oil sands operators like Syncrude and Suncor to keep jetting Atlantic Canadians into and out of Fort McMurray every few weeks, bringing desperately needed money into eastern regions, where fishing and coal mining have ceased to be able to support a flourishing economy. And they're delighted that oil firms are finally giving hope to an Aboriginal population that had for so long seemed to have no prospect of it. Not just hope, of course, but actual jobs, real educational opportunities, and practical job skills training that will without question permanently change the destiny of generations of Aboriginals for the better. Having been unable to do much to help Canadian Aboriginals for the last century or more, Canadian governments can only be relieved that someone else has finally arrived to address one of the country's most pressing social plights.

But we also know what the world's other big oil producers think, the ones that compete with the oil sands to supply the global thirst for energy. They're fervently hoping that the oil sands would somehow just stop. A market share worth trillions of dollars of barrels of oil that should have been theirs – money that could have helped to further arm Nigeria's brutal militias, to fund Iran's hostile nuclear weapons program, to empower Russia's imperialistic warmongering, to prop up Venezuela's failing Marxist experiment and its suppression of citizens' rights, and to allow Saudi Arabia's princes to sponsor more terrorists and buy yet more time for their cruel and decadent regime – is at risk of ending up in Canadian hands instead. Saudi Arabia has already lost a big chunk of market share in the United States – 80 million barrels a year – to Canada, and that trend is only going to grow. Not only is Canadian oil taking money out of the treasuries of OPEC's despots, but bringing oil sands oil to market only adds to the global supply and thus reduces the price of oil that Saudi Arabia and the rest of OPEC gets from the customers that they keep. They can't help but hate that a North American country that prefers peace to conflict will soon dominate an industry that was once the virtual monopoly of the hostile, anti-Western world.

And we know a lot more now about what the environmentalists and self-appointed ethical pundits of the world think. For them, the oil sands represent the greatest opportunity to exploit a particular cause for profit that they've ever encountered. Forget one-dimensional campaigns like Save the Whales and No More Nukes. Those can only take you so far. Never before has an issue been so phenomenally flexible that it could be stretched in ways that could tap into so many fears: water usage, water pollution, wildlife endangerment, forest depredation, air quality, global warming, health dangers, and the jeopardizing of the way of life for Aboriginal peoples. At least no issue that can be exploited from the safety of a democratic, Western country. Greenpeace needs to raise $1 million a day to meet its current budget, and beating up the oil sands is a lot easier than beating up the world's largest polluter, China. You don't go to jail if you criticize the oil sands – even if you are dead wrong about them. You very well could if you criticize the Chinese government's sprawling state-run oil empire. So-called ethical funds can freely abuse the high-minded values of naive investors by badmouthing the oil sands, even as they continue to pump money into them or, worse, into far more environmentally and morally questionable industries.

Where else could you so easily fabricate stories and invent statistics about mutated animals and cancer epidemics, without large numbers of people being able to see the truth for themselves? Northern Alberta may as well be on another planet, so distant is it from the lives of most Westerners.

But what should we think – we who don't have a direct stake in the oil sands, who don't live in Fort McMurray, and who don't work for a company that does business there? Those of us who don't have to keep an eye on Greenpeace's bottom line or have to get maximum return for an ethical fund they manage? We can't tell the difference if our car is fuelled with gasoline made from oil sands oil or conventional oil or even by Saudi oil. What's the most moral stance for us to take on the oil sands?

There is a school of thought that says economic engagement with dictatorships is a better way to make them come around than boycotts or sanctions. Classical economic liberals like the late Frédéric Bastiat argue that if goods don't cross borders, soldiers will. That's a hopeful view, and it is probably true in the case of democratic countries like France and Germany, whose economies are now so closely bound together that another war between them is almost unthinkable. But we have been buying oil from OPEC dictatorships for decades – and at inflated prices for nearly forty years, since the oil shock of 1973 – and, if anything, the moral character of OPEC nations has gotten worse. Saudi Arabia exports jihad around the world; Iran is now a theocracy building nuclear weapons; Venezuela has begun to destabilize its neighbours. And then there are up-and-coming oil exporters like Sudan, who has invested its oil windfalls in weapons, allowing itself to prosecute its wars and internal genocides with a visciousness and power it previously lacked.

By contrast, companies operating in the oil sands include the world's most progressive oil producers; even firms out of China that set up shop in Alberta have to operate by Canada's rules. In the oil sands, PetroChina is learning how to operate while facing accountability for its record of environmental and workers' rights as it never has at home. It actually starts to feel a bit trite to list the democratic differences, and the differences in peace, between Alberta and its biggest competitor, the Middle East. Alberta is quite simply one of the freest, fairest, safest, most liberal jurisdictions in the world. Comparing Alberta's treatment of women, minorities, gays, and Aboriginals to those in OPEC nations is to compare the world's highest standards to the world's worst transgressors. And that's just on the issue of human rights.

Economically, no oil jurisdiction in the world, period, treats workers as well as the oil sands. Where else do people on the lowest rungs of the income ladder have 77 per cent more purchasing power than they would if they lived in the nearest major city? Even the working poor in Fort McMurray are rich compared to the rest of the world. And then there's the massive transfer of wealth through taxes that ends up redistributed across the economy, subsidizing welfare, unemployment

ETHICAL OIL

insurance, health care, schools and university tuitions, training programs, regional development – a fund for helping low-income Canadians that dwarfs anything the companies make by way of profits.

Environmentally, the oil sands are cleaner than any other competing jurisdiction when measured by real pollution – dirty air, dirty water, dirty soil. It's healthier to live downstream from Fort McMurray than downstream from Toronto's CN Tower. That's not government or industry propaganda; that's the collected observations of dozens of countless researchers, constantly combing over the most-inspected industrial site in the world. At any one time, no fewer than ten universities are studying tailings ponds and other environmental challenges in the oil sands – and many more are working in laboratories to improve the technology to eliminate wasteful ideas like tailings ponds altogether. The thought of independent environmental inspections of Saudi or Iranian or Russian oil facilities would be comical if it weren't so depressingly hopeless.

The last-gasp attack on the oil sands is against carbon dioxide, in the name of climate change. Of course human-caused global warming is a theory that isn't uniformly accepted in either the scientific or lay community. But even if one were to take it at face value, the global impact of the oil sands is minuscule. Remember that all this noise, all these crusades and campaigns, all the social and political debates, and the huge amount of psychic space occupied by our incessant agonizing over the oil sands, all of it is about a source of CO_2 that accounts for 0.1 per cent of human carbon emissions every year. It's not that it's not a discussion worth having, but it is something clearly worth keeping in perspective.

So, for that matter, is the fact that new unconventional streams of oil and even many conventional streams, such as in places like Nigeria and Iraq, emit even more CO_2 than the oil sands do today. And while those countries could scarcely be bothered to care about such things (non–First World nations, after all, are consistently exempted from the emissions-limits of climate-change treaties like Kyoto and Copenhagen, and none charge carbon penalties like Alberta does), oil sands producers have only reduced their footprint year after year, investing fortunes into technologies that already have shown themselves capable of stripping down CO_2 to the point where there is scarcely any difference between the carbon impact of oil sands products and the traditional conventional oil coming out of the Middle East. We're at the point where it would be better for many oil consumers to switch *to* oil sands oil than to keep up with the oil they're buying from other sources. These are essential things to keep in perspective, not just because it paints the oil sands in a good light, but because every effort to fight the oil sands by complaining about their carbon impact is not only misleading; every exaggerated portrayal of the environmental risks in Alberta brings us closer to shifting yet more business instead to producers who are so much worse in so many, often horrific ways.

That is the direction that so much hyperbole and deceit by oil sands' enemies is taking us. And each time the oil sands have another victory – a new technology to reduce emissions or a new project to employ Aboriginal workers – you can catch a glimpse of their true, self-serving character. Environmental advocacy groups like Greenpeace have their arguments made even weaker as the oil sands get even cleaner: it makes it harder for them to make their case and get more money out of donors;

ethical funds have a harder time convincing people to avoid their oil sands–investing mutual fund competitors (even if secretly the so-called ethical managers are plowing just as much money into oil sands stocks); someone like Beaver Lake Cree Al Lameman surely knows that it jeopardizes his lawsuit, not to mention that Aboriginals getting real work and providing for themselves, instead of relying on his government's hand-outs, risks undermining his petty empire.

Of course it would be unethical to oppose an industry that brings so much benefit to so many if you are doing so for your own selfish interests, and that's certainly worth keeping in mind when we next hear these various anti–oil sands groups hector-ing us about "morals" and "ethics." But, above all, what's important for us to remember is that, despite the pipe dreams of environmentalists, our carbon-based economy isn't going away. The world isn't throwing out the internal combustion engine anytime soon. In fact, in countries like India, China, and Brazil, the world is buying more cars than ever. So we're stuck with oil for a long time, whether we like it or not. The only question that remains is: if we have to produce oil, and we have to buy oil – and we absolutely must do both – whose oil should we do our best to support? Who can we trust to do it the most morally?

There can be no doubt: Canada does it best. We're an energy superpower. And we're an ethical superpower too, setting inter-national standards for how we treat the environment and how we treat each other. And if our goal as moral citizens is to make the world a better place, then there is only one choice: to pump as much oil as we possibly can out of Fort McMurray. Pump and steam and dig and drill and get that oil out of the sand in any and every way we can. Every drop of oil from Alberta is one less drop from some fascist theocracy, or some brutal warlord; one less cent into the treasuries of Russia's secret police and al-Qaeda's murderers.

Canadian oil sands oil is the most ethical oil in the world, and the people who invest there, work there, and support the oil sands with their patronage and their encouragement should be proud. Whether they realize it or not, they are all, gradually, helping to make the world a more moral, humane, and better place.

Acknowledgements

Let me acknowledge the faith that Doug Pepper of McClelland & Stewart has in me. Thanks to Jenny Bradshaw for her meticulous and patient editing of the book, and to Josh Glover for spreading the word about it. And a big thank you to Kevin Libin, Canada's leading oil-sands journalist, for brainstorming to fact checking and everything in between.

Sources

Introduction

[1] CBC News, "Alberta's oilsands," March 6, 2007.

[2] Canadian Association of Petroleum Producers, "Oil Sands: A Solution to North America's Growing Energy Demands?" September 2009.

[3] American Bird Conservancy

[4] American Wind Energy Association website: awea.org

Chapter 1

[1] Steve Connor. *The Independent*, "Warning: Oil supplies are running out fast," August 3, 2009.

[2] Heavyoilinfo.com. "SEC reconsiders booking of oil sands reserves," January 14, 2008.

[3] U.S. Energy Information Administration. "U.S. Imports by Country of Origin," 2009.

[4] U.S. Geological Survey, World Resources Project, Fact Sheet: "An Estimate of Recoverable Heavy Oil Resources of the Orinoco Oil Belt, Venezuela." October, 2009.

Chapter 2

[1.] U.S. Energy Information Administration. "U.S. Imports by Country of Origin," 2009.

[2.] David Lee and Richard Norton-Taylor. *The Guardian*, "House of Saud looks close to collapse," November 21, 2001.

[3.] CIA. *The World Factbook*. "Saudi Arabia," 2010.

[4.] Amnesty International. "Algeria: Persistent torture by the military security in secret locations," June 10, 2007.

[5.] U.S. Energy Information Administration. "Country Analysis Briefs: Iran," January 1, 2010.

[6.] ForestEthics.org. "Press Release: Whole Foods, Bed Bath & Beyond Reject Canada's Tar Sands," February 10, 2010.

[7.] U.S. Energy Information Administration, Independent Statistics and Analysis. Oil Crude and Petroleum Products Explained. Petroleum Statistics, 2008.

[8.] Dina O'Meara. *Calgary Herald*, "U.S. retailers' oilsands boycott sparks Calgary anger," February 11, 2010.

[9.] Marathon.com. "Exploration and Production," 2008.

[10.] Human Rights Watch. "Saudi Arabia: Women's Rights Promises Broken," July 8, 2009.

[11.] Human Rights Watch. "Saudi Arabia: Drop 'Cross-Dressing' Charges," June 24, 2009.

[12.] Amnesty International. "Saudi Arabian man beheaded and crucified," December 8, 2009.

[13.] Amnesty International. "Juveniles Among Five Men Beheaded in Saudi Arabia," May 12, 2009.

[14.] A.R. Pittaway. *Saudi Aramco World*, "Arabian Forests," July/August 1989. Volume 40, Number 4.

[15.] Human Rights Watch. "Saudi Arabia: Rape Victim Punished for Speaking Out," November 15, 2007.

[16.] Human Rights Watch. "Bad Dreams: Exploitation and Abuse of

Migrant Workers in Saudi Arabia," July 2004.

[17] Human Rights Watch. "'As If I Am Not Human': Abuses against Asian Domestic Workers in Saudi Arabia." July 7, 2008.

[18] Human Rights Watch. "Letter to Ayatollah Larijani on post-election abuses in Iran," August 28, 2009.

[19] Human Rights Watch. "Iran: Alarming spike in executions since disputed presidential election," August 7, 2009.

[20] John Pomfret. Washington Post, "Oil, Ideology Keep China From Joining Push Against Iran," September 30, 2009.

[21] Amnesty International. "Amnesty International Report 2009: Russia," 2009.

[22] Economagic.com. "Crude Oil Production, Russia; Thousand Barrels per Day," 2009.

[23] U.S. Energy Information Administration. "Russia Energy Data, Statistics and Analysis – Oil, Gas, Electricity, Coal," May 2008.

[24] GlobalSecurity.org. "Russian State Budget," September 11, 2008.

[25] Russian Federation 2001 Report. Amnesty International.

[26] Chechnya Overview, Holocaust Memorial Museum, http://www.ushmm.org/genocide/take_action/atrisk/region/chechnya-russia/

[27] Thomson Reuters Foundation. "Chechnya and the North Caucacus," July 28, 2009.

[28] Amnesty International. "Thousands remain displaced a year after Georgia/Russia conflict," August 7, 2009.

[29] BBC News. "Obituary: Anna Politkovskaya," October 7, 2006.

[30] TimesOnline.co.uk. "Anna Politkovskaya's lawyer Stanislav Markelov shot dead in Moscow," January 19, 2009.

[31] Reporters Without Borders. "After Russia awarded 2014 Winter Olympics, authorities should demonstrate a real will to solve murders of journalists," July 10, 2007.

[32] CBC News. "A history of famous poisonings," November 24, 2006.

[33] Human Rights Watch. "Nigeria: Investigate Killings by Security Forces," July 20, 2009.

[34] U.S. Energy Information Administration. "Nigeria Energy Data, Statistics and Analysis – Oil, Gas, Electricity, Coal," May 2009.

[35] The World Bank, "Nigeria: Country Brief," 2010.

[36] *The Telegraph.* "Nigeria comes clean and shows the way for Africa," June 25, 2005.

[37] Based on posted currency exchange rates at the time of writing.

[38] CIA. *The World Factbook.* "Country Comparison: Life Expectancy at Birth," 2009.

[39] U.S. Energy Information Administration. Annual Energy Review 2008. Table 11.5. "World Crude Oil Production, 1960-2008."

[40] Department of Energy, National Energy Technology Laboratory "Consideration of Crude Oil Source in Evaluating Transportation Fuel GHG Emissions," March 20, 2009.

[41] National Energy Technology Laboratory. "An Evaluation of the Extraction, Transport and Refining of Imported Crude Oils and the Impact on Life Cycle Greenhouse Gas Emissions," March 27, 2009.

[42] Human Rights Watch. "Venezuela: Stop Harassing TV Station," May 21, 2009.

[43] Human Rights Watch. "Venezuela: Repeal Measures Aimed at Critics," July 31, 2009.

[44] Amnesty International website. Human Rights in Bolivarian Republic of Venezuela.

[45] Amnesty International. "Amnesty International Report 2009: Venezuela," 2009.

[46] Amnesty International. "Amnesty International Report 2009: Sudan," 2009.

[47] Amnesty International. "African Union refuses to cooperate with Bashir arrest warrant," July 6, 2009.

48. Amnesty International. "Sudan: Amnesty International warns 2.2 million at risk in Darfur after aid agencies expelled," March 5, 2009.

49. Amnesty International. "Amnesty International calls on Sudan to repeal law penalizing women for wearing trousers," September 4, 2009.

50. Agence France-Presse. "Sudan trouser woman 'ready for 40,000 lashes'," August 2, 2009.

51. CNN. "U.N.: 100,000 more dead in Darfur than reported," April 22, 2008.

52. Amnesty International. "Federal Election 2008: Strengthening our Commitment: A Human Rights Agenda for Canada," September 2008.

53. Statistics Canada; *The Daily*. "Canada's Population," Sept. 27, 2006.

54. Ian Munroe. *American Chronicle*, "Canada, biggest climate criminal in the world!" September 5, 2009.

55. Nicholas Kohler. *Maclean's*, "Calgary may label big oil 'unethical'," December 15, 2008.

56. CBC News. "Alberta bishop questions 'moral legitimacy' of oil-sands development," January 26, 2009.

Chapter 3

1. Human Rights Watch. "Sudan, Oil, and Human Rights," 2003.

2. U.S. Energy Information Administration. "Weekly All Countries Spot Price FOB Weighted by Estimated Export Volume (Dollars per Barrel)," April 28, 2010.

3. IndexMundi.com. "Sudan GDP – per capita (PPP)," 2010.

4. U.S. Energy Information Administration. "Country Analysis Briefs: Sudan," September 2009.

5. United States Department of the Treasury. "Effectiveness of U.S. Economic Sanctions with Respect to Sudan," January 2009.

[6.] Churchill, Winston S. *The River War*. Longmans, Green and Co., London; New York. 1899.

[7.] Human Rights Watch. "Sudan, Oil, and Human Rights," 2003.

[8.] U.S. Energy Information Administration. "Country Analysis Briefs: Sudan," September 2009.

[9.] BBC News. "China, Russia bar Sudan sanctions," April 18, 2006.

[10.] Human Rights Watch. "Sudan, Oil, and Human Rights," 2003.

[11.] Ezra Levant. *Financial Post*, "Politics trump human rights in Sudan," June 24, 2002.

[12.] BBC News. "Talisman pulls out of Sudan," March 10, 2003.

[13.] Talisman Energy. "Human Rights: Corporate Responsibility," 2010.

[14.] Human Rights Watch. "Sudan – Entrenching Impunity: Government Responsibility for International Crimes on Darfur," December 2005. Volume 17, No. 17 (A).

[15.] Reg Manhas. *Compact Quarterly*, "Talisman in Sudan: Impacts of Divestment," March 2007.

[16.] U.S. Department of the Treasury. "What You Need To Know About U.S. Sanctions Against Burma (Myanmar)," 2008.

[17.] Total.com. "Total in Myanmar: a sustained commitment," 2008.

Chapter 4

[1.] Suzanne Goldenberg. *The Guardian*, "Canada looks to China to exploit oil sands rejected by U.S.," February 14, 2010.

Chapter 5

[1.] PlatformLondon.org. "Cashing in on Tar Sands: RBS, UK banks and Canada's 'blood oil'."

[2.] "Encana named to Dow Jones Sustainability World Index for fourth consecutive year." Encana news release. Sept. 24, 2009.

[3.] Covalence EthicalQuote.com. "Methodology."

[4.] Covalence EthicalQuote.com. "Team."

[5] Source: FPInfomart search

[6] Saudi Aramco: "EXPEC Advanced Research Center" brochure. 2009.

[7] ExxonMobil. "2008 Summary Annual Report."

[8] Covalence EthicalQuote.com. "Methodology."

[9] Blog: Ella Does Squamish; http://elladoessquamish.blogsome.com/

[10] Ibid.

[11] http://www.covalence.ch/docs/CovalenceEthicalRanking2009_PressRelease_26.01.2010.pdf

[12] Talisman Energy. "2008 Corporate Responsibility Report."

[13] Ibid.

[14] The China National Offshore Oil Corporation. "Social Responsibility Report," 2008.

[15] Ibid.

[16] ExxonMobil. "2008 Worldwide giving report."

[17] William Boot. *The Irrawaddy*, "Chinese Oil Giant Accused of Human Rights Abuses in Burma," October 24, 2008.

[18] Ibid.

[19] Covalence EthicalQuote.com. "Clients."

[20] Management and Excellence website: "Sustainability Ratings."

[21] Management & Excellence. "FAQs."

[22] Management & Excellence. "M&E Ethics Communications Services for Companies."

[23] Management and Excellence website: "Studies and Rankings."

[24] Chris Oliver, "PetroChina tops $1 trillion market cap in debut," MarketWatch. Nov. 5, 2007.

[25] Exxon Valdez Oil Spill Trustee Council. "Questions & Answers."

[26] John S. Patton et al. "Ixtoc 1 oil spill: flaking of surface mousse in the Gulf of Mexico." *Nature*, March 19, 1981.

[27] Exxon Valdez Oil Spill Trustee Council. "Questions & Answers."

[28] David G. Savage. *Los Angeles Times*, "Justices slash Exxon Valdez verdict," June 26, 2008.

29. Antoaneta Bezlova. Asia Times, "China's toxic spillover," December 2, 2005.

30. David Lague. "China Blames Oil Company for Benzene Spill in River," *International Herald Tribune*. Nov. 25, 2005.

31. *Chief Executive*. "Chinese in denial on SARS," March 1, 2004.

32. BBC News. "Chinese papers condemn Harbin 'lies'," November 24, 2005.

33. "Sacked official 'found dead' after Jilin blast," AsiaNews.it. Dec. 7, 2005.

34. BBC News. "Maximum fine over China Pollution," January 25, 2007.

35. Offnews.info. "PetroChina Profit Tops Analyst Estimates; Acquisitions Planned," October 8, 2009.

36. Antoaneta Bezlova. *Asia Times*, "China's toxic spillover," December 2, 2005.

37. Edward Wong. *New York Times*, "In China City, Protesters See Pollution Risk of New Plant," May 6, 2008.

38. Trillium Asset Management. "Divest from PetroChina – BP Amoco."

39. ExxonMobil. "2008 Summary Annual Report."

40. The Tax Foundation. "Summary of Latest Federal Individual Income Tax Data," July 30, 2009.

41. Governor's Budget Summary 2010-11. "Revenue Estimates."

42. Kairos: Canadian Ecumenical Justice Initiatives. "Contact Us."

43. Kairos. "2008 Annual Report."

44. Kairos. "Christian Faith and the Canadian Tar Sands: A KAIROS Reflection on Sustainability and Energy," September 2008.

45. Indian and Northern Affairs Canada. "Notes for an address by The Honourable Jim Prentice, PC, QC, MP Minister of Indian Affairs and Northern Development, and Federal Interlocutor for Métis and Non-status Indians to the Calgary Chamber of Commerce," November 17, 2006.

46. BBC News. "China's Christians suffer for their faith," November 9, 2004.

47. Kairos: Canadian Ecumenical Justice Initiatives. "Economic Advocacy Measures: Options for KAIROS Members for the Promotion of Peace in Palestine and Israel," January 7, 2008.

48. Diocese of St. Paul. "The Integrity of Creation and the Athabasca Oil Sands," January 25, 2009.

Chapter 6

1. Kevin Libin. *National Post*, "British environmentalists link with natives to fight oil sands," September 11, 2009.

2. The Co-operative Investments. www.co-operativeinvestments.co.uk.

3. World Wildlife Fund. "Unconventional Oil: Scraping the Bottom of the Barrel?" 2008.

4. The Co-operative Investments. "Unconventional oil could cost us the earth."

5. Karin Mizgala. *FP Magazine Daily*, "What would Mahatma Gandhi invest in?" July 1, 2009.

6. Investment Company Institute. www.ici.org.

7. The Co-operative Investments. "Our ethical film."

8. The Co-operative Group. "Sustainability Report 2007/08," 2008.

9. The Co-operative Investments. "CIS European Growth Trust," 2009.

10. Total Canada. "About Total E&P Canada."

11. The Co-operative Investments. "CIS Sustainable Leaders Trust," 2009.

12. The Co-operative Investments. "Sustainable Leaders Trust."

13. Amnesty International. "Indonesia must repeal "cruel" new stoning and caning law," September 17, 2009.

14. International Power. "Annual Report 2008."

15. Freedomhouse.org. "Country Report: Map of Freedom 2009," 2009.

[16] International Power. Annual Report 2008.

[17] The Co-operative Investments. "CIS Sustainable Leaders Trust," 2009.

[18] RPS Group web site. "RPS in Canada; Heavy Oil and Bitumen." Accessed July 21, 2010.

[19] The Co-operative Investments. "CIS US Growth," 2009.

[20] ExelonCorp.com. "Nation's Largest Nuclear Fleet," 2010.

[21] ExelonCorp.com. "Three Mile Island," 2010.

[22] Exelon Nuclear. "Three Mile Island Unit 2: Question and Answer."

[23] *The Australian.* "Concern at Three Mile Island leak," November 24, 2009.

[24] Eon.com. "Annual Report Part I/II," 2008.

[25] The Co-operative Investments. "CIS Corporate Income Bond Trust," 2009.

[26] Iberdrola. "Increasing Production, Distributed Energy and Number of Clients," 2009.

[27] The Co-operative Investments. "CIS UK Growth Trust," 2009.

[28] "BP Plans $3 Billion Project to Refine More Canadian Heavy Crude Oil in the U.S. Midwest," BP press release. Sept. 20, 2006.

[29] BG-Group.com. "Canada and Alaska," 2010.

[30] EthicalFunds.com. "Investor Strategy for Reducing Oil Sands Risks Unveiled," October 28, 2008.

[31] EthicalFunds.com. "Focus List 2009," 2010.

[32] EthicalFunds.com. "Changing the World," 2009.

[33] EthicalFunds.com. "Investments," 2010.

[34] "Suncor production averages over 300,000 barrels a day," *Red Deer Advocate.* May 4, 2010.

[35] Fiona Anderson, "Just how responsible is your 'socially responsible' fund?" *Vancouver Sun*, Oct. 20, 2007.

[36] EthicalFunds.com. "Changing the World," 2006.

[37] EthicalFunds.com. "Changing the World," 2007.

38. Power Corporation of Canada. "Corporate Social Responsibility Statement."

39. UN.org. "The Universal Declaration of Human Rights," 1948.

40. EthicalFunds.com. "Changing the World," 2008.

41. EthicalFunds.com. "Changing the World," 2007.

42. "Nortel Technology Threatens Human Rights in China." International Centre for Human Rights and Democratic Development, news release. Oct. 18, 2001.

43. EthicalFunds.com. "Changing the World," 2006.

44. InvestorsGroup.com. "Investments," 2010.

45. Investors Group. "Fund Profile: Investors Summa SRI FundTMA," 2009.

46. TrinidadDrilling.com. "Office Locations," 2008.

47. Investors Group. "Fund Profile: Investors Summa Global SRI A," 2009.

48. BHPBilliton.com. "Our Businesses."

49. Thisisnoblegroup.com. "What is Noble Doing?" 2010.

50. Investors Group, Investors Summa Global SRI C, Fund Profile, 2009.

51. Husky Energy, "Sunrise Oil Sands Project Update," news release. Jan. 20, 2010.

52. Fondsdesjardins.com. "Products and Services," 2010.

53. Fondsdesjardins.com. "Solutions that make your plans happen," 2008.

54. Carrie Tait. *Financial Post*, "EnCana spinoff plans new oil sands project," October 1, 2009. http://www.nationalpost.com/story.html?id=2055150.

55. Fondsdesjardins.com. "Ethical Funds," 2008.

56. AcuityFunds.com. "Summary of Investment Portfolio at March 31, 2010," 2010.

57. Santos.com. "Our Activities: Exploration Acreage," 2010.

58. Santos.com. "About Santos: Key Facts & Statistics," 2009.

59. AcuityFunds.com. "Our Products," 2010.

[60] Oxy.com. Home page.

[61] Oxy.com. "Middle East/North Africa."

[62] Oxy.com. "About Oxy."

[63] Oxy.com. "Human Rights Policy."

[64] Oxy.com. "Climate Change."

[65] AcuityFunds.com. "Quarterly Portfolio Disclosure: Summary of Investment Portfolio at March 31, 2010," 2010.

[66] Petrobank.com. "Sutton, Saskatchewan," 2009.

[67] AcuityFunds.com. "The Acuity Clean Environment Equity Fund," 2010.

[68] Teck.com. "Energy," 2010.

[69] Enbridge. "Alberta Clipper," 2010.

[70] MackenzieFinancial.com. "Mackenzie Universal Sustainable Opportunities Class," 2010.

[71] Petrobras.com. "Petrobras in Numbers," 2009.

[72] Petrobras. "Strategic Plan 2009–2013," January 26, 2009. http://www2.petrobras.com.br/ri/ing/ApresentacoesEventos/ConfTelefonicas/pdf/PN_2009-2013_Ing.pdf

[73] Petrobras.com. "Environmental and Social Responsibility," 2003.

[74] Meritas.ca. "Our Funds," 2010.

[75] Meritas.ca. "Interim Management Report of Fund Performance," 2009.

[76] Ibid.

[77] Meritas. "Semi Annual Report 2009" http://www.meritas.ca/resources/meritas/AllFundsReports/SAR.June.2009.English.pdf

[78] Inhance.ca www.feelgoodinvesting.com

[79] Vancity Circadian Mutual Funds, "Climate Change and the Investment Landscape," brochure. July 31, 2008.

[80] Ibid.

[81] Jason Zweig. MONEY *Magazine*, "What Warren Buffett wants you to know," May 3, 2004.

Chapter 7

[1.] John Donaldson. *A Canoe Quest in the Wake of Canada's "Prince of Explorers": One Day at a Time*. Artful Codger Press: Kingston, ON (2006).

[2.] Agnes Deans Cameron. *The New North*. 2004.

[3.] *New York Times*. "'Hunyadi' Waters," October 14, 1893.

[4.] Agnes Deans Cameron. *The New North*. 2004.

[5.] Greenpeace.org. "Don't make Canada a climate criminal," December 4, 2009.

[6.] Government of Alberta: Energy. "Facts and Statistics," 2010.

[7.] "Ambient Air Quality Trends in Alberta 2008," Government of Alberta. Air Policy and Environmental Health Section Environmental Assurance Division Alberta Environment.

[8.] Casahome.org. http://casahome.org/

[9.] "Ambient Air Quality Trends in Alberta 2008," Government of Alberta. Air Policy and Environmental Health Section Environmental Assurance Division Alberta Environment.

[10.] Casahome.org. http://casahome.org/

[11.] Vancouver.ca. "Becoming the Greenest City," 2010.

[12.] United Nations Environment Program. "IPCC Third Assessment Report: Climate change 2001." 2009.

[13.] John Christy, "The Global Warming Fiasco," *Global Warming and other Eco-Myths*. Edited by Ronald Bailey. Competitive Enterprise Institute, 2002, p.10.

[14.] "The climatic effects of water vapor," *Physics World*, May 1, 2003.

[15.] United Nations Framework Convention on Climate Change. "Summary of GHG Emissions for Canada."

[16.] Environment Canada. "Canada's 2007 Greenhouse Gas Inventory – A Summary of Trends."

[17] U.S. Energy Information Administration. "U.S. Carbon Dioxide Emissions from Energy Sources 2008 Flash Estimate," 2009.

[18] Center for Biological Diversity, "Energy and Global Warming."

[19] U.S. Department of Energy, Carbon Dioxide Information Analysis Center.

[20] Elisabeth Rosenthal. *New York Times*, "China clearly overtakes U.S. as leading emitter of climate-warming gases," June 13, 2008.

[21] Catherine Brahic and Reuters. New Scientist, "China warns of huge rise in emissions," October 22, 2008.

[22] People's Daily Online. "Top firm develops oil shale reserves," December 28, 2005.

[23] Ibid.

[24] Netherlands Environmental Assessment Agency: "Global CO_2 emissions: Annual increase halves in 2008." 2009. http://www.pbl.nl/en/publications/2009/Global-CO2-emissions-annual-increase-halves-in-2008.html

[25] Ibid.

[26] Legget, Jane A. et al. Congressional Research Services, Report for Congress, "China's Greenhouse Gas Emissions and Mitigation Policies," Sept. 10, 2008.

[27] Robert Kunzig. *National Geographic*, "The Canadian Oil Boom," March 2009.

[28] TheGlobeandMail.com. Special Report: "Shifting Sands."

[29] Blog post. Aldyen Donnelly. Energy.ProbeInternational.org, "Attacking Alberta's oil sands reeks of hypocrisy," September 17, 2009.

[30] Carrie Tait. *National Post*, "Canadian Association of Petroleum Producers. "Oil sands not so dirty: study; Emissions average only 10% higher, not 40%," July 24, 2009.

[31] Blog post. Aldyen Donnelly. Energy.ProbeInternational.org, "Attacking Alberta's oil sands reeks of hypocrisy," September 17, 2009.

[32] Robert Collier, "California standards could crimp Canada oil boom / Schwarzenegger's deals might affect Alberta's tar sands," *San Francisco Chronicle*. June 06, 2007.

[33] "Life Cycle Assessment Comparison of North American and Imported Crudes," prepared for Alberta Energy Research Institute, by Jacobs Consultancy, Life Cycle Associates. July 2009.

[34] Blog post. Aldyen Donnelly. Energy.ProbeInternational.org, "Attacking Alberta's oil sands reeks of hypocrisy," September 17, 2009.

[35] Ibid.

[36] E-tenergy.com. "Environmental Advantages," 2010.

[37] Joe Carroll, "Oil Sands May Get Cleaner as Shell, Exxon Bubble Tar to Froth," Bloomberg. Aug. 21, 2009.

[38] Canadian Association of Petroleum Producers. "Recycling Water with Zero Liquid Discharge at Mackay River," 2010.

[39] Canadasoilsands.ca. "Water: What we're doing," 2009.

[40] "Government Protects Oil Sands Industry, Fails to Protect Athabasca River," Pembina Institute news release. March 2, 2007.

[41] Joe Gelt, University of Arizona Water Resources Research Center. "Sharing Colorado River Water: History, Public Policy, and the Colorado River Compact," *Arroyo*, August 1997, Volume 10, No. 1.

[42] Metronews.ca. "Albertans want government to increase environmental education: poll," May 9, 2009.

[43] John Percy. *Globe and Mail*, "Oil-rich Alberta showing shades of Green," February 21, 2008.

[44] Government of Alberta: Energy. "Energy Facts," 2010.

[45] Government of Alberta, Energy, website. "Carbon Capture and Storage." Accessed July 21, 2010.

[46] WBEA.org. "Air Monitoring," 2010.

[47] Alexandra Zabjek. *Edmonton Journal*, "Six hundred birds died at Syncrude site in 1979, court hears," March 19, 2010.

[48.] Alexandra Zabjek. *Edmonton Journal*, "Huge snowfall hampered efforts to scare birds, Syncrude trial hears," March 4, 2010.

[49.] "Syncrude Canada Ltd. Charged For Migratory Bird Deaths," Environment Canada news release. Feb. 9, 2009.

[50.] Dawn Walton and Nathan Vanderklippe. *Globe and Mail*, "Syncrude charged over Alberta duck deaths," February 9, 2009.

[51.] Jim Macdonald. *Toronto Star*, "Syncrude charged after 500 ducks perished on oilsands pond," February 9, 2009.

[52.] MSNBC.com. "U.S., Canada ties get messy with oil sands issue," September 16, 2009.

[53.] The Pembina Institute. "Oil Sands Development Could Claim More Than 160 Million Boreal Birds," December 2, 2008.

[54.] CBC News. "Millions of birds could die from oilsands development: report," December 2, 2008.

[55.] Jeff Wells, Susan Casey-Lefkowitz, Gabriela Chavarria and Simon Dyer. BorealBirds.org, "Danger in the Nursery: Impact on Birds of Tar Sands Oil Development in Canada's Boreal Forest," December 2008.

[56.] BorealBirds.org, "The Global Significance of Canada's Boreal Forest: Quebec."

[57.] Canadian Associate of Petroleum Producers. "Oil Sands," 2010.

[58.] BorealBirds.org. "Boreal Songbird Initiative Staff & Board," 2007.

[59.] The Program on Water Issues, Past Events. http://www.powi.ca/ index_events.php

[60.] Canadasoilsands.ca. "Land use – what we're doing," 2009.

[61.] Robert Bryce. *Wall Street Journal*, "Windmills Are Killing Our Birds," September 7, 2009.

[62.] BCNBirds.org. "Window Collisions," 2006.

[63.] American Wind Energy Association website: awea.org

[64.] Mick Sagrillo. Wind Energy Technical Info, "Putting Wind Power's Effects on Birds in Perspective," 2003.

[65.] Syncrude.ca. "An apology from Syncrude – and a promise to do better," May 2, 2008.

Chapter 8

[1.] World Nuclear Association. "Nuclear Power in China," April 30, 2010.

[2.] "China could become the world leader in wind power, says Greenpeace," Greenpeace news release. Oct. 17, 2005.

[3.] China Guangdong Nuclear Power Group. "General introduction," 2007.

[4.] China Guangdong Nuclear Power Group. "New projects," 2007.

[5.] China Guangdong Nuclear Power Group. "Development of clean energy," 2007.

[6.] Greenpeace.org. "China could become the world leader in wind power, says Greenpeace," October 17, 2005.

[7.] CREIA. "Institutional Structure," 2004.

[8.] Patrick Moore. *Wall Street Journal*, "Why I Left Greenpeace," April 22, 2008.

[9.] Greenpeace.org. "The Founders of Greenpeace," October 29, 2008.

[10.] Greenpeace.org. "Greenpeace Statement On Patrick Moore," October 10, 2008.

[11.] YouTube

[12.] *Washington Post*. "Greenpeace Just Kidding About Armageddon," June 2, 2006.

[13.] Greenpeace.org. "Greenpeace International Annual Report 07," October 16, 2008.

[14.] Greenpeace China's Twitter page. twitter.com/GreenpeaceCn

[15.] Greenpeace China Facebook page. English version. Hong Kong.

[16.] Greenpeace China Facebook page. Beijing.

[17.] Whatblocked.com

[18] Brandon Swain. Christian Crusader Magazine, "Interview with Dr. Patrick Moore."

[19] Vimeo.com. "Solar-tastic in China."

[20] Gershon Grossman, Ofira Ayalon, Yifaat Baron, Debby Kaufman, Samuel Neaman Institute for Advanced Studies in Science and Technology. "Solar energy for the production of heat Summary and recommendations of the 4th assembly of the energy forum at SNI," 2007.

[21] Laura Barnhart. Greenpeace.org, "Climate change tour in Tibet."

[22] Antoaneta Bezlova. Asia Times, "China's Three Gorges Dam comes of age," November 4, 2009.

[23] Greenpeace.org. "Greenpeace Climate Leaders rating: continue to search for Climate Leaders," November 6, 2009.

[24] Vimeo.com. "China's e-waste tragedy: poisoning the poor."

[25] People's Daily Online. "Over 700 million mobile phone users in China," September 3, 2009.

[26] Greenpeace.org. "Wang Jue, director of public projects."

[27] The World Bank. "China Quick Facts," 2010.

[28] Vegan Fitness home page. www.veganfitness.net/

[29] Pembina Institute, 2006

[30] Pembina Institute, for Canadian Physicians for the Prevention of Nuclear War, 1989

[31] *Toronto Star.* "Canada called on to join renewable-energy agency," June 16, 2009.

[32] PembinaFoundation.org. "A Donor Bill of Rights."

[33] PembinaFoundation.org. "About," 2007.

[34] Samantha Smith. *Goddess Earth: Exposing the Pagan Agenda of the Environmental Movement.* Huntington House: U.S.A. (1994).

[35] Greenlearning.ca.

[36] Takepart.com. "AIT in the Classroom," 2006.

[37] PembinaFoundation.org. "Annual Report, 2008."

38. http://ecards.greenlearning.ca

39. Taylor, Amy et al. "When the Government is the Landlord,"
Pembina Institute publication. July 2004.

40. Greenlearning.ca. "Introducing e-cards-to-Copenhagen," 2010.

41. PembinaFoundation.org. "Annual Report, 2008."

42. Ibid.

43. Office of the Commissioner of Lobbying of Canada.

44. Oilsandswatch.org. "Clearing the Air on Oil Sands Myths."

45. Claudia Cattaneo. *National Post*, "An environmental quagmire,"
May 17, 2008.

46. PembinaFoundation.org. "Annual Report, 2008."

47. Kevin Libin. *National Post*, "Carbon report's bloody portent,"
October 30, 2009.

48. Claudia Cattaneo. *National Post*, "Green groups ramp up attacks
on oil sands," November 19, 2008.

Chapter 9

1. www.downstreamdoc.com

2. CBC News web site. "In Depth: Fort Chipewyan,"
http://www.cbc.ca/edmonton/features/fort-chipewyan/in-depth.html.
Accessed July 21, 2010.

3. *Cancer Incidence in Fort Chipewyan, Alberta 1995–2006*. Alberta
Cancer Board Division of Population Health and Information
Surveillance, Feb. 2009.

4. Carol Christian. *Fort McMurray Today*, "Health Canada mum on
O'Connor complaint," 2009.

5. Kevin Libin. "Cancer clusters: Fluke or cause for concern?"
National Post, Feb. 14, 2009.

6. CanWest News Service, "Feds target medical whistleblower: doctor
claims," Nov. 12, 2007.

7. *Cancer Incidence in Fort Chipewyan, Alberta 1995-2006*, Alberta Cancer Board, Division of Population Health and Information Surveillance. Feb. 2009.

8. Ibid.

9. Laura Eggertson. "High Cancer Rates Among Fort Chipewyan Residents," *Canadian Medical Association Journal*, February 25, 2009. www.cmaj.ca

10. Kevin Libin. "Still a 'whistle-blower' to oil sands activists," *National Post*, Nov. 10, 2009.

11. Florence Loyie. *Edmonton Journal*, "Doctor who suggested oil-sands-cancer link cleared of misconduct charge," November 8, 2009.

12. CBC News. "Fort Chip doc cleared of complaints," November 6, 2009.

13. Kevin Libin. "Still a 'whistle-blower' to oil sands activists," *National Post*, Nov. 10, 2009.

14. College of Physicians and Surgeons of Alberta, Investigation Report, File No. 070059, November 4, 2009.

15. Kevin Libin. *National Post*, "Nothing fishy about this specimen," March 12, 2009.

16. Ibid.

17. Angela Brunschot. *See Magazine*, "Beauty and the Beast; Delegates at the Third Keepers of the Water Conference saw 'Both sides of Fort Chip,'" August 21, 2008.

18. Kelly Cryderman, "Fish with double jaw sparks eco interest," *Edmonton Journal*, Aug. 20, 2008.

19. Ibid.

20. *Fort McMurray Today*, Nov. 9, 2007"New report finds elevated arsenic risk in Fort Chipewyan".

21. *Edmonton Sun*, Nov. 9, 2007 "High levels of poisons found in water downstream of oil sands"

22. Kevin Timoney. *The Trumpeter*, "On Being Natural," 1993.

23. Kevin Timoney. *Fish Deformities in the Vicinity of Fort Chipewyan, Alberta*. February, 2009. www.borealbirds.org/resources/report-timoney-fishmutation.pdf

24. Regional Aquatics Monitoring Program, Technical Report, 2008. http://www.rampalberta.org/UserFiles/File/AnnualReports/2008/2008_RAMP_Technical_Report-Main.zip

25. U.S. Food and Drug Administration. "Product-Specific Information," 2009.

Chapter 10

1. CBC Radio-Canada. "Policy 1.1.12: Free Travel," 1994.

2. http://www.cbc.radio-canada.ca/docs/policies/journalistic/socio.shtml

3. "Greenpeace takes anti-oilsands message to oil companies' homes," Richard Warnica, Oct. 11, 2009 http://www.canada.com/business/Greenpeace+takes+anti+oilsands+message+companies+homes/2091969/story.html

4. Andrew Nikiforuk. *Toronto Star*, "A public tarring in Saudi Canada," June 28, 2009.

5. "The word on 'dirty' oil," *Calgary Herald*. November 2, 2008

Chapter 11

1. U.S. Energy Information Administration. "U.S. Imports by Country of Origin," 2009.

2. Cera.com. "Press Releases: Oil Sands Move from the "Fringe to Center" of Energy Supply," May 18, 2009.

3. U.S. Energy Information Administration. "U.S. Imports by Country of Origin," 2009.

4. Deborah Yedlin. CBC News, "The Saudis badmouth Alberta's oilsands," November 15, 2007.

[5.] Carol Christian. *Fort McMurray Today*, "Oilsands targeted by new U.S. law," March 26, 2008.

[6.] Co-operativecampaigns.co.uk. "Contact your MP."

[7.] Carol Christian. *Fort McMurray Today*, "Oilsands targeted by new U.S. law," March 26, 2008.

[8.] Youssef Ibrahim. *New York Sun*, "Israel's Lobby's Pull Pales Next to Evil Saudi Input," September 25, 2007.

[9.] Kevin Bogardus, The Center for Public Integrity. "Saudis Drop Big Bucks for Washington Influence," 2008.

[10.] John Solomon and Jeffrey H. Bimbaum. *Washington Post*, "Clinton Library Got Funds from Abroad," December 15, 2007.

[11.] Don Van Natta Jr., Jo Becker and Mike McIntire. *New York Times*, "In Charity and Politics, Clinton Donors Overlap," December 20, 2007.

[12.] John Solomon and Jeffrey H. Bimbaum. *Washington Post*, "Clinton Library Got Funds from Abroad," December 15, 2007.

[13.] http://www.nydailynews.com/opinions/2008/04/27/2008-04-27_to_see_jimmy_carters_true_allegiances_ju.html

[14.] United Nations Economic and Social Commission for Asia and the Pacific. "Addressing Climate Change Through Market Mechanism."

[15.] Reuters. "FACTBOX: Saudi Arabia's oil refining capacity," April 13, 2010.

[16.] United Nations Framework Convention on Climate Change. "List of Non-Annex I Parties to the Convention."

[17.] "Saudis want aid if world cuts oil dependence," Associated Press. Oct. 8, 2009.

[18.] Meghan Clyne. *New York Sun*, "Report Links Brooklyn Mosque to Saudi Hate Material," January 31, 2005.

[19.] Paul Michael Wihbey, Frederick Cedoz, Robert E. Heiler, Cecelia Messing. Gwest.net. "The Global Politics of Energy," March 2006.

[20.] Ibid.

[21.] Michelle Nichols, "Gore urges civil disobedience to stop coal plants," Reuters. Sept. 24, 2008.

[22.] Marcia Stepanek. MSNBC.com, "Clinton summit warns on global warming," September 25, 2008.

[23.] Sara Bongiorni. *Christian Science Monitor*, "A year without 'Made in China'," December 20, 2005.

[24.] *The Encyclopedia of Arkansas History & Culture*. "Wesley Kanne Clark," 2008.

[25.] WesPAC. "Mission Statement." http://securingamerica.com/mission

[26.] Reuters. "Growth Energy Launches Nationwide Campaign to Require Country of Origin Labeling...," 2010.

[27.] www.citgoboycott.org

[28.] Reuters. "Growth Energy Launches Nationwide Campaign to Require Country of Origin Labeling...," 2010.

[29.] BBC News. "US pulls out of Saudi Arabia," April 29, 2003.

[30.] GlobalSecurity.org. "Ahmed Al Jaber Air Base," 2005.

[31.] GlobalSecurity.org. "Iraq Facilities," 2005.

[32.] Jules Dufour, GlobalResearch.ca. "The Worldwide Network of US Military Bases," July 1, 2007.

[33.] "Jordan: New US base to train Iraqis and Palestinians, says report," AND Kronos International. Oct 10, 2008.

[34.] Justin Huggler. *The Independent*, "US soldiers are 'using Jordan to enter Iraq'," March 28, 2003.

[35.] BBC News. "US military aid for Middle East," July 30, 2007.

[36.] Dr. Edward J. Marolda. "The United States Navy and the Persian Gulf."

[37.] Ibid.

[38.] Jean-Paul Rodrigue. *Les Cahiers de Geographie du Quebec*, "Straits, Passages and Chokepoints: A Maritime Geostrategy of Petroleum Distribution," 2004.

[39] U.S. Energy Information Administration. "U.S. Imports by Country of Origin," 2009.

[40] Ibid.

[41] Inflationdata.com. "Historical Crude Oil Prices (Table)," 2010.

[42] Dawn Walton. *Globe and Mail*, "Protests dog Alberta PR campaign to Cover Up Tar Sands Disaster," April 27, 2008.

[43] Greenpages.ca. "Tar Sands Oil Remains Dirty." July 2009.

[44] CTV Montreal. "Environmental activists protest Stelmach's U.S. visit," January 16, 2008.

Chapter 12

[1] *Vancouver Province*, "Green jobs to offset climate layoffs: UN," December 7, 2007.

[2] Jim Harris. *National Post*, "Green jobs will pay for themselves," October 2, 2009.

[3] CBS News. "Obama Hits Ohio," January 16, 2009.

[4] Speech by President Obama at the Edison Electric Vehicle Technical Centre, March 19, 2009; Political Transcript Wire.

[5] CIA. *The World Factbook*

[6] Gabriel Calzada Álvarez et al, Universidad Rey Juan Carlos. "Study of the effects on employment of public aid to renewable energy sources," 2009.

[7] Ibid.

[8] Kevin Libin. *National Post*, "'Real Warriors Hold Jobs'," February 20, 2008.

[9] Deloitte.com. "Critical talent issues for the oil industry," 2006.

[10] Suncor.com. "Aboriginal Relations at Suncor."

[11] Juliette Jowit. *The Guardian*, "Indigenous people in legal challenge against oil firms over tar sand project," February 26, 2009.

[12] Beaver Lake Cree Nation. Statement of Claim.

[13] Beaver Lake Cree Nation. "Kétuskéno Declaration," 2008.

14. Statistics Canada, 2006 census data.

15. Kevin Libin. *National Post*, "'Real Warriors Hold Jobs'," February 20, 2008.

16. Beaver Lake Cree web site: Chief and Council. http://beaverlakecreenation.ca/default.aspx?ID=2-2. Accessed July 21, 2010.

17. Ibid.

18. Beaver Lake Cree website: Beaver Lake Administration. http://beaverlakecreenation.ca/default.aspx?ID=2-3. Accessed July 21, 2010.

19. Statistics Canada, census 2006, Beaver Lake Cree Nation band profile.

20. Roland Cilliers. *Fort McMurray Today*, "Local unemployment Alberta's lowest," 2010.

21. John O'Connor. *Halifax Chronicle-Herald*, "Letter to the Editor," December 30, 2007.

22. "Measuring a sustainable community," Regional Municipality of Wood Buffalo news release. Jan. 26, 2006.

23. Regional Municipality of Wood Buffalo, "Municipal Census 2008."

24. MoneySense. "Best places to live – economic," 2007.

25. "Fort McMurray Leads the Nation Again!" United Way news release. April 29, 2009.

26. Sylvia LeRoy, Todd Gabel and Niels Veldhius, Fraser Forum. "Comparing Charitable Giving in Canada & the United States: Canada's Generosity Gap," December 2003.

27. Regional Municipality of Wood Buffalo. "Suncor Community Leisure Centre set for October 30 opening," August 20, 2009.

28. Nichols Applied Management. "Sustainable Community Indicators: Summary Report," January 2006.

29. Regional Municipality of Wood Buffalo, "Summer set to sizzle with programs and events for Wood Buffalo residents," June 5, 2009.

[30] Regional Municipality of Wood Buffalo, "Regional Profile 2003."

[31] Regional Municipality of Wood Buffalo, "Redevelopment of MacDonald Island continues," April 29, 2009.

[32] Regional Municipality of Wood Buffalo, "More than 8,000 residents pitching in for Community Clean Up," April 24, 2009.

[33] Canadian Energy Research Institute. "About Ceri."

[34] Canadian Energy Research Institute. "Economic Impacts of the Petroleum Industry in Canada: Summary Report," July 2009.

[35] Canadian Association of Petroleum Producers. "The Outlook for Canada's Oil and Gas Sector," October 21, 2009.

[36] Statistics Canada, *The Daily*, Nov. 6, 2009. "Labour force characteristics by province."

[37] CAW/TCA Canada. "Membership Profile," 2007.

[38] Jim Harris, Green Party of Canada. "US Automakers shed 16,587 Ontario jobs between 1999-2009 despite $1B subsidy," November 2, 2007.

[39] Statistics Canada.

[40] Canadian Energy Research Institute. "Economic Impacts of the Petroleum Industry in Canada: Summary Report," July 2009.

Conclusion

[1] Terry Macalister. *The Guardian*, "Thin smile from Shell as it sells Sakhalin stake," April 19, 2007. Conclusion.

[2] Andrew Meier. *New York Times*, "Who Fears a Free Mikhail Khodorkovsky?" November 18, 2009.

[3] Tyler Bridges. *Miami Herald*, "Chavez's expropriation of oil firms could spark labor unrest," June 12, 2009.